Navigating the 21st Century Business World
Case Studies in Management

Edited by
Dorottya Sallai and Alexander Pepper

LSE Press

Published by
LSE Press
10 Portugal Street
London
WC2A 2HD
press.lse.ac.uk

ISBN (Paperback): 978-1-911712-38-1
ISBN (PDF): 978-1-911712-39-8
ISBN (EPUB): 978-1-911712-40-4
ISBN (Mobi): 978-1-911712-41-1

DOI: https://doi.org/10.31389/lsepress.nbw

This book has been peer-reviewed to ensure high academic standards. For our full publishing ethics policies, see https://press.lse.ac.uk

To read the free, open access version of this book online, visit https://doi.org/10.31389/lsepress.nbw or scan this QR code with your mobile device:

Contents

PART 1: INTRODUCTION

1. Business cases: what are they, why do we use them and how should you go about doing a case analysis?

In this introductory capture we consider the history of case teaching in US business schools, the difference between the 'Harvard' and 'Chicago' approaches to management education, why at London School of Economics and Political Science (LSE) we find merit in both approaches, how the application of theory helps to elucidate cases, and how cases provide a laboratory for exploring management decision-making. We go on to explain the Introduction–Facts–Theory–Analysis–Conclusion approach to writing a case analysis.

PART 2: STRATEGY AND GENERAL MANAGEMENT

2. Corporate strategy in the UK vehicle components industry: a comparison of Lucas Industries and GKN

The story of how Lucas Industries and GKN responded to the changing economic environment during the years of industrial decline in the UK is one of the classic cases of business strategy. Lucas Industries and GKN, manufacturers of automotive and aerospace industry components, were in their heyday two of the UK's largest listed industrial companies. Yet, while GKN managed successfully to negotiate the rapidly changing economic and industrial scene of the 1980s–1990s, Lucas Industries struggled to adapt and was eventually forced to merge with the North American Varity Corporation in what many commentators regarded as an effective takeover.

3. The collapse of Carillion plc

This case examines the collapse of Carillion plc, an outsourcing company. It describes how outsourcing became a common business model in the 1990s, how being the lowest-cost provider is not by itself a sustainable long-term business strategy and how optimistic assumptions about the profitability of long-term contracts can lead to financial failure.

4. On what matters: Unilever plc – purpose or performance?

Shareholder primacy, socially responsible business, corporate purpose and sustainability are examined in this case about Unilever's evolving business strategy over the period from 2017, following an attempted takeover by Kraft Heinz Company, to 2024 with the appointment of a new chief executive officer from outside the group.

PART 3: GOVERNANCE, ACCOUNTING AND CONTROL

5. Asset allocation and governance at the Imperial Tobacco pension fund in the mid-20th century

This case is concerned with exploring the relationship between the practice of management as an internal set of rules and management as interacting and advocating standards that relate to external rules relating to governance. It highlights the reasons that managers engage with professional standards as part of their management practice. More generally, the case is an opportunity to consider cultural changes in the approach to governance.

6. The fall of the Maxwell empire

This is a 'raw case' which draws on a number of independent reports on Robert Maxwell's business practices and flotation of Mirror Group Newspapers, videos and other secondary material to examine the rise and fall of the Maxwell empire. It can be used to teach how corporate governance in the UK has developed since 1990, the role of auditors and directors, the significance of pension funds in the capital markets, developments in pensions law, and the strengths and risks of a 'productive narcissist' CEO.

PART 5: HUMAN RESOURCE MANAGEMENT AND ORGANISATIONAL BEHAVIOUR

PART 6: PUBLIC MANAGEMENT

This case study explores how socio-economic background – often referred to as social class – impacts career progression within the UK Civil Service. Despite ongoing efforts to promote diversity and inclusion, evidence indicates that an individual's class background significantly shapes their career trajectory within the public sector. The case of career progression within the UK Civil Service provides a unique perspective on social mobility and equal opportunities. It shows how individuals from various economic and social classes navigate their career paths, highlighting both the explicit and subtle ways in which class influences professional advancement.

List of figures and tables

Figures

Tables

Editors and contributors

Editors

Dorottya Sallai is an Associate Professor of Management (Education) at the London School of Economics and Political Science (LSE), where she has received consistent recognition for teaching excellence, including LSE's Outstanding Teaching Award. Her research has been published in leading peer-reviewed journals. Beyond her academic work, she serves as an expert consultant to the European Commission and provides strategic consultancy to public and private sector organisations.

Alexander Pepper (better known as Sandy) is Emeritus Professor of Management Practice at LSE, where he taught and carried out research from 2008 to 2023. He was previously a partner at PwC, where he held various senior management roles, including as global leader of the human resources tax and legal services business from 2002 to 2006.

Contributors

Vida Amani is a corporate reward expert with over 14 years' experience gained in the pharmaceuticals, media and oil industries, working in the UK and US. She is a Fellow of the CIPD and a guest speaker at LSE in reward management.

Luciano Andrenacci is Associate Professor and Director of the Master's Degree in Public Policy Planning and Evaluation at the School of Politics and Government of the National University of San Martín (Buenos Aires) and Professor and Academic Coordinator of the Human Development Program at FLACSO, Argentina Branch. He earned a doctorate in Latin American Social Studies from the Sorbonne-Nouvelle University (Paris III, France) and is a teacher, researcher and national and regional consultant on issues of citizenship, social policy and public management.

Yally Avrahampour is Associate Professor (Education) in the Department of Management at LSE and joint programme director of the MSc Social Innovation and Entrepreneurship. Yally is also a director of the Pensions Archive Trust, a charity. The Pensions Archive Trust exists to ensure that important information about the history of occupational pensions is not lost to history but is retained and made available to any who wish to learn from the successes and failures of the past.

Michael Barzelay is Professor of Public Management at LSE and member of the Department of Management since its establishment. He is author of seven books on public policy and public management, including *Public Management as a Design-Oriented Professional Discipline* (2019) and the forthcoming *Public Management: Recovering Designs through Case Study Research*. He has written and taught cases since the 1980s, when he was a junior faculty member at the Harvard Kennedy School of Government, specialising in public management.

Rebecca Campbell is Associate Professor (Education) at LSE and programme Director of the Global Master's in Management. Her research interests include pay and pensions. She is currently course leader for MSc courses in foundations of management, strategic reward and business ethics. Prior to her career in academia, Rebecca worked as a director of a womenswear fashion business.

Aurelie Cnop is a guest teacher and researcher at LSE and Imperial College London. She has over a decade of experience teaching negotiation skills and managing people and teams, blending practical and theoretical knowledge. She holds an MSc in Business Engineering from the University of Louvain and an MSc and PhD in Organisational Behaviour from LSE. Aurelie's research focuses on leadership, individual and team motivation and wellbeing in high-pressure environments. She has over 15 years' experience in strategy consulting, working for global firms like Novartis and DHL.

Christine Côté is Associate Professor (Education) at LSE and Academic Director of the CEMS Master's in International Management. She holds a PhD in International Political Economy from LSE, an MPA in Economic Policy from Harvard's Kennedy School of Government, an MBA in Finance and Strategic Management from London Business School and a BA in Economics and Politics from McGill University. She was previously an international trade negotiator with the Canadian Department of Foreign Affairs and International Trade, and a strategy, policy and economics consultant with PricewaterhouseCoopers in London.

Ellie Cumpsty is an Executive at EY Parthenon, specialising in Turnaround and Restructuring. A graduate of LSE, she earned first-class honours in Management in 2021. Following her graduation, Ellie worked as a research assistant during the summer of 2021, where she contributed to various projects before starting her role at EY. She furthered her expertise by completing the ACA qualification, qualifying in 2024. Outside of her professional commitments, Ellie is passionate about sports, particularly sailing and netball, where she thrives on competition and teamwork.

Saul Estrin is Emeritus Professor of Managerial Economics and Strategy at LSE and was the founding Head of the Department of Management in 2006. He was formerly Adecco Professor of Business and Society and Associate Dean (Faculty and Research) at London Business School. He is a Fellow of the British Academy and a Fellow of the Academy of International Business. Saul's research covers a range of subjects in international business and entrepreneurship, with particular reference to emerging economies.

Roger Fon is an Assistant Professor of International Business at Newcastle Business School, Northumbria University. Previously he was a Fellow in Management at LSE. Roger's research focuses on the internationalisation strategies of firms from developing countries with particular emphasis on the African context. His research has been nominated for and received prestigious awards including the 2018 Danny Van Den Bulcke Best Paper Award at the Annual Conference of the European International Business Academy and nominated for the 2023 International Management Division GWU-CI-BER Best Paper in Emerging Markets Award at the Annual Conference of the Academy of Management.

Ian Hill is an academic education pathway scholar specialising in Human Resource Management and Employment Relations at King's Business School, King's College London. Ian is also a Fellow of the Higher Education Academy and a Certified Management and Business Educator. He recently completed his PhD (2025) at Loughborough London's campus and has been teaching within higher education institutions in the UK for almost 15 years. He won the 2022 Innovation in Education Dean's award at King's Business School and in May 2025 his co-edited (with Professor Sally Everett) textbook, *Diversity, Equity and Inclusion for Business and Management* was published by Sage.

Alfred Jasansky is a business analyst at McKinsey & Company. He read classics at Durham University and completed his Global Master's in Management at LSE in 2024, with an exchange semester at the University of Chicago Booth School of Business.

Karin A. King is a Fellow in the Department of Management at LSE. Following a professional career in global human resource management and management consulting, Karin received her PhD in Management from LSE. Her research focus includes global talent management and talent strategy effectiveness. She works with organisations on executive development, leadership and talent management, strategic human resource management, negotiations and leading change.

Lauren Oddoye is a product manager at Meta. Lauren graduated with distinction from the Global Master's in Management MSc programme at LSE in 2020. She also has a Master's in International Management awarded by the CEMS Global Alliance in Management Education and a first-class Bachelor's degree in philosophy from the University of East Anglia.

Sir Geoffrey Owen is visiting Professor of Practice in the Department of Management at LSE and Head of Industrial Policy at Policy Exchange. The larger part of his career has been spent at the *Financial Times*, where he was deputy editor from 1973 to 1980 and editor from 1981 to 1990.

Daniel Shapiro joined Simon Frazer University in Vancouver, Canada in 1991 and served as dean of SFU Beedie School of Business from 2008 to 2014. Over his remarkable career, he demonstrated a steadfast commitment to academic excellence and leadership. As a teacher, Danny was unparalleled, receiving the TD Canada Trust Teaching Award twice – in 1995 and 2002 – and earning the prestigious Academy of International Business (AIB) Fellows International Educator of the Year Award in 2014. Over his distinguished 40-year career, Danny authored five books and more than 150 scholarly publications, including 10 articles following his retirement in 2022. His latest was published in the *Journal of International Business Studies* (December 2024). His research, cited over 14,000 times, spanned international business and strategy, corporate ownership and governance, foreign investment and emerging markets, and public policy, earning him international acclaim.

Emma Soane is an Associate Professor in the Department of Management at LSE where she has been working since 2008. She teaches organisational behaviour, leadership and risk to postgraduate students and executives. Emma has extensive experience of studying public and private sector organisations, including government departments, NHS hospitals, manufacturing, IT and investment banks.

Janna Wirth is a graduate of the LSE Global Master's in Management programme and earned a CEMS Master's in Management degree from LSE and Cornell University. She previously graduated with distinction from the University of Mannheim with a BSc in Business Administration. Janna has experience in deal advisory and strategy consulting.

Part 1
Introduction

1. Business cases: what are they, why do we use them and how should you go about doing a case analysis?

Dorottya Sallai and Alexander Pepper

Introduction

In the 1970s, economists used to distinguish between the 'Saltwater school' of macroeconomics associated with economists from universities on the east and west coasts of the United States, especially Harvard and MIT in Cambridge, Massachusetts, including Princeton and Yale, as well as Berkeley in California, and the 'Freshwater school' centred on the Chicago School of Economics and other universities located around the Great Lakes. Saltwater economists typically aligned with the approach to macroeconomics first set out by John Maynard Keynes, in its classic Keynesian or neo-Keynesian versions, and were critical of high theory based on assumptions about free markets, perfect competition and rational expectations. Freshwater economists emphasised the significance of the rational expectations model in economic decision-making and the importance of building a strong theoretical connection between how individuals and firms interact in markets when building theories intended to account for aggregate macroeconomic phenomena.[1]

In much the same way as Saltwater and Freshwater economics, there have been two traditions in management scholarship: the Harvard Business School approach to teaching, which makes extensive use of cases, and the Chicago Booth School of Business approach, which espouses the primacy of theory.[2] Another parallel is with the 'two cultures' thesis advanced by British natural scientist and novelist C.P. Snow in the 1950s, who, in his Rede Lecture at the University of Cambridge in 1959, famously argued that the intellectual life of western society had become split between the two cultures of science and the humanities and that this division was a major handicap to solving global problems[3] – for the use of business cases in management teaching, think 'humanities' and for the approach which advocates the primacy of theory and quantitative techniques think 'science'. Both have their place.

How to cite this book chapter:

Sallai, Dorottya and Pepper, Alexander (2025) 'Business cases: what are they, why do we use them and how should you go about doing a case analysis?', in: Sallai, Dorottya and Pepper, Alexander (ed) *Navigating the 21st Century Business World: Case Studies in Management*, London: LSE Press, pp. 1–13. https://doi.org/10.31389/lsepress.nbw.a

What then is the approach to management education taken at LSE? The answer – as you might expect, given the antecedents of the Department of Management in economics, finance and accounting – is that there is a strong focus on theory and quantitative techniques. But the Department of Management also has its roots in teaching industrial relations, international business, organisational behaviour, leadership, change management, ethics and the sociology of information systems – subjects that are more closely associated with qualitative research. In these areas case studies have always been an essential part of the curriculum.

Someone once said (or perhaps it is apocryphal): 'Business is the art of making irrevocable decisions based on incomplete information.' Business cases have great value because of how they imitate real life: they contain lots of information – more than you need – and teach you to focus on what is important and relevant; several interpretations are usually possible, depending on what information you take to be most relevant; and they lack a single, compelling answer to the question of what to do next. At the same time, the application of theory and the examination of numerical data using quantitative techniques and financial analysis mean that the level of critical case analysis moves a long way beyond the bland, superficial and anecdotal of some 'problem-oriented' case teaching. Case analysis taught in an analytical way provides students with critical thinking skills that will be essential in their future careers.

What is the purpose of this book?

The case studies in our collection encompass a wide range of industries, including health, tech, media, oil and gas sectors, fast fashion, financial services and the public sector. All cases were written by LSE's Department of Management's faculty members (some with co-authors). With a focus on curriculum enhancement, *Navigating the 21st Century Business World: Case Studies in Management* is intended to serve as a source of inspiration for teaching management theories.

Why *Navigating the 21st Century Business World* you might ask? Certainly, many of the issues dealt with in the collection are decidedly modern – notably corporate purpose (Chapter 4 on Unilever), climate change and sustainability (Chapter 11 about 'Big Oil' and Chapter 12 on fast fashion), AI and the digital revolution (Chapter 15 about transformation in the automotive sector). But some of the cases raise issues which predate the start of the new millennium (for example, Maxwell [Chapter 6], Chapter 2 on Lucas Industries/GKN and the Imperial Tobacco pension fund [examined in Chapter 5]). We make no apologies for including these historical cases, which we continue to use in our teaching. History matters, in business as in other spheres of life. The Nobel prize-winning economic historian Douglass North has demonstrated how path dependencies mean that the past does affect the future. Patterns do repeat themselves. Two of the older cases in the collection, Lucas Industries/

GKN and the Maxwell case, provide valuable lessons – the former as a way of comparing the positioning and resource-based views of business strategy, the latter to help understand why good corporate governance is critically important as security against misrule.

Business schools still teach strategic positioning and the resource-based view – classically illustrated by the Lucas/GKN case, even if industrial engineering has noticeably declined in the United Kingdom. There is much to be learned from the Maxwell case about the bad corporate governance and the dangers of narcissistic leadership – which sadly continues to be a 21st-century phenomenon. The American philosopher George Santayana said that those who forget the past are condemned to repeat it – or was it Winston Churchill? No matter the source, the sentiments are perennial, in business as elsewhere. Better to learn vicariously from the mistakes of others – indeed that is one of the things which case study teaching and learning is all about.

We anticipate that the knowledge gained from these practical situations will enable current and future management students and leaders to navigate the intricacies of the corporate world with confidence, flexibility, critical thinking and adaptability.

Types of case

The cases found in this selection are of three kinds:

- short cases intended primarily for class discussion and designed to shed light on a particular idea or theory;
- classic cases, first developed by the faculty at Harvard Business School – who invented the case method as a way of illustrating real-world challenges facing organisations – place the student in the shoes of a key decision-maker;
- 'raw cases', as pioneered by Yale School of Management. These are open-ended, multi-perspective studies with many pages of relevant material that students must analyse, such as statutory documents, analyst reports, news articles, stock charts and interviews with key players. This format reflects the way managers must access and analyse information to make informed business decisions. The raw case study method allows students to wander through real-time information with a specific assignment that prompts them to 'discover, evaluate, analyse, decide and communicate, similarly to how managerial decisions are made in the real world of international business.'[4]

In Table 1.1 we have set out the types of cases in this collection and provide a number of key words to identify important themes which are explored in each case.

Table 1.1: Types of cases and issues covered

	TYPE OF CASE	ISSUES COVERED
Part 2: Strategy and general management		
2. Corporate strategy in the UK vehicle components industry: a comparison of Lucas Industries and GKN	Classic case	Britain's industrial decline, product diversification, corporate strategy, resource-based view, strategic positioning
3. The Collapse of Carillion plc	Classic case	Accounting for long-term contracts, business strategy, mergers and acquisitions, outsourcing, transaction cost economics
4. On what matters: Unilever plc – purpose or performance?	Classic case	Shareholder primacy, socially responsible business, corporate purpose, sustainability
Part 3: Governance, accounting and control		
5. Asset allocation and governance at the Imperial Tobacco pension fund in the mid-20th century	Classic case	Governance, professional standards
6. The fall of the Maxwell empire	Raw case	Auditors, corporate governance, directors, narcissistic leaders, pension funds
7. Activist investors: Alliance Trust and Elliott International	Classic case	Activist investors, corporate governance, leadership, measuring financial performance
8. The failure of the Royal Bank of Scotland	Raw case	Corporate governance, global financial crisis, managerial decision-making, mergers and acquisitions, narcissistic leaders
Part 4: Economics, politics and the business environment		
9. China National Petroleum Company in Sudan	Classic case	Chinese state-owned enterprises, emerging markets, government-investor relations, international business
10. The Oyu Tolgoi copper mine and the obsolescing bargain in Mongolia	Classic case	Emerging markets, international business, multinationals
11. Activist investors versus Big Oil: How should ExxonMobil and British Petroleum respond?	Classic case	Corporate purpose, the social responsibility of business

12. Environmental impact: why fast fashion is bad for the environment	Raw case	Environment, fashion industry, marketing, change management
Part 5: Human resource management and organisational behaviour		
13. The UK's National Health Service: teams, conflict and performance	Short case	Conflict, conflict management, diversity, team-building
14. Redesigning a performance management system	Classic case	Pay, performance management systems
15. Transformation in the automotive sector: the management challenges of AI and the digital revolution	Classic case	Digital transformation, job design, future of work
16. auticon: promoting a neuro-diverse workforce	Classic case	Diversity and inclusion, neurodiversity, human resource management, environmental, social, and governance (ESG)
Part 6: Public management		
17. Planning and programming for a government-hosted mass gathering event in India: the 2019 Prayagraj Kumbh Mela	Classic case	Design science, leadership, systems change
18. Socio-economic background and career progression within the UK Civil Service	Short case	Socio-economic class, human resource management, diversity and inclusion, organisational behaviour

As well as the three types of cases (classic, short, and raw) we asked contributors to write the cases studies in this collection in their own style and voice, not to a prescribed formula. We regard this kind of diversity as a strength.

Who is this book for?

This collection is intended to be a useful resource for academics and students in higher education as well as practitioners at various levels of their management careers. In today's fast-paced business environment – when volatility, uncertainty, complexity and ambiguity are the norms – rather than teaching students what to do, we should prepare them to navigate their environment with an open mind and the necessary skills that enable them to critically assess different options and make decisions in high-stakes, high-pressure situations. The capacity to critically evaluate large amounts of information and effectively solve complex challenges and dilemmas is essential for university students as well as future leaders.

The case studies provide business scenarios to inspire debates and discussion not only for students aspiring to enter the field of management but also for seasoned executives aiming to enhance their leadership skills and entrepreneurs who are constantly looking for a competitive advantage. Each case study gives an in-depth look at the wide range of challenges faced by organisations and business leaders in various industries and geographical areas.

Mostly for students...

How do business cases work?

The basic structure of a standard case study presents:

- a decision-maker with a dilemma;
- background information, often including financial and other quantitative data, setting up the basis of the current situation and the dilemma;
- a set of choices, goals or issues that need to be resolved, which form the basis for the case discussion.

Thus, we can derive three generic questions:

- What is the nature of the problem?
- What factors explain the situation as we now find it?
- What are the choices going forward, and their likely consequences?

These questions mirror our mission to teach the uses of theory: applying general understandings about the 'causes of things' in order to:

- explain the shape of the present; and
- predict the likely consequences of possible interventions.

What are you aiming for in preparing a case discussion?

You are ready for a case discussion when you can answer each of the questions posed in class in a cogent and complete manner when called upon to do so. You should have a clear statement (thesis) and be able to argue it using facts from the case. Preparation should take time – hours, not minutes. If you cannot do this, you are not adequately prepared for the case class – instead, you will be relying on others to have done the work on your behalf that is required for the group to carry the discussion forward. You will also be running several steps behind the discussion and will only grasp a small percentage of what is going on.

What do you need to do?

You will sometimes be given specific instructions about the task, but the default is simply 'to write a case analysis'. To do this, you need to work out what the main issues are, before deciding what specific questions you need to answer to address these issues. Sometimes your instructor will help you by providing a list of some of the questions that the case analysis should cover.

You need to be a detective. Look for clues, infer, fill in the blanks, look for patterns. Be curious. Interrogate the data and ask the questions that you would want to know answers to, as if you were a manager with a problem to solve in practice. You need to be able to draw conclusions and justify them. Get to the bottom-line answer in as simple a form as possible, but make sure you can support your answer with arguments, facts and data. Can you answer the main question in one sentence?

Ways to do this include:

- Make a first pass of the facts and the data. Read the case and make lots of notes in the margins. Summarise the takeaway from each important paragraph. Note details and interpretations.
- Think. What is the big picture? What frameworks and theories help to explain the phenomena you are trying to understand? How would they explain the 'causes of things' in the case?
- Examine the data in the exhibits (figures, tables and other exhibits). Start asking questions – what can you do with this information? What is relevant and what is irrelevant to the question at hand? Case writers often provide lots of data to encourage you to sift through and work out what is important.
- Look at the specific questions you have been set, if any. Use any of the generic questions set out in the case. Answer them directly and clearly. If no specific question is set, think about what the main question might be. Why have you been set this particular case? Before you can give a good answer, you need to be clear about what the critical question is.

Can I use information outside the written case?

The basic rule is – 'No', particularly in short cases and classic cases. Generally speaking, all the information you need will be contained in the case notes and exhibits. It is not particularly helpful to use evidence that you glean from Wikipedia or using Google, for example, about what actually happened next in the real case. However, there are some exceptions to this rule.

In 'raw cases' you are encouraged to search for additional information to help you develop your research skills. You should weigh the validity of different sources carefully. Peer-reviewed academic journal articles and independent reports commissioned by the government or international organisations are a good starting point. Company reports and accounts are an important source of financial information and other data but be careful to distinguish between material required by statute, which has been audited by independent third-party auditors, and other material which is essentially no more than corporate PR. Newspaper articles can be good for facts and data, but you might need to triangulate by comparing two or more different sources. Be careful to distinguish between facts and opinions.

Be aware of potential biases. In the UK, *The Guardian* has traditionally adopted a left-of-centre political perspective, compared with *The Times* and *The Daily Telegraph*'s more predominant right-of-centre perspective. The *Financial Times* and *The Economist* are typically well researched and rigorously edited, but do be aware of their editorial stance, which is based on classical, social and economic liberalism, particularly advocacy of free trade and free markets. In the US, *The Wall Street Journal*, *The Washington Post* and *The New York Times* are generally reliable sources of information. Most other countries have a leading newspaper focused on financial journalism equivalent to the *Financial Times* and *The Wall Street Journal*. Blogs, consultancy reports and papers produced by think tanks can also be sources of useful information but do remember to assess the validity and reliability of published material very carefully, and always be careful to distinguish between facts and opinions.

In summary, you must carefully follow the instructions you are given – your teachers will not be impressed if you spend a lot of time searching for additional information when they want you to focus on developing your analytical skills or if you rely upon relatively thin information when they are expecting you to do additional research.

Writing up a case analysis

As well as discussing cases in class, you may be asked to write a case analysis as part of a formative or summative assignment. There are many ways of doing this, and your instructor will guide you on what they are expecting. An approach sometimes used at LSE is the Introduction – Facts – Theory – Analysis – Conclusion, or 'IFTAC' framework. This is a systematic approach to case analysis, intended to encourage you to identify the key facts in the case, to identify relevant theory, to apply theory to the key facts as part of your critical analysis of the case, and to draw conclusions that answer the questions you have been set. More information about the IFTAC framework is set out below.

- Introduction. Provide some context. Think about why you have been set this particular case. What is the main question you are being asked to answer?
- Facts. What are the key facts? Summarise the main points – this part of the assignment is, in some ways, an old-fashioned exercise in comprehension. What story is the data telling? Be as concise as possible and make selective use of any of the quantitative (for example, financial) data that really stands out. Depending on the case, your summary

of the facts might be best structured chronologically, focusing on key events or thematical, focusing on the key themes which are apparent in the written case.

- Theory. What is the theoretical framework for your analysis? What are the main theories that are relevant to your analysis of the data? Again, be selective and concise. This is not an opportunity for you to write at length about a particular theory, or to provide blanket coverage of all the theories that you think might be tangentially relevant to the case. It is a chance to think hard about the key theory or theories that are the main tools in your critical analysis.
- Analysis. This is the engine room of your assignment. By applying your theoretical framework to the data you have summarised at the start, how do you explain the data – what is going on?
- Conclusion. Make sure you have answered the specific question or questions asked in the case. What is the main takeaway? Also remember the importance of reaching balanced conclusions. The facts in a case study provide evidence, not a proof. Your conclusions are probabilistic ('more likely than not', 'likely', 'very likely') rather than absolutely certain. It is unwise to generalise from a single case – the fact that a particular outcome has resulted in a particular set of circumstances does not mean that, given the same circumstances in another case, the same outcome will inevitably occur. 'Business is the art of making irrevocable decisions based on incomplete information' – is also about taking risks on a timely basis after weighing the best available evidence.

Most of all, make your case write-up interesting. Tell the story of the case in a way that becomes an 'analytical narrative', an intelligent study demonstrating your academic credentials, not mere tabloid journalism.

Mostly for instructors...

Different cases for different purposes

The versatility of case studies is demonstrated by how some of our contributors have used them in their courses. For example, the Maxwell case has proven particularly valuable in a Masters in Management course to teach students about corporate governance. Students worked in groups over a three-week period investigating corporate governance in public companies and the lessons learned from Maxwell, the governance of occupational pension funds in the post-Maxwell period as well as the role of non-executive directors and auditors in business. Similarly, the Lucas Industries and GKN case was used to teach the classic tools of business strategy, such as strategic positioning and the resource-based view, within the context of Britain's industrial decline in the 1980s–1990s.

Cases are also great tools to assess students' learning. The Royal Bank of Scotland case, for example, was designed as the basis of a 3500-word summative assignment for postgraduate Masters in Management students at the conclusion of a course on business ethics, corporate governance and ethical leadership. The Carillion and the 'Alliance Trust and Elliott International' cases have been successfully used for both formative and summative assessments at the postgraduate level, typically through 2000-word analytical assignments. Their complexity and scope make them equally suitable for MBA courses and third-year undergraduate management courses.

Teaching at the advent of generative artificial intelligence (GenAI)

Case studies are particularly well-suited to learning and assessment of learning in the era of AI. The management theorist W. Edwards Deming once said that the key to providing a good solution is to ensure that you ask the right questions – or was it Plato, or Einstein, or Carl Jung or somebody else that said this? Either way, the key insight is that, when presented with a vast amount of information – some of which is relevant, and some not – writing a good case analysis requires the analyst to craft the right questions to ask, as well as the ability to process and summarise the data. GenAI tools such as ChatGPT or Copilot are becoming better and better at processing information and answering even critical questions.

However, GenAI is not as well adapted to the messy world of business cases when it is necessary to work out what the right questions are in the first place. The skills that students develop and cannot yet effectively 'outsource' to GenAI tools are those that require thinking, emotional intelligence, self-reflection and going beyond the mere facts. To successfully analyse and draw useful insights from case analysis, students need to explore the human side of situations, such as the understanding of political motivations, stakeholder dynamics, ethical dilemmas, power relations within organisations, the nature of change and how people go through it.

Even though most students are already using GenAI tools in their learning and assessments,[5] we believe that cases still provide a useful laboratory for developing managerial skills in the classroom. While reliance on GenAI tools among students may be helpful for reducing the effort required to get through long readings, relying on chatbots without proper guidance can lead students to miss developing essential critical thinking and problem-solving skills.[6] Students may accept chatbots' responses unquestioningly, mistaking authoritative tones for factual accuracy and failing to use their own common sense and hence miss important human dynamics.[7]

Sandy set the Royal Bank of Scotland (RBS) case study as his final assignment for second-year Masters in Management students before retiring from full-time teaching. The task was: 'To write an extended case analysis of the Royal Bank of Scotland case, making particular use of theories and concepts which have been covered in the course.' After marking 80 3500-word case analyses, he decided to set ChatGPT the same task. But first he had to formulate a question: 'Why did Royal Bank of Scotland fail?' ChatGPT's answer was concise, well structured and well written. It covered much of the ground that many of the students did and would have warranted a pass grade. However, it ignored certain important issues, especially business ethics. It was under-referenced, made up some of the references it did cite, and – most importantly – lacked a critical perspective. At least two-thirds of the student cohort wrote better assignments.

Indeed, the use of GenAI in university courses can be both exciting and daunting for course convenors as well as students. The potential for time-saving and increased efficiency is attractive, but we should not underestimate the impact it has on teaching and learning. Similarly to how business leaders grapple with managing and adapting to change in their jobs, the integration of GenAI in classrooms is a change journey for all as well. AI-enabled technologies have an accelerated impact on students' learning experiences, the overall dynamics of higher education teaching, and the outcomes of case discussions, regardless of whether educators openly and actively embrace or approve them, or whether students rely on them without their professors' awareness.[8]

Future employees in professional jobs will rely on skills that cannot efficiently be substituted by machines. Case studies, if used as intended – with or without the help of GenAI tools – provide excellent opportunities to develop problem-solving, emotional intelligence, as well as political and negotiation skills. We believe that GenAI tools, if used with purpose – instead of 'mindlessly' to substitute learning – can effectively enhance and augment students' skills and boost their creativity, leaving them more time for critical thinking and the evaluation of human dynamics.[9]

What are the key lessons for us from this?

The ability to identify the most important issues that are embedded in all the noisy details of a good business case, and then to frame the right questions to ask, are the key skills students need to learn. It is this ability to think critically which is important.

For the instructor this means carefully constructing the assignment instructions and being prepared to re-evaluate their assessments or re-explore students' learning process. In the cases contained in this book you will find some illustrative questions which are designed to help give some general guidance, but are not intended to be exhaustive. You can decide whether, and how, you want to use these questions. But do think about encouraging students to work out what the case is all about by formulating key questions themselves, perhaps as a preliminary assignment before the main event.

Teaching notes

Teaching notes are available to bona fide educators from a number of the individual case writers. You will find further details at the beginning of each chapter. Please make any requests by email from a work email address containing a link to an academic website confirming your status as a bona fide educator. The teaching notes are not written to a prescribed format and are typically the notes that the case writer wrote for themselves prior to teaching the case. Please do use them responsibly – it would defeat the object of the exercise if they were to be circulated widely among students.

References

[1] See Warsh, D. (2006) *Knowledge and the Wealth of Nations – A Story of Economic Discovery*. New York: W.W. Norton & Company.

[2] See Augier, M., and March, J. (2011) *The Roots, Rituals, and Rhetorics of Change – North American Business Schools After the Second World War*. Stanford, CA: Stanford University Press.

[3] Snow expanded upon the lecture in his book entitled *The Two Cultures and the Scientific Revolution*, published by Cambridge University Press in 1959 and illustrated it in his sequence of novels *Stranger and Brothers*.

[4] Shi, Yuwei and Dow, Sandra (2019) 'International business education at the interface: the raw case study method', *Journal of Teaching in International Business*, vol. 30, no. 3, pp. 246–268. https://doi.org/10.1080/08975930.2019.1698392

[5] Sallai, Dorottya (2024) 'Assessment and curriculum design can't ignore how students use AI', *Management with Impact Blog*, 9 August. LSE's Management Department. https://blogs.lse.ac.uk/management/2024/08/09/assessment-and-curriculum-design-cant-ignore-how-students-use-ai/

[6] Sallai, Dorottya (2024) 'Assessment and curriculum design can't ignore how students use AI', *Times Higher Education*, 23 July. https://www.timeshighereducation.com/blog/assessment-and-curriculum-design-cant-ignore-how-students-use-ai

[7] Sallai, Dorottya, Cardoso Silva, Jonathan and Barreto, Marcos (2024) 'Approach Generative AI Tools Proactively or Risk Bypassing the Learning Process in Higher Education'. http://dx.doi.org/10.2139/ssrn.4886015

8 Sallai, Dorottya, Gyger, Annina C, Francisco, Julio Ignacio Benitez, Chaudhuri, Arundhati, Benghan, Solomon, Farley, Meagan, Nwokedi, Ada Onyinye and Singh, Rashmi (2024) 'Embracing GenAI in Higher Education: A Change Journey Through the Eyes of Educators and Students', *Management with Impact Blog*, 1 August. LSE's Management Department. https://blogs.lse.ac.uk/management/2024/08/01/embracing-genai-in-higher-ed-an-emotional-journey-through-the-eyes-of-educators-and-students/

9 Sallai, Dorottya (2024) 'A Human-Centred Approach to AI Transformation', *Management with Impact Blog*, 9 May. LSE's Management Department. https://blogs.lse.ac.uk/management/2024/05/09/a-human-centred-approach-to-ai-transformation/

Part 2
Strategy and general management

2. Corporate strategy in the UK vehicle components industry: a comparison of Lucas Industries and GKN

Sir Geoffrey Owen

The stories of how Lucas Industries and GKN responded to the changing economic environment during the years of industrial decline in
the UK is one of the classic cases of business strategy. Lucas Industries
and GKN, manufacturers of automotive and aerospace industry components, were, in their heyday, two of the UK's largest listed industrial
companies. Yet, while GKN managed successfully to negotiate the
rapidly changing economic and industrial scene of the 1980s–1990s,
Lucas Industries struggled to adapt and was eventually forced to
merge with the North American Varity Corporation, in what many
commentators regarded as effectively a takeover.

This classic comparative case study is an opportunity to apply key
concepts from the positioning and resource-based views of business
strategy in developing a case analysis.

Guidance on how to write a case analysis can be found in Chapter 1,
'Business cases: what are they, why do we use them and how should
you go about doing a case analysis?'.

Introduction

In 1980, Lucas Industries and GKN were two of the biggest manufacturers
of vehicle components in the UK. Although both companies had other businesses, vehicle components represented the largest part of their turnover
– about 80 per cent in the case of Lucas, 50 per cent for GKN. Both companies, especially Lucas, were also substantially reliant on UK-based vehicle
assemblers, principally British Leyland, Ford and General Motors (Vauxhall).
During the 1970s this had become an increasingly precarious customer base,
following the near-collapse of British Leyland in 1974 and the decision by the

---

How to cite this book chapter:

Owen, Geoffrey (2025) 'Corporate strategy in the UK vehicle components industry: a
comparison of Lucas Industries and GKN', in: Sallai, Dorottya and Pepper, Alexander (ed) *Navigating the 21st Century Business World: Case Studies in Management*, London: LSE Press, pp. 17–38. https://doi.org/10.31389/lsepress.nbw.b

two American-owned assemblers to concentrate most of their new invest-ment in continental Europe.

Thus, Lucas and GKN were faced at the start of the 1980s with two strategic issues. One was how to strengthen their position in the world vehicle components industry, which was then in the early stages of a shift from a nationally based structure (national component makers supplying national vehicle assemblers) to global sourcing. The world's leading car and truck manufacturers were beginning to restrict their component purchases to suppliers that were capable of meeting their needs throughout the world, and to delegate to them a larger responsibility for complete systems or subsystems, rather than discrete components.

To keep pace with these developments, Lucas and GKN needed to ensure that their products were competitive in cost, quality and technology, and to establish manufacturing facilities in the world's major vehicle-producing regions – continental Europe, North America and the Far East – whether through direct investment, acquisitions, joint ventures or licensing arrange-ments.

The second strategic issue was to decide whether, and, if so, to what extent, they should build up non-automotive businesses to offset their dependence on the motor industry. If they chose to diversify, should they focus on activi-ties which had some sort of 'synergy' with vehicle components, or should they go for entirely different industries?

Resolving these issues became more pressing as a result of the severe UK recession of 1980–1981, when both GKN and Lucas made losses (Table 2.1) and their survival as independent companies looked in doubt. The two com-panies dealt with their problems in different ways, and the outcome at the end of the 1990s was that Lucas had disappeared as an independent company (although several of its businesses survived under different ownership), while GKN seemed well placed to maintain its position both in vehicle components and in the other sector – aerospace – into which it had diversified.

This section describes the strategic decisions taken by the two companies during the 1980s and 1990s, and considers the implications of their experi-ence for theories of strategy. A chronology of the main events is set out in the Exhibits section.

Table 2.1: Pre-tax profits at Lucas Industries and GKN 1979–1995 (figures in £m)

Lucas			GKN		
	£m			£m	
1979–80	41		1979	126	
1980–81	(21)	loss	1980	(1.2)	loss
1981–82	20		1981	35	
1982–83	2		1982	41	
1983–84	33		1983	88	
1984–85	58		1984	120	
1985–86	95		1985	133	
1986–87	115		1986	132	
1987–88	146		1987	147	
1988–89	187		1988	178	
1989–90	191		1989	215	
1990–91	84		1990	172	
1991–92	23		1991	95	
1992–93	50		1992	122	
1993–94	(130)	loss	1993	98	
1994–95	30		1994	200	
1995–96	180	*	1995	322	

* In 1996 Lucas merged with Varity of the US to become LucasVarity
Source: Company annual reports

Lucas Industries

Origins and early growth

The original Lucas business was founded in Birmingham in 1872 by Joseph Lucas, an apprenticed silversmith, to make pressed metal goods, including ship, coach and carriage lamps; he later became a leading supplier of lamps and other components to the bicycle industry. The company went public in 1897, but the Lucas family continued to play a large role in the management. The founder's son, Harry, was chair from 1902 to 1918, and his grandson, Oliver, served as joint managing director and deputy chair in the inter-war years.[1]

With the growth of car production after the turn of the 20th century, Lucas turned its attention to vehicle components, and established a close relationship with some of the emerging car manufacturers, notably William Morris in Oxford. In addition to lighting, the company made a wide range of other mechanical and electrical components. The range was extended at the start of the First World War to include magnetos (a type of electrical generator). Supplies of this device, an essential component both for motor vehicles and for aircraft, had hitherto come almost entirely from a German company, Robert Bosch, whose founder had invented the magneto in 1886; the British government urgently needed a domestic supplier for military purposes. Lucas took over Thomson-Bennett, a small Birmingham firm which made a copy of the original Bosch magneto and transferred production to its main factory at Great King Street in Birmingham. This transaction also gave Lucas a foothold in the aircraft industry, which became an important customer during the war.

The inter-war years saw considerable growth in UK car and truck production, as well as an increase in the number of electrically operated components, including electric starters, electric horns and electric windscreen wipers. The vehicle assemblers bought most of their components from outside suppliers, and Lucas became the leading manufacturer in its field. This was achieved partly by buying out its competitors. In the mid-1920s Lucas acquired its two main rivals in electrical components, C.A. Vandervell (later CAV) and Rotax, and by the end of the decade it had a virtual monopoly in starting, lighting and ignition equipment.[2]

Lucas also protected its position in the UK through market-sharing agreements with its overseas counterparts. In the case of Bosch, a wide-ranging agreement was concluded in 1931, which barred Bosch from selling electrical equipment in Britain and British Overseas Territories, while Lucas stayed out of Germany. This arrangement provided for the creation of a jointly owned company, CAV-Bosch, to make diesel engine fuel injection equipment to Bosch's design. This was a time when manufacturers of commercial vehicles and farm tractors were beginning to switch from petrol to diesel engines, and CAV was to become one of the world leaders in this field. Lucas bought out Bosch's interest in the joint company in 1937 and acquired full control on the outbreak of the Second World War.

A similar agreement was made with Auto-Lite, one of the leading American suppliers of electrical components (later acquired by Ford). This involved the supply of technical know-how to Lucas as well as an agreement to stay out of each other's territory. Lucas had a close link with another American company, Bendix, which made brakes as well as electrical equipment. Lucas made Bendix starters under licence, and in 1932 it bought a majority stake in Bendix's UK brake factory. This side of Lucas' business was enlarged 10 years later with the acquisition of Girling, a leading British-owned brake manufacturer.

Much of Lucas' technology came from its foreign partners. Its forte was production engineering, not innovation. According to one account, Lucas 'copied the designs of others, principally American, German and sometimes French competition, most often under licence, but sometimes by skilful adaptation in a way that made the design amenable to large batch, flow-line production methods.'[3] Lucas' senior executives, notably Oliver Lucas, were enthusiastic admirers of US management, and used an American consulting firm, Bedaux, to reorganise the Great King Street factory in the 1930s.

The Second World War, like the first, brought a big expansion of Lucas' business, especially in aircraft components. Some of the company's standard automotive products were adapted for military use, and Lucas made a variety of other war-related equipment, including gun turrets, aircraft wing sections, fuses and bombs. Rotax, now focused almost entirely on the aircraft industry, made magnetos for Rolls-Royce Merlin engines, the start of a long association with the leading British aero-engine builder.

Post-war prosperity

At the end of the Second World War, Lucas had some 40,000 employees and was one of the largest engineering groups in Britain. With the death of Oliver Lucas in 1948, the founding family was no longer directly involved in the management, but the family tradition lived on in a paternalistic approach to employees. Bertram Waring, chair from 1951 to 1969, was steeped in the Lucas culture. He had joined the company as an accountant in 1922 and later served as personal assistant to Oliver Lucas.

For the first 20 years after the war, Lucas enjoyed steady growth in sales and profits. There were no new entrants to disturb its monopoly, and, although most of the pre-war cartels had been dissolved, informal market-sharing arrangements tended to preserve national markets for national suppliers.

The heart of the business was the Lucas Electrical Company, accounting for some 75 per cent of the UK market for automotive electrical components. This subsidiary saw some important technical changes, including the replacement of the dynamo by the alternator, and, in the 1960s, the introduction of electronics into ignition systems and other products. Lucas, now committing more resources to research and development (a central laboratory was set up in 1957), was one of the first British companies to make a sizeable commitment to semiconductors and integrated circuits.

CAV, making diesel fuel injection equipment, continued to benefit from the shift from petrol to diesel by the commercial vehicle manufacturers, and the scale of production increased considerably after the war. One of the biggest investments was a new factory at Sudbury, Suffolk, to make fuel injectors. Described as 'unsurpassed in the world for making small, very high-precision components', this plant was producing some 450,000 injectors a month by the mid-1970s, and exporting 70 per cent of its output.[4] As before the war, acquisitions played a part in the growth of this business. Lucas bought Bryce Berger from Hawker Siddeley in 1960, and eight years later acquired Simms, its last remaining competitor in diesel fuel injection equipment. The takeover was partly prompted by the fear that Simms might have been sold to Bosch.

The other big automotive subsidiary, Girling, strengthened its position in the UK with the development of disc brakes, and began to win business elsewhere in Europe. A factory was built at Koblenz, Germany, in 1961 to supply Ford and Daimler-Benz, despite strenuous opposition from Teves, the leading German brake manufacturer. A few years later a similar facility was built in France to supply Peugeot.

The aircraft components business, dependent on the unpredictable demands of the UK Ministry of Defence, was more volatile. The cancellation of the TSR-2 in 1965 and the bankruptcy of Rolls-Royce in 1971 forced Lucas to make sizeable write-offs and redundancies. Yet it continued to add to its interests in this field, and Lucas was seen by the Labour government of 1964–1969 as a suitable rationaliser of a fragmented sector; with the help of a £3m loan from the Industrial Reorganisation Corporation, it bought English Electric's aircraft component businesses. However, in the mid-1970s, Lucas Aerospace, as the division was now called, was making a negligible contribution to profits (Table 2.2).

Table 2.2: Lucas Industries in 1975: divisions' sales and surplus

	Sales (£m)	Trading surplus (£m)
Vehicle components	455	35
Aircraft equipment	71	0.9
Industrial products	43	2.5

Source: Lucas 1975 annual report

The 1970s slowdown

In 1972 Lucas was judged by the French business magazine, *L'Expansion*, to be the most dynamic company in Europe, as measured by growth in sales and profits. But the business outlook in the UK was darkening. The principal worry was the poor performance of the British motor industry. British Leyland, one of Lucas' biggest customers, was in the throes of what turned out to be a terminal decline – it was saved from bankruptcy by the government in 1974 – and car production in the UK was stagnating. Output reached a peak of 1.9m vehicles in 1972, only marginally higher than 10 years earlier; over the same period French production had doubled, from 1.4m to 2.9m, while German production had risen from 2.7m to 3.6m units. Car imports were rising rapidly, and international component suppliers, both European and Japanese, were setting up plants in the UK. It was clear that Lucas had to make itself less dependent on the domestic market.

Like most British engineering firms, Lucas had traditionally derived the bulk of its business from the UK and the Empire. However, the growth of car production in Europe during the 1950s, together with the formation of the Common Market at the end of the decade, prompted moves to establish a European presence. Waring set up a committee at the end of the 1950s to study the European market, and this led to a joint venture in France to make fuel injection equipment, followed by the Girling factories in Germany and France. However, the internationalisation of Lucas Electrical, the largest part of the group, was more problematic.

Lucas had a long-standing association with Ducellier, the leading French supplier of electrical components, which was partly controlled by Bendix. This arrangement was extended in 1962 when Lucas bought a 40 per cent stake in the French company. Bernard Scott, who became chair of Lucas in 1974, was keen to go further, and in 1977 the Lucas shareholding in Ducellier was increased to 49 per cent. Scott then opened negotiations with Bendix to acquire the remaining 51 per cent.

The idea was that a Lucas-Ducellier combination could be the nucleus for a powerful European electrical components group (which might include other firms, such as Marelli in Italy, at a later stage), and act as a counterweight to Bosch. Unexpectedly, this plan ran into opposition from the French government, which wanted a greater degree of national ownership in the vehicle components sector. Bendix was persuaded to sell its Ducellier shares to a French component manufacturer, Societe Francaise du Ferodo (SFF), which later became part of the Valeo group. The new shareholding structure was Lucas with 50 per cent and SFF with 48 per cent, with 2 per cent held by a French bank.

In the US, Lucas had some export business in the early 1970s, but no manufacturing operations. The first move towards a stronger US presence came in 1977, when it opened a plant in South Carolina to make fuel injection equipment for diesel engines. This was to serve the needs of a large British customer, Perkins Engines, which had started to manufacture diesel engines in the US. However, a bigger opportunity for fuel injection equipment soon materialised. This was a time of growing concern in the US about fuel economy, and some companies, notably General Motors (GM), believed that diesel-powered cars would take an increasing share of the market. In 1977 the American company began talking to Lucas about a device known as a microjector, a fuel injection device for diesel cars which Lucas had developed some years earlier. This led to a firm order, and the indications were that GM would need 1.36m microinjectors a year for five years from 1979. The South Carolina plant was expanded to meet this demand.

Thus, by the end of the 1970s an international strategy for vehicle components was beginning to take shape, but Lucas was still dependent on the UK both as a manufacturing base and as a market. The fragility of this situation was exposed by the recession of the early 1980s. Pre-tax profits, which had reached a peak of £77m in 1976–1977, fell to £41m in the following year, and 1980–1981 saw the first loss in the company's history.

The 1980s shock

The recession coincided with a change of management at the top. Godfrey Messervy took over as chair and chief executive from Bernard Scott in 1980. The new chair, like Scott, had spent his entire career with Lucas, and he stood for continuity rather than radical change. He delegated a good deal of authority to two joint managing directors, Tony Gill and Jeffrey Wilkinson, who were given responsibility for different parts of the business – Gill for Girling, CAV and Aerospace, Wilkinson for Lucas Electrical and its associated subsidiaries, Lucas World Service and the industrial division. This division of roles was to cause a good deal of friction.

The immediate response to the crisis was a drastic programme of cost reduction in the UK factories, coupled with renewed efforts to build up sales in Europe and the US. Looking further ahead, the plan was to develop a new source of profit in what was called the Industrial Products division – a collection of industrial businesses which had come into the group through acquisition and were seen as a 'third leg', diluting Lucas' dependence on the automotive and aircraft industries. The goal was to reduce the proportion of sales coming from automotive components to no more than 60 per cent, with aerospace and industrial products each providing 20 per cent of the total.

The biggest loss-maker in the early 1980s was Lucas Electrical, which was more dependent on the UK than either CAV or Girling; less than 10 per cent of its production was exported. Several factories within this division were closed between 1980 and 1983, but the UK operations continued to make heavy losses. This increased the urgency of doing a deal with the French over Ducellier; the hope was that an integrated Lucas-Ducellier company would not only cement Lucas' links with the French motor industry, but also permit rationalisation between the French and British plants. However, the French authorities continued to obstruct any deal that gave Lucas majority control. In 1983, an outline agreement was reached whereby Ducellier would be divided between Lucas and Valeo, the former taking electronics, lighting and ignition, while the latter took starters and alternators. Lucas planned to build on this with other acquisitions and alliances. However, the agreement was never finalised. In 1984, Lucas disposed of its stake in Ducellier, acquiring in return a small shareholding in Valeo which was later sold.

As the Ducellier negotiations stalled, Messervy and Wilkinson looked for other ways of strengthening Lucas Electrical. This led to the decision to acquire control of the electrical instrumentation business of Smiths Industries. Smiths, originally a clock and watch manufacturer which had diversified into vehicle instruments before the war, had decided to opt out of this business. It had seen the need for heavy investment to acquire the electronics expertise which it lacked, and the deal with Lucas was a convenient exit route. For Lucas, the case for the deal was much more questionable. Messervy justified it on the grounds that the combined group would offer a complete range of electronic control systems and cut out duplication in research and product development.[5] However, the effect was to make Lucas Electrical even more dependent on the UK.

Overseas, Lucas' fortunes in the early 1980s were mixed. Girling scored a notable success when it secured a contract from Ford in the US; a brake factory was set up in Cincinnati in 1982 to supply the American company. However, this was offset by a setback on the diesel injection side. By the end of 1981 it was clear that GM's projections for diesel-powered cars in the US had been too optimistic; there were also technical problems in converting the engine of one of its models, the Oldsmobile, from petrol to diesel. Orders from Lucas were sharply reduced, to the point where the South Carolina plant was no longer viable.

Meanwhile, in the UK the cost-cutting continued – employment in the UK fell by a third, from 70,000 to 47,000, between 1979 and 1983 – but, with the UK economy improving, Lucas gradually regained some financial flexibility. In 1985 it launched a £89m rights issue, the purpose of which was to finance acquisitions in the aerospace and industrial divisions. Lucas also took advantage of the surplus in its pension fund to take a pensions' 'holiday', suspending contributions to their pension scheme for two years. Pre-tax profits rose to £95m in 1985–1986, surpassing the previous peak in 1977.

Yet the underlying problems had not been solved. Lucas still had too many businesses, especially within Lucas Electrical, that were not internationally competitive. The aerospace division was too dependent on the UK, and on Rolls-Royce in particular; and diversification through what was now called Lucas Industrial Systems had been half-hearted and lacking in direction.

By this time, the leading figure in the company was Tony Gill, who became sole managing director in 1984 (Wilkinson had resigned after the collapse of the Ducellier negotiations). He succeeded Messervy as chair three years later. Gill was an engineer who had come into the group through the Bryce Berger acquisition in 1960, and, prior to his appointment as joint managing director, had been in charge of CAV.

1986–1996: the search for a defensible position

A more forceful personality than his predecessor, Gill saw that productivity in the UK was still too low, particularly in relation to the Japanese factories, which were now seen as the benchmark. An early decision was to introduce what were called 'Competitiveness Achievement Plans', measuring each plant against its best competitors and setting a clear timetable within which improvements were to be implemented. The programme was led by John Parnaby, an engineering academic who was hired in 1983 to be group director of manufacturing technology. Parnaby was well informed about Japanese manufacturing methods and sought to spread them around the group.

Gill also took a more radical line in streamlining the product portfolio. The termination of the Ducellier negotiations had removed any remaining chance that Lucas could be a major force in the European electrical equipment market. Apart from electronics-based systems, Gill regarded most of the old Lucas Electrical as low-technology, commodity-type business which Lucas should get out of. In the second half of the 1980s several of these operations, including lighting, starters and batteries, were closed down, put into joint ventures or sold. Among the divestments were most of the instruments companies that had been bought from Smiths Industries in 1983.

The strongest of the automotive businesses were Girling and CAV, but even here there were some problems. Although Girling had a strong worldwide position in disc brakes, it had missed out on the trend towards fully electronic anti-lock brakes. It had developed its own electro-mechanical anti-lock braking system (ABS), which for a while looked the most likely contender for mass-produced cars, but the take-up of fully electronic systems came quicker than Girling had expected. By the end of the decade its main international competitors – Bosch, Teves and Bendix – were well ahead in ABS.

Meanwhile, Gill was determined to build up the non-automotive divisions, and this was the stated purpose of the £163m rights issue launched in 1988. In aerospace the aim was to reduce the group's dependence on Rolls-Royce by building a larger business in the US, principally through acquisition; some $300m was spent on buying American companies between 1985 and 1990. Ambitious targets were also set for the industrial division, now known as Lucas Applied Technology. The main focus was on measurement and control systems, but there was some uncertainty as to whether the role of this division was to be a completely separate profit centre or a provider of technology and other support to the automotive and aerospace businesses. There was also concern towards the end of the decade about whether the division's acquisition programme, mainly involving small and medium-sized companies, was absorbing money and management time that could be better used in Lucas' core activities.

Thus, at the start of the 1990s the strategic problems which had faced Lucas 10 years earlier had been only partially resolved. Automotive now accounted for only 59 per cent of total sales against 72 per cent in 1981, and the proportion of sales made in the UK had come down from 46 per cent to 32 per cent (Table 2.3). But there were still weaknesses on the automotive side, and, while the aerospace division was now more strongly placed, the return on the acquisitions that had been made in Applied Technology had been poor.

Hence Lucas was not well placed to withstand what turned out to be an exceptionally severe recession in the early 1990s; operating profits in vehicle components fell by more than half between 1990 and 1991. In September 1992, the share price fell to its lowest level for seven years, valuing the group at some £550m, less than half its pre-recession peak. To make matters worse, there was uncertainty over the succession to Gill; a new group managing director, Tony Edwards, who had been running the aerospace division, was appointed in February 1992, but he lost the confidence of the board and left the company eight months later.

Table 2.3: Lucas sales in 1981 and 1991 (per cent of total sales)

By destination	1981	1991
UK	46	32
Rest of Europe	29	38
North America	6	21
Rest of world	19	9

By sector	1981	1991
Automotive	72	59
Aerospace	19	30
Applied Technology	9	11

Source: Lucas 1992 Annual Report

Some of the non-executive directors believed that the right way forward for Lucas was to make a transforming acquisition which would radically alter the balance of the group, making it less dependent on automotive and aerospace. Several possible candidates were identified, including a large American manufacturer of process control equipment, a field in which Lucas already had some experience. Such a deal might also have solved the succession problem, since the chief executive of the target company seemed well qualified to take over as chief executive from Gill. However, the proposal was turned down by the board early in 1993.

The succession issue was eventually resolved by the appointment as chief executive of George Simpson, a well-regarded manager who was widely credited with reviving the Rover car company over the previous decade. He took up his post in April 1994 and Sir Brian Pearse, formerly head of Midland Bank, was brought in as non-executive chair.

Within a few months of his arrival, Simpson concluded that Lucas needed to go further and faster in focusing on its core activities, and in disposing of underperforming businesses. Several divestments and closures took place, the effect of which was to incur exceptional costs of over £200m in the 1993–1994 financial year. Most of these costs related to acquisitions that had been made over the previous five years. In 1995, the Applied Technology division was disbanded, with its residual operations transferred to other parts of the group. In that year the automotive content of group sales had gone back up to 75 per cent, and its share of profits was even higher.

By this time the recession was easing, but Simpson still had doubts as to whether Lucas could make it on its own. In his view, the world vehicle components industry would soon be consolidated in the hands of a small number of 'super-integrators', serving vehicle manufacturers worldwide. These companies would either be broad integrators capable of providing a range of systems, such as Delphi in the US, Bosch in Europe and Nippondenso in Japan, or more specialised firms offering individual subsystems, such as Valeo in France. One option for Lucas was to join forces with one of the bigger groups. Another was to merge with, or acquire, a components company of comparable size.

While these options were being debated, the company was faced with an unexpected problem – that of the succession to George Simpson. Within a few months of his arrival at Lucas, Simpson had been approached by GEC (General Electric Company) as a possible successor to Lord Weinstock as managing director of that company; by the start of 1995 he had decided to accept the offer. The choice of successor then became a matter of urgency, and it was resolved in an unconventional way. This was a merger with Varity, a US-based engineering group whose businesses included Kelsey-Hayes, a leading US brake manufacturer.

Lucas had considered making an offer for Kelsey-Hayes when it had been put on the market some years earlier – it would have been a good fit with Girling – but had felt unable to match the price paid by Varity. Now a full-scale merger with Varity offered the prospect not only of strengthening Girling's position in the US, but also of solving the Lucas succession problem. The Varity chief executive, Victor Rice, was an obvious candidate to take over from Simpson and run the enlarged group.

The merger went through in May 1996. Rice became chief executive of the merged group, and most of the other key positions were filled by Varity executives. This led City commentators to complain that the deal had been a reverse takeover, not a merger, and that Varity had achieved this without paying a premium. The City was further upset in 1998, when Rice tried to shift the domicile of LucasVarity from the UK to the US; shareholders rejected this plan by a narrow majority.

In the following year, Victor Rice, apparently believing that the company was still not big enough, negotiated a merger between LucasVarity and another American components manufacturer, TRW. TRW subsequently sold the diesel injection business to Delphi, keeping brakes and electronic systems; the Lucas aerospace business was sold to Goodrich. Thus, although several of Lucas' businesses survived under different ownership, the original parent ceased to exist.

GKN

Origins and early development

In 1900, John Guest, whose family owned one of the largest iron and steel producers in South Wales, merged his business with a Birmingham manufacturer of nuts and bolts, controlled by Arthur Keen. Two years later the combined group joined forces with another Midlands company, Nettlefolds, which made screws and fasteners. The three-way merger which created Guest, Keen & Nettlefolds was an early example of vertical integration between steelmaking and steel-using industries, and the new group was one of Britain's largest industrial companies, employing some 12,500 workers.

GKN continued to expand by merger and takeover before and after the First World War. Two of the biggest acquisitions were F.W. Cotterill, a rival manufacturer of nuts and bolts which also owned Garringtons, a drop-forging business, and, in 1920, John Lysaght, which made sheet steel. The latter included Sankey, which made wheels, chassis frames and body pressings for the motor industry. This industry became an important customer for other GKN companies in the inter-war period, but at this stage GKN was predominantly a supplier of semi-finished materials – forgings, castings and pressings – rather than the proprietary components in which Lucas specialised.

The strategy of vertical integration and growth by acquisition continued after 1945. The acquisitions included a number of vehicle component companies, starting with BRD, a manufacturer of propeller shafts in 1956. At the time of this purchase British Motor Corporation (BMC) was developing the Mini, a revolutionary small car which incorporated a front-wheel-drive design, and it was looking for a new type of drive shaft which would transmit torque from the engine to the wheels. BRD competed for the order, but the preferred supplier was Hardy Spicer, a subsidiary of the Birfield group, whose patented technology in constant velocity joints (CVJs) fitted BMC's requirements. Birfield became the sole supplier of CVJs for the Mini and for BMC's subsequent front-wheel-drive cars.

In 1966, GKN acquired Birfield, and this proved to be a hugely significant move. In addition to its special position in CVJs, Birfield had a 39.5 per cent stake in Uni-Cardan, a German company which had similar technology and supplied components to Volkswagen and other continental assemblers. GKN had traditionally been geared to Commonwealth markets, and the Uni-Cardan stake provided a European dimension which other British vehicle component makers (including Lucas) lacked.

GKN bought other British vehicle components businesses during the 1960s, including Vandervell Products, a manufacturer of engine bearings, and it was also diversifying in other directions. It entered the plastics industry, for example, both as a processor of plastic materials and as a manufacturer of plastics machinery. However, the heart of GKN remained steelmaking, and its raison d'etre was vertical integration; in the mid-1960s it was using 2.5m tons of steel a year, 12.5 per cent of UK steel production. That strategic core, which had dominated GKN since its creation, was removed in 1967 when the Labour Government nationalised the steel industry, and GKN had to look in new directions.

For the first few years after nationalisation the redirection of GKN proceeded in a halting and uncertain manner. Several acquisitions were made, mostly of engineering companies loosely linked to GKN's existing activities.

The acquired firms were allowed to continue as independent businesses, and there was no attempt to weld them into an integrated group. Moreover, the company's senior managers, most of whom had spent their working lives in the company, continued to regard themselves as steelmakers. One of the old GKN mills, at Brymbo in Wales, was bought back from the nationalised British Steel Corporation in 1973, and a new rod mill was built at Cardiff.

By the mid-1970s GKN had become an engineering conglomerate, with over 100,000 employees spread around a large number of mostly unrelated businesses, all competing for resources and management time. A sharp fall in profits in the second half of the decade prompted a reappraisal of policy, in which 'new men', less emotionally committed to GKN's heritage, played an important part. An influential figure was Trevor Holdsworth, an accountant who had joined the group in 1963, having previously worked for Bowater, the papermaker. Holdsworth climbed up the GKN ladder on the finance side, before becoming deputy chair of the group in 1974; he was appointed managing director in 1977 and chair in 1980.

Holdsworth's view of GKN in the mid-1970s, as set out in a subsequent speech, was that the company represented 'the quintessence of the British problem: a manufacturer of mature engineering products, largely a sub-contractor, predominantly in Britain with a large commitment to the troubled and reducing British motor industry. Its international involvement was based upon following the flag round the Commonwealth. Although we had adopted all the then fashionable techniques of corporate planning and every year produced large volumes of divisional and group plans, we were drifting uncertainly into the future without a clear strategy.'[6]

Out of this rethinking came a four-point plan: not to be a steel company (though GKN might still make steel on a small scale to support downstream operations); to build up the automotive components business; to dilute the dependence on the automotive market, and on manufacturing in general, by investing in wholesale distribution; and to invest internationally.

The choice of vehicle components as the main avenue for growth was logical. Many of the world's vehicle manufacturers, responding to the growing demand for small, fuel-efficient cars after the first oil crisis, were switching to front-wheel-drive and GKN was well placed to supply a key component, the CVJ. At the end of the 1970s, Ford in the US decided to buy CVJs from an outside supplier rather than make them in-house. As it was not prepared to rely on CVJs imported from Europe, Ford encouraged GKN to build a plant in the US. Thanks to this contract, together with the expansion of Uni-Cardan in continental Europe, GKN by the end of the 1970s was on the way to becoming an international vehicle component supplier. Additional shares in Uni-Cardan were acquired during this period, giving GKN majority control.

GKN was looking for growth in other sectors of the vehicle component business during this period. In 1979, it bought Sheepbridge Engineering, and its piston business was put together with Vandervell to form GKN Engine Parts Division. GKN also tried to buy Sachs, a German company whose principal subsidiary, Fichtel and Sachs, was the leading German clutch manufacturer, but this was blocked by the German competition authorities.

The move into wholesale distribution was to be achieved largely by acquisition, and several companies were bought in the 1970s. In addition, GKN formed what proved to a profitable joint venture with Brambles, an Australian company which had built up a pallet-pooling operation in Australia. The partnership was called CHEP (the Commonwealth Handling Equipment Pool), and it was extended in 1981 to include Cleanaway, a waste management business.

Thus, by the end of the 1970s, GKN's situation was better than that of Lucas to the extent that its vehicle component business had become less dependent on the UK. However, it was still widely diversified, as a result of the unfocused acquisition policies of the preceding two decades. It had several 'heritage' businesses, such as nuts and bolts, which were either losing money or had little growth potential; the cartel arrangements which had protected these businesses in the past had broken down, and import competition was increasing. Moreover, apart from the joint venture with Brambles, most of the distribution businesses that had been acquired proved to be disappointing or worse. The group as a whole was not in good shape to withstand the recession of the early 1980s.

The Thatcher shock

As in the case of Lucas, the loss that GKN reported in the 1980–1981 financial year was a traumatic event and prompted a strenuous effort to cut costs; GKN's UK labour force dropped from 70,000 to less than 25,000 during the 1980s. However, the strategic redirection which took place in the first half of the decade was more comprehensive than at Lucas, and involved a sharper break with the past.

With Holdsworth and a few like-minded colleagues now firmly in charge – most of the 'old guard' had retired – drastic action was taken to clean up the portfolio. Many of the peripheral businesses, including the two original ones, nuts and bolts and fasteners, were sold and GKN rethought its approach to distribution. Holdsworth and his colleagues realised that what they had bought were mostly collections of small businesses, more suitable for ownership by an owner-entrepreneur than a big industrial group. A series of disposals left the Brambles joint venture as the main asset in what was now called the industrial services division, although the car aftermarket business was retained.

The 1980–1981 recession also underlined the urgency of getting out of steel. The first step came in 1981, when GKN's Cardiff-based wire and rod interests were pooled with those of the state-owned British Steel Corporation to form a separate company, Allied Steel and Wire; this company was later floated on the stock exchange. A similar deal, covering GKN's engineering steels, was agreed with British Steel in 1986; again, a new company was formed, United Engineering Steels (UES), with GKN retaining a minority interest.

Profits from vehicle components, especially Uni-Cardan, kept the group afloat in the early 1980s, and the prospects for the CVJ business looked good. However, Holdsworth believed that CVJs on their own were not enough to ensure GKN's survival in the vehicle components industry. To establish a broader base, GKN attempted in 1983 to enlarge its stake in engine components by making a takeover bid for AE (formerly Associated Engineering), the leading UK manufacturer of bearings, pistons and cylinder liners; the bid was blocked by the Monopolies Commission on competition grounds. Two years later, Holdsworth briefly pursued the idea of a merger with Lucas, but this did not find favour with the Lucas managers; they could see no benefit of linking their vehicle components business with what they saw as GKN's distinctly low-technology operations.

Arguably the failure to take over AE (and to merge with Lucas) was a fortunate outcome for GKN. The engine components sector was more competitive and more crowded than CVJs, and although the combination of GKN and AE would have yielded some scale economies, neither company was strong in continental Europe or the US. As it was, GKN was able to concentrate single-mindedly on CVJs, where it had a clear technical advantage. (GKN's engine components division was subsequently sold to another British components manufacturer, T & N.)

By the time of Holdsworth's retirement in 1988, GKN had been extensively reshaped and had made an impressive recovery since the slump in profits at the start of the decade. Although there was some tidying-up to be done – GKN still had a substantial stake in automotive parts distribution – the two main pillars of the group were now vehicle components (mainly CVJs) and industrial services (mainly the joint ventures with Brambles) (Table 2.4).

Table 2.4: GKN pre-tax profits by sector in 1987 (£m)

	£m
Automotive and defence	92
Industrial services	35
Automotive parts distribution	11
Related companies	38
Net interest	(29)
Total	147

1988–2002: specialisation plus opportunism

Holdsworth's successor as chair and chief executive was David Lees, who had previously been finance director. While the change at the top brought no immediate change in strategy, Lees believed that GKN had an opportunity to develop a profitable 'third leg', which would be complementary to its two existing businesses.

GKN had a long history as a supplier to the Ministry of Defence, most recently as the manufacturer (through Sankey) of a fighting vehicle, the FV432. In 1985 GKN won a contract to build a new armoured personnel carrier, the Warrior. Lees believed that defence contracting could be expanded to the point where it made roughly the same profit contribution as vehicle components and industrial services.[7] He thought that GKN, with its expertise in light armoured vehicles, could capitalise on the trend within NATO towards mobile equipment suitable for a 'rapid reaction' strategy. This led him to consider the helicopter industry as a suitable area for diversification.

In 1988, GKN acquired a 29.9 per cent equity stake in Westland, the British helicopter manufacturer. (The shares were acquired from Fiat and Hanson, both of which had bought the shares during the Westland crisis of 1986.) Westland had a technical partnership with Sikorsky, the American helicopter maker; its parent, United Technologies, held an 8 per cent stake in Westland.

Lees made it clear at the time of this purchase that his ultimate aim was to acquire majority control, and that the helicopter company formed part of his plan to make GKN a major defence contractor; he wanted a position in army weapons systems akin to that of British Aerospace in air systems and Vickers Shipbuilding and Engineering in ships and submarines.[8] In 1994, United Technologies decided to sell its stake, and GKN used this opportunity to make an offer for the whole of the company.

At the time of the takeover, Westland was one of three competing European helicopter manufacturers in a market which was not big enough to sustain more than two; the others were Eurocopter (a partnership between Aerospatiale of France and MBB of Germany, and now part of EADS [European Aeronautic Defence and Space Company]) and Agusta of Italy. A logical step, since GKN and Agusta were already collaborating on a major European project, the EH101 military helicopter, was for these two companies to join forces. An agreement was reached to create a new company, AgustaWestland, which would be owned on 50-50 basis.

One of the attractions of Westland to GKN was that, in addition to helicopters, it had a separate business making aerospace structures and components for airframes and aero-engines. Following a trend which was already under way in the motor industry, the big aircraft manufacturers were beginning to delegate more responsibility to their suppliers, and Lees saw this as an opportunity for GKN to establish itself as a 'tier one' aerospace component supplier. An important step in this direction came in 2000, when GKN announced the acquisition of the fabrication operations of Boeing's Military Aircraft and Missile Systems Group.

Thus, by 2001 GKN's 'third leg' was substantially larger than it had been 10 years earlier, and different in composition. The armoured vehicles business was sold in 1998 to Alvis, another UK company which specialised in tanks and armoured personnel carriers; in return GKN obtained a 29.9 per cent stake in Alvis. In 2001 GKN's aerospace division – consisting of aerospace services (structures, components and design services for aircraft and aero-engine manufacturers) and the joint venture with Agusta – reported an operating profit of £119m on sales of £1.5bn; this compared with profits of £187m in the automotive division, on sales of £2.8bn.

GKN continued to expand in CVJs, helped by the increasing popularity of four-wheel-drive vehicles which also relied on this component. Although this business was no longer protected by patents, GKN had a first-mover advantage which made it difficult for other component makers to catch up, and most of the vehicle assemblers, although they had the technical capacity to make CVJs in-house, were content to buy from GKN because of its advantages in scale, cost and technology. By the end of the 1990s GKN's share of the world CVJ market was just under 40 per cent.

There was still some debate within GKN as to whether the group should diversify into other parts of the vehicle components industry. One possibility was to merge with T & N, which had acquired AE in 1988 and had become a major world player in engine components. However, T & N had heavy financial liabilities arising from its previous involvement with asbestos, and this was a deterrent to any potential acquirer. Thus, GKN decided to concentrate on CVJs and on closely related products.

Its only major diversification within vehicle components, but outside CVJs, was in powder metallurgy, a process for making lightweight components more economically than could be achieved through conventional forging and machining methods. This was a fragmented sector, and GKN believed that through acquisitions and organic growth it could become the dominant player. GKN made two large acquisitions in the US, and by 2001 sales by the Powder Metallurgy division had reached some £600m – still small compared to the Automotive Driveline division (£1.8bn), but growing fast.

As for industrial services, growth continued in the 1980s, and at the end of the decade the important decision was taken to establish CHEP into the US. When it did so, there was no national pallet pool in existence, and a substantial investment was necessary to build a nationwide presence. By the end of 1992, CHEP USA had a pool of over 2m pallets operating from four regional centres and supported by a national network of over 130 depots.

David Lees remained chair and chief executive of GKN until 1997; in that year he became non-executive chair and was succeeded as chief executive by C.K. Chow. Under Lees' leadership GKN had concentrated on three areas – vehicle components, industrial services and aerospace (Table 2.5).

Table 2.5: GKN sales by business in 1997 (£m)

	£m
Automotive	2049
Industrial services	430
Aerospace and special vehicles	904

The final withdrawal from steelmaking had taken place in 1995, when GKN's stake in United Engineering Steels was sold to British Steel. In the same year, the sale of the US automotive aftermarket distribution business was announced. Lees described these transactions as the last in a series of divestments of strategically peripheral businesses, leaving GKN fully focused on its core activities. The cash raised by the divestments, he said, would not be used for diversification. 'The business strategy is to go deeper, not wider, and therefore the plan is to use the cash for bolt-on acquisitions rather than to expand into new businesses.'[9]

Over the next few years an important change took place in GKN's portfolio. The relationship between GKN and Brambles, though profitable to both partners, was complicated by the fact that the joint venture had become an increasingly important part of Brambles' business. CHEP was a big international company in its own right, and the 50-50 ownership, requiring both parents to agree on major decisions, was no longer an appropriate arrangement. As Lees commented later, 'Running a fast-moving growth business like CHEP in a joint venture was really putting pressure on the system and impacting on its efficiency.'[10] In 2001, the two companies agreed on a scheme whereby CHEP and Cleanaway would be demerged from GKN into Brambles, and GKN shareholders would acquire 43 per cent of the enlarged Brambles Group.

The outcome was to narrow GKN's portfolio to two legs – automotive and aerospace – both of which were seen as capable of profitable growth.

Preparing the case

In preparing the case analysis you might like to consider three specific questions in particular:

- Compare and contrast the ways in which Lucas Industries and GKN handled their vehicle component businesses, and how they handled their diversification outside vehicle components.
- What insights does the positioning approach to business strategy provide in the case of Lucas Industries and GKN?
- Is the resource-based theory of strategy relevant to this story?

Postscript

While GKN survived as independent company through the 1980s, 1990s and early part of the 21st century, it was eventually acquired in a hostile and highly controversial takeover by 2018 Melrose Industries, a relative upstart in the engineering industry which had been founded by corporate financiers David Roper, Christopher Miller and Simon Peckham in 2003. Melrose's business strategy was to buy and turn around underperforming businesses. In March 2023, Melrose announced its decision to demerge parts of the former GKN business into Dowlais Group plc, a pure-play automotive component supplier.

Following a series of disposals and the demerger of its automotive business, Melrose is now focused on the former GKN aerospace operation. Roper stood down as executive vice-chair of the industrial conglomerate in May 2020, leaving with shares worth £30m.[11] In March 2024, Miller and Peckham both stepped down from the board after more than two decades of dealmaking. They were the biggest beneficiaries of a £180m bonus pot declared prior to their departure.[12]

Further reading

Barney, J. (1991) 'Firm resources and sustained competitive advantage'. *Journal of Management,* vol. 17, no. 1, pp. 99–120. https://doi.org/10.1177/014920639101700108

Owen, G. (1999) *From Empire to Europe: The Decline and Revival of British Industry Since the Second World War.* London: HarperCollins.

Porter, M. (1979) 'How competitive forces shape strategy'. *Harvard Business Review,* vol. 57, no. 2, pp. 137–145.

Porter, M. (1996) 'What is strategy'. *Harvard Business Review,* vol. 74, no. 6, pp. 61–78.

Exhibits

GKN chronology

1900–1902	Three-way merger creates Guest, Keen & Nettlefolds
1919	Acquires F.W. Cotterill
1920	Acquires John Lysaght
1948	Acquires Brymbo Steel Works
	Acquires 50 per cent stake in BRD (automotive components)
1955	Acquires Lincoln Electric (welding machinery)
	Acquires full control of BRD
1962	Acquires Acton Bolt (nuts and bolts)
1966	Acquires Birfield (vehicle components)
1967	Steel nationalisation
	Acquires Vandervell Products (vehicle components)
1969	Acquires R.H. Windsor (plastics machinery)
1973	Buys back Brymbo from British Steel Corporation

1974	Forms joint venture with Brambles in industrial services
1979	Acquires Sheepbridge Engineering (vehicle components)
1980	Trevor Holdsworth appointed chair
1983	Bids for Associated Engineering, rejected by Monopolies Commission
1987	David Lees appointed group managing director, succeeds Holdsworth as chair in the following year
1988	Acquires stake in Westland
1994	Acquires full control of Westland
1995	Sells minority stake in UES Holdings to British Steel
1996	Sells US automotive parts business
1997	Lees becomes non-executive chair, succeeded as Chief Executive by C.K. Chow
2001	Puts Westland into joint venture with Agusta
2001	Demerges industrial services business into Brambles

Lucas chronology

1872	Joseph Lucas founds the business in Birmingham
1897	Becomes a public company
1914	Acquires Thomson-Bennett, manufacturer of magnetos
1926	Acquires C.A. Vandervell (later known as CAV)
	Acquires Rotax
1929	Acquires Rist
1943	Acquires Girling (brakes)
1959	Forms joint venture with Ducellier in France to make fuel injection equipment
1960	Opens Girling factory in Germany
1962	Acquires 40 per cent stake in Ducellier
1977	Builds factory in the US for fuel injection equipment
1980	Godfrey Messervy appointed chair
1983	Buys control of Smiths Industries' instrumentation business
1984	Sells holding in Ducellier
1986	Sells starters and alternators to Magneti Marelli, lighting to Fausto Carello
1987	Tony Gill appointed chair and chief executive
1994	George Simpson succeeds Gill as chief executive, Brian Pearse appointed non-executive chair
1996	Merges with Varity to form LucasVarity
1999	LucasVarity acquired by TRW
	TRW sells CAV to Delphi
2001	TRW sells Lucas Aerospace to Goodrich
2002	Northrop Grumman announces plan to take over TRW, together with the sale of TRW's vehicle components business to the Blackstone group

References

[1] Nockolds, Harold (1976) *Lucas: The First Hundred Years, Vol 1, The King Of The Road.* Newton Abbot: David & Charles.

[2] Monopolies Commission (1963) *Report On The Supply Of Electrical Equipment For Mechanically Propelled Land Vehicles* London: HMSO.

[3] Loveridge, Ray (1988) 'Lucas Industries, a study in strategic domain and discourse', Work Organisation Research Centre, Aston University, Working paper no 32.

[4] Nockolds, Harold (1983) *Lucas, The First 100 Years, Vol 2, The Successors.* Newton Abbot: David & Charles, p. 233.

[5] *Financial Times*, 8 January, 1983.

[6] Holdsworth, Trevor (1990) Speech to Institute of Chartered Accountants in Scotland, September.

[7] *Financial Times*, 10 March, 1988.

[8] *Financial Times*, 4 October, 1988.

[9] *Financial Times*, 7 December, 1995.

[10] *Sunday Times*, 22 April, 2001.

[11] *The Times*, May 2019.

[12] *Financial Times*, 3 June, 2024.

3. The collapse of Carillion plc

Lauren Oddoye and Alexander Pepper[1]

This case examines the collapse of Carillion plc, an outsourcing company. It describes how outsourcing became a common business model in the 1990s, how being the lowest cost provider is not by itself a sustainable long-term business strategy, and how optimistic assumptions about the profitability of long-term contracts can lead to financial failure. Carillion provides a rich source of material for exploring a wide range of management, governance, finance and accounting questions. The issues explored in the case include:

- industry structure – the market for construction and facilities management services, the business of outsourcing, especially with public sector customers;

- Carillion's strategy and business model;

- the upsides and downsides of growth through mergers and acquisitions;

- managerial decision-making – agency theory, groupthink and the winner's curse;

- the difficulties in accounting for long-term contracts;

- the role and responsibilities of auditors;

- corporate governance – why good corporate governance is important for preventing agency problems and poor managerial decision-making, and the 'presenting issue' of high executive pay;

How to cite this book chapter:

Oddoye, Lauren and Pepper, Alexander (2025) 'The Collapse of Carillion plc', in: Sallai, Dorottya and Pepper, Alexander (ed) *Navigating the 21st Century Business World: Case Studies in Management*, London: LSE Press, pp. 39–56. https://doi.org/10.31389/lsepress.nbw.c

- the 'financialisation thesis' advanced by Greta Krippner, Gerry Davis and others – the increasing influence of financial considerations in the management of large corporations in the late 20th and early 21st centuries.

Guidance on how to write a case analysis can be found in Chapter 1, 'Business cases: what are they, why do we use them and how should you go about doing a case analysis?'.

A teaching note for this case is available to bona fide educators. To request a copy please email a.a.pepper@lse.ac.uk

Introduction

'There are some failures where the ramifications are so enormous that the industry feels as if it's been felled as well. Losing Carillion was a disaster.'[2]

In July 1999, Carillion plc demerged from Tarmac plc to form a construction company specialising in facilities management and construction services. Through a series of mergers and acquisitions the company grew into a multinational group, operating across the UK, Canada and the Middle East. Carillion made most of its revenue (74 per cent or £3.8 billion in 2016) in the UK and the company eventually rose to become the UK's second largest facilities management and construction services business, with government contracts accounting for 33 per cent of its total revenues and 45 per cent of its UK business. The value of these contracts made Carillion the sixth largest strategic supplier to the UK government in 2017. Contracted services included facilities management, catering, road and rail maintenance, accommodation, consultancy and construction. These services were provided to support the armed forces, prisons, transport, hospitals and schools across the UK. In June 2017, the company reported total annual revenues of £5.2 billion and £146.7 million in profit before tax for the year ended 31 December 2016, before paying its highest dividends ever (£55 million).

Just one month later, Carillion issued a profit warning and reduced the value of several major contracts by £845 million. Shortly after this, an additional £200 million was also written off, cancelling out the previous seven years' profits and leaving Carillion with over £405 million in liabilities. Between 7 and 12 July 2017, the share price plummeted from 197p to 57p per share. In that year, Carillion reported debts of over £900 million as well as a pension fund deficit of £587 million (a figure later thought to be understated by an independent pensions consultant, who speculated that the real pension deficit could be closer to £800 million). On 15 January 2018, Carillion was forced into mandatory liquidation because it had 'no real assets left to sell'; by this time its shares were valued at just 14p. At that time Carillion employed around 45,000 people, and as a trusted strategic government supplier, held around 420 UK public sector contracts.

All companies have a natural life cycle, but Carillion's collapse was not natural. Its rapid decline brought into question whether the entity, so strong on paper, had ever had any real substance. In the words of the joint Department of Work and Pensions and Business, Energy and Industrial Strategy parliamentary committees, 'The mystery is not that [Carillion] collapsed, but how it kept going so long.'[3]

Formation

In 1999, Tarmac plc, a British construction company, demerged its construction contracting and facilities management arms to create Carillion plc. Having previously expanded into facilities management and construction services through mergers, Tarmac was hit hard by the housing recession of the early 1990s. To survive the economic downturn, Tarmac's board decided to downsize and to return the company to its roots in heavy building materials. The firm's construction contracting and professional services businesses officially became Carillion plc in July 1999.

As a construction services business, Carillion had to acquire profitable new contracts in order to build scale. Once a contract had been negotiated and signed, it became Carillion's responsibility to ensure that the work was completed within the agreed terms of the contract. Carillion would do this by hiring multiple suppliers and subcontractors to complete the various parts of the project. Once construction was complete, Carillion might also be obliged to provide ongoing facilities management services for the facility in question. For example, after constructing a school Carillion might be contractually obligated to provide such services as catering for pupils, cleaning the school buildings and maintaining the grounds. Carillion's construction services and facilities management obligations varied, depending on the terms of individual contracts. Because of its inheritance from Tarmac, Carillion was immediately responsible for a number of high-profile public projects, including the renovation of the Royal Opera House and transformation of the derelict Bankside Power Station into the famous Tate Modern art gallery. On paper, its business model looked simple but effective.

Over the years that followed, the business grew larger and more complex until the company careered progressively out of control from beneath the feet of its senior management. To understand why Carillion collapsed, we need to go back to the beginning of its corporate story, to take a closer look at Carillion's early years of rapid growth, ask questions about its corporate governance, and examine exactly how its business model was implemented in practice. The story begins by examining a long list of mergers and acquisitions, arguably the start of Carillion's problems.

Mergers and acquisitions

In 2001 Carillion, already specialising in construction contracting, expanded aggressively into facilities management. The board was keen to establish Carillion as a major player in the facilities management industry and therefore implemented an aggressive growth strategy. Carillion's growth was initially achieved through mergers and acquisitions of companies with strategically important areas of specialism in the contracting industry. For example, Carillion added railway maintenance to its portfolio of service offerings by acquiring the remaining 51 per cent share of GT Rail Maintenance it did not already own, creating Carillion Rail in September 2001. This helped the company to bid for large Network Rail contracts. Recognising a connection between its acquisitions and its ability to secure new contracts, Carillion sought to strengthen its service offering and reduce competition by acquiring major rivals. In addition, mergers potentially offered cost savings through scale and synergies.

The first major acquisition was of one of the UK's largest construction and civil engineering companies, Mowlem, which Carillion successfully bought for £350 million in 2006. Acquisitions were typically funded by debt rather than equity, thus increasing the company's gearing. Debt was offset in Carillion's balance sheet by goodwill arising on acquisition. When purchasing a company, the difference between the net value of tangible assets and the actual amount paid is referred to as 'goodwill'. In part, goodwill represents intangible assets, such as brands, know-how and client-contacts. There may also have been a premium for 'strategic fit' between the acquiring and acquired companies. The balance sheet value of goodwill is therefore highly judgemental. The purchase price of Mowlem significantly exceeded the value of its net tangible assets, resulting in a substantial goodwill element of £431 million. Some commentators thought that Carillion had overpaid, but this did not appear to cause much concern to Carillion's management for a number of reasons. First, they regarded the acquisition as a strategic move designed to reduce competition, which it did. Secondly, Carillion's profits that year were not affected. Finally, they were able to persuade the company's financial advisers to capitalise any acquisition premium as goodwill. Given the difficulty in determining how many extra contracts Carillion acquired per year as a direct result of the acquisition, or the exact value of cost savings which it benefited from, it was difficult to say whether the acquisition of Mowlem was a financial success or not.

Emboldened by the increase in revenues and the size of its balance sheet, Carillion continued to make acquisitions. In 2008 it acquired Alfred McAlpine, a major road builder which had constructed over 10 per cent of Britain's motorways, for £565 million. By 2009, Carillion had become one of the UK's largest construction services firms, second only to Balfour Beatty. Next, Carillion set its sights on Eaga, a British supplier of energy efficiency products. Unfortunately, Carillion's purchase of Eaga for £298 million in 2011 resulted in five years of losses worth £260 million, completely wiping out Carillion's cash reserves. Undeterred, in 2014 Carillion sought to become the UK's biggest construction firm by proposing an 'opportunistic' £3 billion merger with Balfour Beatty. Balfour Beatty's board rejected the proposal, suspicious of Carillion's predicted cost savings of at least £175 million a year by 2016. The rejection marked the end of Carillion's strategy of expansion via mergers and acquisitions.

Public finance initiative

Carillion derived a significant proportion of its total revenues from government contracts and, as a company receiving over £100m in revenue per year from public sector contracts, was classified as a 'strategic supplier' to the UK government. In order to understand Carillion's business model, we must first examine the government's position as a major client and provider of contracts to Carillion. The government has a responsibility to provide national infrastructure and public services at the lowest reasonable cost to taxpayers. Since the mid-1980s it has been common for the UK government to achieve this by outsourcing through 'public-private partnership' projects (PPPs). This is known as the Private Finance Initiative (PFI). PPPs are contracts between public sector bodies and construction firms, under which private sector firms take responsibility for the provision of public infrastructure projects and their associated long-term support services, in exchange for a predetermined contract price.

Carillion was able to win a significant number of valuable PPP contracts. It became one of the leading suppliers of rail infrastructure services in the UK, consistently featuring as one of Network Rail's top suppliers. For example, in 2013, Carillion won two contracts worth £122 million for the integration of the new Crossrail service with Network Rail's existing infrastructure. Carillion also won contracts to build some urgently needed and highly specialised public buildings such as the Royal Liverpool and Midland Metropolitan hospitals. They also won contracts with the Ministry of Defence, such as a joint venture contract to support the Army Bases Programme. This involved designing, constructing and providing facilities management services to the Salisbury Plain Training Area and to army bases in Aldershot, work valued at over £1.1 billion. Carillion also managed several local government school meals contracts.

Government contracts are typically awarded through a descending-price or 'Dutch' auction process: contractors bid for projects at the lowest contract price for which they are willing to work, and the company proposing the lowest amount wins the contract, thus guaranteeing the government the best price. Carillion's strategy for securing contracts was to undercut competitors' bids. Though apparently successful, winning Carillion its strategic government supplier status and 450 governmental contracts worth £2 billion, this was not a sound strategy. Government contracts are very price-sensitive, so consistently bidding lower than the next lowest bidder inevitably results in razor thin profit margins. For example, the facilities management services Carillion provided to central government typically had operating margins of around 1 per cent. Though local government contracts were generally more profitable (operating margins of 13–15 per cent), these were offset by several of Carillion's high-profile PPP projects, which incurred significant losses.

One such PPP contract was the Royal Liverpool Hospital, which began haemorrhaging money. The contract, to design and construct the hospital over a five-year period, was signed on 13 December 2013 for a contract price of £235 million. Construction began in February 2014 and the first phase was due to be completed by the end of March 2017. In May 2015, reports of asbestos on the old site led to extensive delays. Nevertheless, a major project status report published in October 2015 estimated a final profit margin of 5.5 per cent, 2 per cent higher than the initial forecast before delays. In November 2016, cracks were discovered in two of the hospital's concrete beams. A further review revealed smaller cracks in six further beams. Richard Howson, Carillion's chief executive, announced that Carillion would fix all the beams at an extra cost to the company of over £20 million, even though he also said that 'those beams would probably never [have failed] in their cracked state'. The director of the hospital company begged to differ, stating five of the eight defective beams could have failed under the load of a fully operational hospital, resulting in an unsafe work environment and potentially causing injury or loss of life. Fixing the problem required three virtually finished floors to be removed to allow new steel beams to be inserted.

A peer review of the contract in November 2016 concluded that additional costs would result in losses of 12.7 per cent, but Carillion's senior management disagreed and continued to record an expected profit margin of 4.9 per cent. Because of the contract accounting method used by Carillion, this resulted in approximately £53 million in additional revenues being recognised in the 2016 accounts (see further comments below under the heading 'Aggressive accounting'). It is interesting to note that this is the same amount that the company eventually made provision for in its July 2017 profit warning.

The Royal Liverpool Hospital contract's problems did not end with Carillion's eventual insolvency. Further issues were uncovered in the aftermath of Carillion's collapse. A quarter of the hospital's exterior cladding which had been installed by Carillion did not meet fire regulations and had to be replaced. The government had to underwrite all excess costs following the collapse of Carillion. The contract was due to be completed five years late and more than £200 million over budget. Additional costs include over £1 million for essential maintenance of the dilapidated old hospital, which in 2018 suffered eight floods and several related electrical failures.

Rising debt

Over the eight years from December 2009 to January 2018, the total owed by Carillion in loans increased from £242 million to an estimated £1.3 billion – more than five times the value at the beginning of the decade; see Figure 3.1.

Figure 3.1: Carillion's loans: total owed (£ millions) 2009–2018

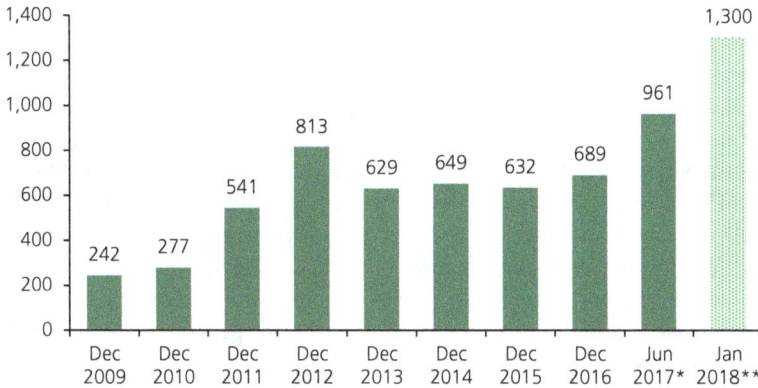

Source: Mor *et al* (2018) p.15, reproduced under the Open Parliament Licence v3.0.[4] Data from Carillion's annual financial statements; * Interim financial statement for the six months ended 30 June 2017; ** from *Financial Times* (16 Jan 2017)

In December 2015, Standard Life Investments began selling shares in Carillion. In its letter to the Parliamentary Work and Pensions Committee regarding its decision, the investment company cited its concern about the UK's shrinking construction market, Carillion's defective corporate governance, its widening pension deficit, low levels of cash, high dividend pay-outs and even higher levels of debt. In early 2015, UBS claimed that Carillion's total debt levels were higher than the company was stating in its reports, prompting more and more investors to bet against Carillion's shares.

Although Carillion's board acknowledged the company's debt levels were significant, the company's loans seemed to be of little concern to the directors. While giving oral evidence to a parliamentary committee in February 2017, Keith Cochrane, non-executive director from July 2015 and interim chief executive from July 2017, would later reflect that, although the board was aware of shareholders' concerns raised in 2015 regarding the debt position and pension deficit, these were considered as being among the company's 'lesser concerns'. He admitted that it was not until 2016 that the board would rather belatedly recognise the importance of addressing these issues.

Pension schemes

There are two types of occupational pension scheme: defined benefit pension schemes (DBs) and defined contribution schemes (DCs). DB schemes guarantee a certain pay-out at retirement, dependent on the employee's tenure and salary. DC schemes provide a pay-out at retirement based on the amount of money contributed by the employee and the employer, and the success of the investment vehicle used. With a DC pension plan it is the employee's responsibility to ensure they have paid sufficient contributions to purchase an adequate retirement annuity. With a DB scheme it is the employer's responsibility to ensure sufficient funds have been raised to cover pension liabilities owed to their employees on retirement. At any one time, therefore, DB schemes may be in surplus or in deficit, depending on the level of its assets and liabilities. In the UK, private sector occupational pension schemes are typically 'funded', established separately from the sponsor company and held in trust by a body of trustees appointed by the company and pension scheme members.

As well as its own DB pension scheme, which it inherited on the demerger from Tarmac, Carillion also acquired various other pension schemes on its acquisition of Mowlem, Alfred McAlpine and Eaga. All these schemes were in deficit. Under the 'Scheme Specific Funding Regime' introduced in the Pensions Act 2004, trustees must have a statutory funding objective – to ensure there are 'sufficient and appropriate assets to cover their technical provisions' (or liabilities). They must obtain triennial actuarial valuations, and where a scheme is in deficit, they must prepare a recovery plan setting out the steps that will be taken to meet the funding objective, and over what time. A copy of the plan is sent to the Pensions Regulator. The trustees expected the valuation of the various Carillion schemes to have a cumulative deficit of £990 million

Figure 3.2 Carillion's pension deficit (IAS 19) gross of taxation (£ millions)

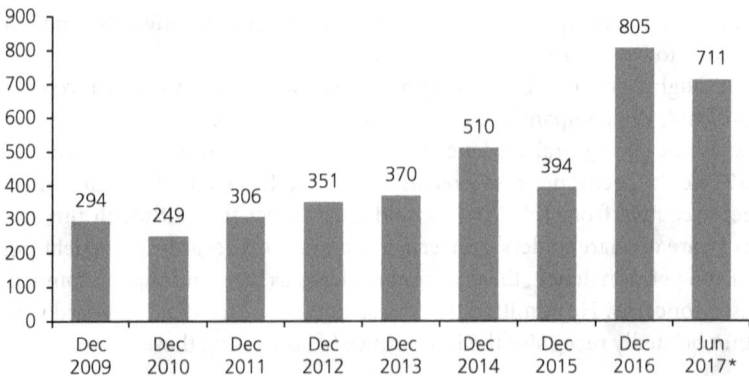

Source: Mor *et al* (2018) p.22, reproduced under the Open Parliament Licence v3.0.[5]
* Interim financial statement for the six months ended 30 June 2017

as at 31 December 2016. The reason for the increase since 2013 (see Figure 3.2) was the significant reduction in interest rates over those three years. At the end of December 2013, the same schemes were 76 per cent funded. A recovery plan was agreed, under which recovery payments could continue until 2029. The total size of the deficits is shown in Figure 3.2.

In 2007, Richard Adam, Carillion's finance director had refused to invest in the pension schemes, describing them as a waste of money. In April 2009, under Adam's leadership, Carillion closed its DB schemes for future accruals, replacing them with a more cost-effective DC plan. However, it was still required to honour all DB pension entitlements that had accumulated until that date, and the deficits on the various schemes continued to increase as asset values failed to match rising pension liabilities.

Expansion into new markets

Carillion's acquisitions policy had increased the company's debt levels and exhausted its cash reserves. To survive, Carillion desperately needed to increase its profits by securing new contracts. By 2014, the Carillion board had concluded that the company could no longer increase its market share by acquiring further competitors, and that its best option was to expand into new markets. This led to several largely disastrous expansions into Canada, the Caribbean and the Middle East. In the words of Richard Howson, chief executive from January 2012 to July 2017:

> We did not have any money to buy competitors, as we had done in the past. We had to win our work organically. We had to bid and we had to win …[6]

Carillion commenced bidding on a large number of contracts, particularly in the Middle East. Although, according to Carillion's own research, the Dubai market outlook was given a relatively poor rating, in Carillion's 2010 annual report the company stated it would 'target new work selectively' in Dubai and other parts of the United Arab Emirates. Despite a poor understanding of the local property market, Carillion proceeded to aggressively bid for 13 new contracts in Qatar between 2010 and 2014. Although Carillion was largely unsuccessful in winning work in Qatar, the one contract the company was able to secure went on to become notorious as Carillion struggled to adapt to local business practices and to manage the contract profitably. The Msheireb Properties contract involved building hotels, offices and residential buildings in Doha. Although it was due to be completed in 2014, the project remained unfinished in 2018. The directors of Carillion and Msheireb Properties each claimed that the other party owed them £200 million. Carillion's auditors were unable to determine what the reality of the situation was. Even after being sacked as chief executive in July 2017, Richard Howson was retained by the company in a new role devoted solely to negotiating payment for failing contracts in the Middle East. In an interview with the parliamentary committee following Carillion's collapse, Howson expressed relief that Carillion had 'thankfully' only won one construction project in Qatar. In their report, the parliamentary committee concluded that:

> …[Carillion's] expansions into overseas markets were driven by optimism rather than any strategic expertise. Carillion's directors blamed a few rogue contracts in alien business environments, such as with Msheireb Properties in Qatar, for the company's demise. But if they had had their way, they would have won 13 contracts in that country.[7]

Aggressive accounting

Accounting for construction contracts is inherently difficult as, under the accrual basis of accounting, revenues are accounted for when they are earned rather than received. This means that construction companies are able to account for future revenues on long-term contracts at the start of a project rather than when cash is received and expenditure incurred. To accomplish this, construction companies typically deduct forecast costs from predicted revenues in order to determine profits. However, when a construction project is not due to be completed for many years, the difficulties in assessing how far from completion the project is and what costs will be incurred in future make profit recognition a matter of judgement and often highly subjective. It is also a requirement that losses should be recognised in the accounts when they are first anticipated.

According to board minutes, Andrew Dougal, chair of the audit committee, identified a reluctance on the part of management to acknowledge the losses incurred on the major Royal Liverpool Hospital project. In an August 2017 board meeting, Keith Cochrane also observed that long-serving Carillion staff tended to adopt a rather cavalier attitude towards profit recognition. Andrew Dougal described the finance director, Richard Adam, as 'defensive in relation to some challenges in board meetings', and as someone who 'exercised tight control over the entire finance function, [and] had extensive influence throughout the Group'. Nevertheless, the non-executive directors failed to challenge Carillion's accounting and risk management process.[8]

Carillion was widely criticised for its aggressive accounting. Aggressive accounting is the practice of declaring revenue and profits based on optimistic forecasts, before the money has actually been made. All is well if the forecasts are correct, but if costs rise and revenues fall (say, because of delays and defects), expected profits turn into actual losses. Because aggressive accounting means declaring profits before receiving the money, it shows up in company accounts as a fall in the actual cash that the company makes, compared with the profits it declares. Carillion's accounts shown in Figure 3.3 are a case in point.

Figure 3.3: Declared profit vs cash generated, from operations (£ millions)

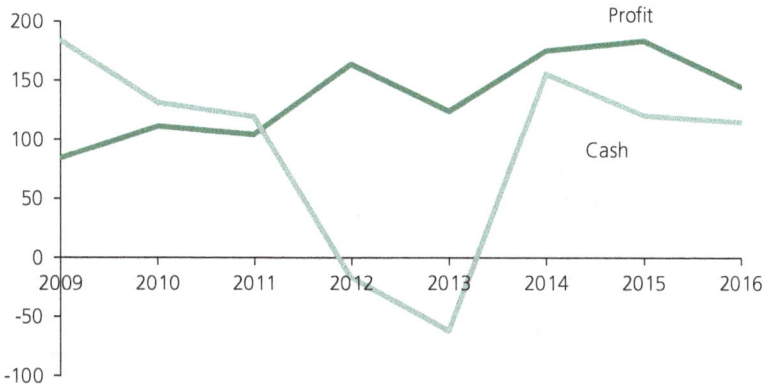

Mor *et al* (2018) p.17, reproduced under the Open Parliament Licence v3.0[9]

Richard Adam's decision to leave the company in 2016, before problems began to emerge in 2017, is perhaps significant. He received a final payment of £1.1 million in December 2016. His decision to immediately offload his shares after leaving is also noteworthy. He sold all his shares on the day the 2016 accounts were published, then cashed in his 2014 long-term performance award on the day that it matured in May 2017. In total, he profited by an amount of £776,000 between March 2017 and May 2017, before the share price fell to 57p in mid-July.

Dividends

Despite Carillion's ever increasing debt levels and pension scheme deficits, dividend payments increased every year from the company's inception in 1999. The board announced that dividend payments were increasing in line with earnings per share. Nevertheless, cash from operations and profits varied significantly between 2011 and 2016. In both 2012 and 2013, operational cash flow was negative as construction volumes decreased. However, despite the net cash outflow, dividends continued to be paid. Carillion's first profit warning was issued in July 2017, yet its highest dividends of over £55 million were paid just one month prior to this on 9 June 2017. In January 2017, Zafar Khan, the new finance director, proposed withholding the June dividend payment in order to reduce debt and conserve cash, but faced strong opposition from other board members, and was eventually over-ruled. Andrew Dougal, chair of the audit committee, and Keith Cochrane, then senior independent non-executive director and later interim chief executive, worried about the message that withholding dividends would send to the market. Some investors, such as BlackRock, made investment decisions on a passive basis, using tracking indices. These indices are reactive to events such as the suspension of dividends and significant falls in share price, which trigger an automatic obligation to sell shares. Withholding or reducing dividends would have been likely to cause a fall in the share price, triggering automatic selling. However, a number of active investors saw high levels of dividend payments as red flags and chose to sell their shares. In their letter to the parliamentary committee which examined the collapse of Carillion, Standard Life Aberdeen cited 'unsustainable dividends' as one of many reasons why they chose to divest from Carillion in December 2015.[10] They believed it was indicative of Carillion's failure to manage its debt levels in favour of paying dividends. The board rejected the idea that dividends were prioritised over other financial obligations. Richard Adam claimed that Carillion's dividends policy 'balanced the needs of many stakeholders', including pensioners, staff and shareholders.[11] Nevertheless, between 2011 and 2016, while Carillion made only £246 million in pension scheme deficit recovery payments, it paid dividends of £441 million. Richard Adam argued that dividends increased by only 12 per cent during this period, while pension payments increased by 50 per cent. However, during his tenure as finance director, deficit recovery payments increased by only 1 per cent, while dividend payments rose substantially.

The Carillion board clearly took pride in the company's dividend track record and upheld it in spite of the company's erratic financial performance. Many commentators have subsequently argued that this showed scant regard for other stakeholders or the sustainability and long-term future of the company.

Board of directors

According to the UK Corporate Governance Code, the 'underlying principles of good governance [are] accountability, transparency, probity and a focus on the sustainable success of an entity over the longer term'.[12] By this standard Carillion lacked meaningful corporate governance. The chief executive of the Insolvency Service, Sarah Albon, remarked that the company's 'incredibly poor standards' made it difficult to pin down even simple information, such as an up-to-date list of directors.[13] In his presentation to the board on 22 August 2017, Keith Cochrane identified 'continued challenges in quality, accessibility and integrity of data, particularly profitability at contract level'.[14] While conducting a strategic review of Carillion, EY quickly identified a 'lack of accountability … professionalism and expertise', as well as an 'inward looking culture' of 'non-compliance'.[15] It is the responsibility of a company's board to govern the practices which determine its culture. Something appears to have gone wrong.

Before July 2017, the board consisted of seven members, including the chief executive, finance director and five non-executive directors. The executive directors were Richard Howson (chief executive) and Zafar Khan (finance director). Non-executives were Philip Green (chair), Keith Cochrane, Andrew

Dougal, Alison Horner and Baroness Morgan of Huyton. By the time that the company collapsed Richard Howson and Zafar Khan had been replaced by Keith Cochrane and Emma Mercer respectively. With the exception of Emma Mercer and Zafar Khan, none of the board members seemed to grasp the reality of Carillion's financial situation even after it had failed. The non-executive directors, who were responsible for scrutinising executive management's decisions, appeared to do little to challenge the board.

Richard Howson and Philip Green both underestimated the challenges facing Carillion. In one interview, Mr Howson claimed that 'but for a few very challenging contracts, predominantly in the Oman and one in Qatar, ... Carillion would have survived.'[16] He further argued that 'the business was in a sustainable position' based on the support it was receiving from banks. Even after being stripped of his role as chief executive, he appeared to remain convinced of his own effectiveness. Philip Green seemed to be equally misguided. Even as the company was collapsing on Wednesday 5 July 2017, just five days before the profit warning on Monday 10 July, in which Carillion announced a write-down of £845 million, the Carillion board minutes recorded:

In conclusion, the Chairman noted that work continued toward a positive and upbeat announcement for Monday, focusing on the strength of the business as a compelling and attractive proposition ... [17]

In the words of the parliamentary committee, 'it is difficult to believe the Chairman was not aware of the seriousness of the situation, but equally difficult to comprehend his [unerringly optimistic] assessment if he was.'[18]

Keith Cochrane was appointed senior independent non-executive director in July 2016. He already had extensive board-level experience, but soon seemed to adapt to the Carillion board's culture of passive optimism. Although aware of shareholder concerns about the pensions deficit and rising debt, the board failed to pursue these issues until the first profit warning. Mr Cochrane claimed that he challenged executives 'in an appropriate manner', and believed there was 'no basis' in 2016 for 'not accepting the view that management put forward'. In an interview post-liquidation, Mr Cochrane asked himself 'should the board have been asking further, more probing questions?', but even with hindsight, could only concede 'perhaps'.[19] After Richard Howson was removed from his role as chief executive in July 2017, Keith Cochrane was asked to take over as interim chief executive until a permanent CEO could be found. During his period of tenure, he gave 'limited and vague' answers to 'fairly fundamental questions', thus reinforcing external shareholders' concerns, and exacerbating the selling of shares. A new CEO was scheduled to join the company in January 2018, but by this time Carillion would already be in liquidation.

The other non-executive directors claimed that they were effective in their roles. 'We challenged; we probed; we asked', said Philip Green, citing the company's level of debt in 2016 and 2017 as an example. 'The board consistently challenged management on debt, and management then developed a so-called self-help plan to reduce debt'.[20] However, the debt actually rose from £689 million to £961 million over the same period. Mr Green also referenced the non-executive directors' challenges regarding contract mismanagement, although he later named large contract mismanagement as a 'very significant factor' in Carillion's collapse. Former Carillion shareholder Murdo Murchison of Kiltearn Partners questioned whether the non-executive directors exercised 'any effective check on the executive management team'. Non-executive directors are vital in challenging a company's risk management and strategy, but as Mr Murchison suggested 'it appears that they were hoodwinked as much as anybody else'.[21]

Remuneration committee

Carillion's remuneration committee (RemCo) was responsible for determining senior executive salaries, bonuses and share awards. RemCos typically investigate the remuneration for particular jobs within an industry, then set their own remuneration levels for equivalent jobs in the company. According to the chair of Carillion's RemCo, Alison Horner, the company's executive remuneration policy was to pay the industry median. Carillion commissioned Deloitte to carry out a pay benchmarking analysis for this purpose in 2015. Their research suggested that Carillion's chief executive's remuneration package was lower than average. To correct this apparent inconsistency, the RemCo agreed to raise Richard Howson's salary by 8 per cent in 2015 and 9 per cent in 2016. As such, Richard Howson's basic salary increased from some £1.1million up to £1.5million by 2016. Other board members also received pay rises based on the benchmarking exercise. For example, Philip Green, chair of the board, received a 10 per cent increase in the amount of his remuneration from £193,000 to £215,000. At the same time Carillion's workforce received only a 2 per cent pay increase in 2016.

In a meeting in March 2015, some executives expressed concerns that their bonuses might be clawed back because of declining profits and said that any such decision should not include 'retrospective judgements on views taken on contracts in good faith'. Nevertheless, the RemCo went ahead to approve potential bonuses for senior executives of up to 100 per cent of basic pay. For example, Richard Howson was awarded a bonus of £245,000 (37 per cent of his salary) in 2016 despite meeting none of his financial performance targets.

The RemCo failed to reclaim bonuses as Carillion's situation deteriorated. Clawback terms had been introduced in 2015, but the terms were defined in such a way that the RemCo was not able to recoup bonuses even at the time of the £845 million write-down in July 2017. In September 2017, the RemCo briefly considered asking directors to return their bonuses, but failed to make the case for the return of bonuses even as the company collapsed.

External auditors

One of the noteworthy features of the Carillion case is that all of the Big 4 auditing and accounting firms were involved with the company in some way. KPMG were Carillion's external auditors. Deloitte had a contract to provide internal audit services. EY were Carillion's external financial advisers for the six-month period prior to the company's failure. PricewaterhouseCoopers were appointed as special managers in the company's liquidation.

Although it is the directors of a company who are responsible for producing its annual financial statements, it is the external auditor's responsibility to confirm the validity of these documents and flag up any evidence of misinformation. KPMG served as the Carillion's external auditors from the company's formation in 1999 until it was forced into liquidation in 2018. Some commentators argue that such long relationships between companies and auditors cast doubt over the auditor's impartiality and objectivity. KPMG eventually accepted that in Carillion's case that the length of the relationship was too long to be impartial.

The subsequent review of Carillion's accounts revealed that the external auditors could have raised concerns for any number of reasons. For example, at no stage was there an impairment charge in respect of goodwill carried in Carillion's accounts. This seems hard to justify in the case of the Eaga acquisition, which resulted in the creation of goodwill of £330 million, but was followed by five consecutive years of losses.

Internal auditors

Carillion outsourced its internal auditing services to Deloitte. Carillion used two internal processes to verify margins on projects: first, through monthly project review meetings (PRMs), at which management appraised contracts and made reasonable adjustments; second, by peer reviews, whereby an external party conducted a similar assessment. Between July and August 2017, Deloitte reviewed the peer reviews for contracts from January 2015 to July 2017. They found that internal PRM appraisals generally reported higher profit margins than peer reviews. While peer reviews did sometimes recommend higher margins than the PRM appraisals (14 per cent of cases), management recommended higher margins than peer reviews on three times as many occasions (42 per cent of cases). The impact on the accounts was significant, as the PRM values were included in annual reports. In the case of the Royal Liverpool University Hospital contract, Carillion's 2016 report and accounts recognised an additional £53 million in profits compared with the peer review, which proposed losses of 12.7 per cent rather than a profit margin of 4.9 per cent. Carillion's July 2017 profit warning would later include a provision of £53 million against the same contract. Andrew Dougal, chair of Carillion's audit committee, expressed concern about these variances when they were first revealed to him, but this happened too late for the audit committee to avert the crisis.

Collapse

The retirement in December 2016 of Richard Adam, the 'architect of Carillion's aggressive accounting policies' according to the parliamentary committee, marked the beginning of the end for Carillion. The company issued its first profit warning on 10 July 2017, announcing it would reduce the value of several major contracts by £845 million. The announcement was unexpected, given Carillion had paid its highest ever dividends just one month before. An additional £200 million was subsequently written off, cancelling out profits for the last seven years and leaving Carillion with £405 million in liabilities. Borrowing rose to £961 million, goodwill on Carillion's balance sheet was reduced by £134 million, and its level of working capital fell to a dangerously low level. Between 7 July and 12 July 2017, the share price plummeted from 197p to 57p. By 15 January 2018, when Carillion was forced into liquidation, its shares were valued at only 14p.

At the time of its collapse, Carillion was responsible for providing essential public services to the UK's NHS, national defence, education, energy and prison sectors, all of which were left vulnerable given the speed of Carillion's demise. In particular, two urgently needed hospitals, the Midland Metropolitan Hospital and the Royal Liverpool, had to be rescued by the government. Carillion's supply chain included hundreds of small companies, many of which were placed in a perilous financial position because of extended credit terms imposed by Carillion and the non-payment of debts. The eventual liquidation of the construction group raised big questions about outsourcing, bank lending, governance and auditing. MPs singled out a number of parties who played a role in the demise of the outsourcing firm.

The politicians – from the joint inquiry by the Business, Energy and Industrial Strategy Committee, and Work and Pensions Committee – said the collapse of Carillion was a 'story of recklessness, hubris and greed', and pulled no punches in their findings as to what led to the firm's failure, which put 20,000 jobs at risk. Carillion's board of directors bore the brunt of the responsibility, the report of the joint parliamentary committee found, but many others were involved in the behaviour that ultimately pushed the company over the edge.

Preparing the case

In preparing the case analysis you might like to consider three specific questions in particular:

1. *Business model.* Explain Carillion's business model in the light of transaction cost economics, Porter's generic business strategies and the resource-based view of the firm. You should focus primarily on Carillion's facilities management (support services) and public-private partnership projects businesses.

2. *Managerial decision-making.* What insights can be gained from the literature on organisational decision-making on the activities of Carillion's board of directors, senior management team and auditors? You should base your analysis primarily on evidence contained in the case documentation, rather than speculating about what may or may not have taken place.

3. *Case analysis.* To what extent is the formation, growth and eventual collapse of Carillion explainable in terms of the 'financialisation thesis'?[22]

Further reading

Barney, J. (1991) 'Firm resources and sustained competitive advantage'. *Journal of Management,* vol. 17, no. 1, pp. 99–120. https://doi.org/10.1177/014920639101700108

Coase, R. (1937) 'The nature of the firm'. *Economica,* vol. 4, no. 16, pp. 386–405. https://doi.org/10.1111/j.1468-0335.1937.tb00002.x

Davis, G. F. (2009) *Managed by Markets: How Finance Re-Shaped America.* Oxford: Oxford University Press.

Janis, I. L. (1982) *Groupthink.* 2nd ed. Boston, MA: Houghton Mifflin.

Thaler, R. H. (1992) *The Winner's Curse: Paradoxes and Anomalies of Economic Life.* New York: The Free Press.

References

[1] The case was written by Lauren Oddoye under the supervision of Professor Alexander Pepper.

[2] Rogers, D. (2018) 'Carillion analysis: the fall of the titan'. Building. https://perma.cc/42GJ-HCNB

[3] House of Commons (2018) 'Second Joint report from Business, Energy and Industrial Strategy and Work and Pensions Committees', HC 769, p.16, paragraph 14. https://publications.parliament.uk/pa/cm201719/cmselect/cmworpen/769/769.pdf

[4] Mor, Federico; Conway, Lorraine; Thurley, Djuna and Booth, Lorna (2018) 'The Collapse of Carillion', House of Commons Library Briefing Paper, Number 8206,14 March, p.15. https://researchbriefings.files.parliament.uk/documents/CBP-8206/CBP-8206.pdf. Figure reproduced under the Open Parliament Licence v3.0. https://www.parliament.uk/site-information/copyright-parliament/open-parliament-licence/

[5] Mor *et al* (2018), p.22. See Note 4 licence information.

[6] House of Commons (2018) HC 769 p.15. paragraph 10.

[7] House of Commons (2018) HC 769, p.16, paragraph 14.

[8] House of Commons (2018) HC 769, p.46, paragraph 103.

[9] Mor *et al* (2018), p.17. See Note 4 for licence information.

[10] House of Commons (2018) HC 769, p.18, paragraph 19.

[11] House of Commons (2018) HC 769, p.18, paragraph 18.

[12] House of Commons (2018) HC 769. p.26, paragraph 44.

[13] House of Commons (2018) HC 769. p.27, paragraph 47.

[14] House of Commons (2018) HC 769. p.27, paragraph 46.

[15] House of Commons (2018) HC 769. p.27, paragraph 45.

[16] House of Commons (2018) HC 769. p.28, paragraph 51.

[17] House of Commons (2018) HC 769. p.31, paragraph 62.

[18] House of Commons (2018) HC 769. p.31, paragraph 62.

[19] House of Commons (2018) HC 769. p.29, paragraph 54.

[20] House of Commons (2018) HC 769. p.30, paragraph 58.

[21] House of Commons (2018) HC 769. p.30, paragraph 58.

[22] See Krippner, G. R. (2005) 'The Financialization of the American Economy.' *Socio-Economic Review*, vol. 3, no. 2, pp. 173–208; and Davis, G.F. (2009) *Managed by Markets: How Finance Re-Shaped America*. Oxford: Oxford University Press.

4. On what matters: Unilever plc – purpose or performance?

Alexander Pepper

Shareholder primacy, socially responsible business, corporate purpose and sustainability are examined in this case about Unilever's evolving business strategy over the period from 2017, following an attempted takeover by Kraft Heinz Company, to 2024 with the appointment of a new chief executive officer from outside the group.

The case addresses important questions about the views of investors about corporate strategy, whether 'net positive' business outcomes will only be achieved if demanded by consumers, what happens if socially responsible business practices and corporate performance come into conflict, and what responsibility companies have to provide leadership when it comes to sustainability, climate change and socially responsible business.

Guidance on how to write a case analysis can be found in Chapter 1, 'Business cases: what are they, why do we use them and how should you go about doing a case analysis?'.

A teaching note for this case is available to bona fide educators. To request a copy please email a.a.pepper@lse.ac.uk

Introduction

We concluded that the purpose of business is to solve the problems of people and planet profitably, and not profit from causing problems. We proposed a framework for 21st century business based on corporate purposes; commitments to trustworthiness; and ethical corporate cultures.[1]

How to cite this book chapter:

Pepper, Alexander (2025) 'On what matters: Unilever plc – purpose or performance?', in: Sallai, Dorottya and Pepper, Alexander (ed) *Navigating the 21st Century Business World: Case Studies in Management*, London: LSE Press, pp. 57–67. https://doi.org/10.31389/lsepress.nbw.d

In February 2017, Kraft Heinz Company launched a hostile takeover bid for Unilever, one of the world's largest fast-moving consumer goods companies. The offer was for $50 per share, valuing the company at $143 billion, an 18 per cent premium over Unilever's share price. Kraft Heinz's bid was characterised by some commentators as pitting red-in-tooth-and-claw capitalism against green purposeful business.

Kraft Heinz Company

The American company had form when it came to hostile acquisitions of socially responsible companies. In 2010 Kraft had acquired Cadbury Schweppes in a controversial takeover. Cadbury came from a long tradition of ethical British businesses with roots in the Quaker movement. These included Rowntree's the chocolate manufacturer, Clarks the shoemaker, and Reckitt & Sons, makers and distributors of household products. Following the acquisition of Cadbury, Kraft reneged on a number of its promises, including to stick with Cadbury's commitment to using Fairtrade cocoa beans to produce its chocolate, confirming the suspicions of many UK-based business commentators that the American company was 'only in it for the money'. One journalist described the controversial takeover as 'how one of Britain's best-loved brands went from a force for social good to the worst example of corporate capitalism.'[2]

Kraft was itself to be acquired in 2015 by Brazilian-based 3G Capital, in a deal which had been partly financed by Berkshire Hathaway, the investment company chaired by the iconic American investor Warren Buffett. This mega-merger involved combining 3G's subsidiary H.J. Heinz with Kraft to form Kraft Heinz Company. 3G had a well-established business strategy of generating rapid returns from company acquisitions by cutting costs and improving cash flow using zero-based budgeting. It believed this strategy could be successfully applied to Unilever to enhance shareholder value and accelerate growth prospects.[3]

Unilever

Unilever has a long history. It was created in 1929 through the merger of Margarine Unie, a collection of Dutch companies and the British firm of Lever Brothers. The merger was a climax of a series of amalgamations over many years between companies which were involved in the production of oils and fat – tropical plantations, Arctic whaling, oil mills, refineries, hardening plants, soap and margarine factories, and retail stores.[4] The company's products include baby food, beauty products, bottled water, breakfast cereals, cleaning agents, energy drinks, healthcare, hygiene products, consumer pharmaceuticals, instant coffee, tea, soft drinks and ice cream. These are organised in five brand families: beauty and wellbeing, personal care, home care, nutrition and ice cream. Some of the company's leading brands include Domestos, Dove, Lifebuoy, Lux, Hellman's, Horlicks, Omo, Radiant, Surf, Magnum and

Walls. The iconic ice cream company Ben & Jerry's, famous for its progressive values, was a notable addition to the ice cream division when it was acquired by Unilever in 2000. As part of the deal, Ben & Jerry's was allowed by Unilever to continue to operate semi-independently.

At the time, Unilever, like Royal Dutch Shell – another multinational Anglo-Dutch company – had a very complex corporate structure involving two separate holding companies, Unilever NV based in the Netherlands and Unilever PLC based in London, as well as hundreds of subsidiaries. Many analysts believed, not unreasonably, that this complex corporate structure added significantly to Unilever's cost base.

The Polman era

Unilever's CEO at the time of the Kraft Heinz Company bid was Paul Polman, a Dutch businessman who worked for Proctor & Gamble for 27 years before joining Nestlé in 2006 as chief financial officer. Polman succeeded Patrick Cescau as CEO of Unilever in 2009 and was to continue as chief executive for nearly a decade. Polman was a champion of socially responsible business. Under the headline 'The parable of St Paul', *The Economist* newspaper described his corporate philosophy in the following terms:

> PAUL POLMAN runs Europe's seventh-most valuable company, Unilever, worth $176bn, but he is not a typical big cheese. A Dutch-man who once considered becoming a priest, he believes that selling shampoo around the world can be a higher calling and detests the Anglo-Saxon doctrine of shareholder primacy, which holds that a firm's chief purpose is to enrich its owners. Instead Mr Polman preaches that companies should be run 'sustainably' – by investing, paying staff fairly and by making healthy products with as little damage as possible to the environment. This is actually better for profits in the long run, he argues: society and shareholders need not be in conflict.[5]

Polman put sustainability at the centre of Unilever's strategy, launching the 'Unilever Sustainable Living Plan' in 2010. This had goals which included halving the environmental impact of Unilever's products, supporting the health and wellbeing of consumers and suppliers, developing ethical supply chains, and paying a living wage to employees across the world.

The Unilever board rejected Kraft Heinz's bid, arguing that it fundamentally undervalued the Anglo-Dutch company, and saying that they saw 'no merit, either financial or strategic, for Unilever's shareholders.'[6] Investors sided with Unilever and, as a result, Kraft Heinz announced it would not pursue a hostile deal. However, Unilever was forced to announce a series of measures designed to enhance long-term shareholder value as part of its takeover defence. These included improving operating margins from 16.5 per cent to 20 per cent by

2020, repurchasing stock in order to enhance earnings per share, reducing advertising costs, spinning-off a number of underperforming businesses, and selectively seeking earnings-enhancing bolt-on corporate acquisitions.

In 2018, Unilever announced its intention to simplify its corporate structure by merging the two legal entities into a single Dutch company with its headquarters in Rotterdam. However, in October 2018 the plan was abandoned because of objections by institutional shareholders, who were concerned about the tax consequences and the implications of Unilever's shares dropping out of the FTSE 100 index.

In November 2018, Polman announced that he would step down as CEO of Unilever at the end of the year. He has continued to work on sustainability, climate change, and inequality, and is leading proponent of 'net positive' business, the subject of a book co-authored with Andrew Winston, called *Net Positive: How Courageous Companies Thrive By Giving More Than They Take*, published in October 2021.

Unilever after Polman

Polman was succeeded as CEO of Unilever by Alan Jope, an internal continuity candidate. Jope joined Unilever in 1985 as a graduate trainee after a doing a business degree at the University of Edinburgh Business School. He was to continue with Polman's strategic focus on sustainable business, reconfirming that Unilever's corporate purpose was 'to make sustainable living commonplace'.[7]

In November 2020 Jope successfully managed to unify the Unilever group under one parent company, but importantly with the single holding company now based in the UK rather than the Netherlands, thus allaying the concern of institutional shareholders. During that year, Unilever faced turbulent times as a result of the Covid-19 global pandemic, which caused very dramatic falls in sales in food services and the beauty and personal care divisions. Underlying sales growth in 2020 was broadly flat, which many believed represented a good performance in the circumstances, but operating margins fell and were significantly down on the levels that had been achieved in 2018.

In 2021, Unilever made a bold strategic move, attempting to buy the consumer health arm of GSK for £50bn. Jope believed that this would accelerate the company's presence in a fast-developing market and re-energise Unilever's overall growth prospects. However, shareholders were not persuaded by the strategy behind the plan, and many voiced strong opposition to the size and timing of the deal, which was eventually unsuccessful. One major shareholder, Terry Smith, called the failed bid 'a near death experience', echoing words which Paul Polman had previously used to describe Kraft Heinz's attempt to acquire Unilever in 2017.[8] Smith set out his views on behalf of his investment company, Fundsmith, in a wide-ranging letter which cited Unilever management's 'penchant for corporate gobbledegook'.[9] Smith had previously written, 'Unilever seems to be labouring under the weight of a management which is obsessed with publicly displaying sustainability credentials at the expense of focusing on the fundamentals of the business.'[10]

The views of Smith and other investors were the result of their analysis of Unilever's historical performance in comparison with its global peers – see the Exhibits section for more details.

Jope was to retire as chief executive at the end of 2023, following investor discontent over the misconceived bid for GSK's consumer pharmaceutical business and the company's perceived lacklustre financial performance. His replacement, Hein Schumacher, had also begun his career as a graduate trainee with Unilever, but subsequently worked for H.J. Heinz for over a decade. He had led the successful turnaround of Kraft Heinz's AsiaPacific business, before becoming CEO of Royal FrieslandCampina, a Dutch multinational dairy cooperative, in 2018.

In October 2023, Schumacher set out his new strategy for Unilever, focusing on faster growth, increased productivity and building a performance culture. He said that the global consumer group's results were not matching its potential, as he announced a major overhaul of the group's leadership team. While Unilever's new CEO believed that for some brands, purpose was central to the marketing and positioning to consumers, this was not true for others and had become an 'unwelcome distraction'. He added that the time and investment the company had put into sustainability had had a negative impact on its financial performance.[11]

In March 2024, Unilever announced that it was to demerge its ice cream business and cut 7500 jobs. The company said its productivity programme would deliver savings of about €800mn over the next three years, 'more than offsetting operational dis-synergies' from the separation of ice cream.[12] This appeared to be the first step in Schumacher's drive to turn around the financial performance of the business.

Preparing the case

In preparing the case analysis you might like to consider three specific questions in particular:

1. How important are the views of investors when it comes to questions about corporate strategy?
2. What do you think about Hein Schumacher's comment that, while in some cases purpose is central to product marketing and positioning with consumers, this is not true for all brands? Will 'net positive' only be achieved if demanded by consumers?
3. If socially responsible business practices and corporate performance come into conflict, is it inevitable that socially responsible business practices will give way? What responsibility do companies have to provide leadership when it comes to sustainability, climate change and socially responsible business?

Further reading

Polman, P., and Winston, A. (2022) *Net Positive – How Courageous Companies Thrive By Giving More Than They Take*. Boston, MA: Harvard Business Review Press

Exhibits

Sources for exhibits: Statista, Company annual reports, Morningstar, Macrotrends.

Table 4.1: Comparative financial information

Year	2014	2015	2016	2017	2018	2019	2020	2021	2022	2023
Unilever										
Worldwide revenue (€ billion)	48.4	53.3	52.7	53.7	51.0	52.0	50.7	52.4	60.1	59.6
Worldwide operating profit (€ billion)	8.0	7.5	7.8	8.9	12.5	8.7	8.3	8.7	10.8	9.8
Operating margin (%)	16.5%	14.1%	14.8%	16.5%	24.6%	16.8%	16.4%	16.6%	17.9%	16.4%
Employee numbers ('000s)	173	171	169	165	155	150	149	148	138	128
Nestlé										
Worldwide revenue (CHF billion)	91.6	88.8	89.5	89.6	91.4	92.6	84.3	87.1	94.4	93.0
Worldwide operating profit (CHF billion)	14.5	9.1	8.5	7.2	10.1	12.6	12.2	16.9	9.3	11.2
Operating margin (%)	15.8%	10.2%	9.5%	8.0%	11.1%	13.6%	14.5%	19.4%	9.8%	12.1%
Employee numbers ('000s)	339	335	328	323	308	291	273	276	275	270
Proctor & Gamble										
Worldwide revenue (US$ billion)	74.4	70.7	65.3	65.1	66.8	67.7	71.0	76.1	80.2	82.0
Worldwide operating profit (US$ billion)	13.9	11.0	13.3	13.8	13.4	5.5	15.7	18.0	17.8	18.1
Operating margin (%)	18.7%	15.6%	20.3%	21.2%	20.0%	8.1%	22.1%	23.6%	22.2%	22.1%
Employee numbers ('000s)	118	110	105	95	92	97	99	101	106	107
Mondelez*										
Worldwide revenue (US$ billion)	34.2	29.6	25.9	25.9	25.9	25.9	26.6	28.7	31.5	36.0
Worldwide operating profit (US$ billion)	3.2	8.9	3.1	3.5	3.3	3.8	3.9	4.7	3.5	5.5
Operating margin (%)	9.5%	30.0%	12.0%	13.4%	12.8%	14.9%	14.5%	16.2%	11.2%	15.3%
Employee numbers ('000s)	104	99	90	83	80	80	79	79	91	91

Year	2014	2015	2016	2017	2018	2019	2020	2021	2022	2023
Kraft Heinz Company										
Worldwide revenue (US$ billion)	10.9	18.3	26.3	26.1	26.3	25.0	26.2	26.0	26.5	26.6
Worldwide operating profit (US$ billion)	1.6	2.6	6.1	6.1	(10.2)	3.1	2.1	3.5	3.6	4.6
Operating margin (%)	14.4%	14.4%	23.4%	23.2%	-38.8%	12.3%	8.1%	13.3%	13.7%	17.2%
Employee numbers ('000s)	43	42	41	39	38	37	38	36	37	36
Exchange rates										
€/$	1.22	1.09	1.05	1.20	1.15	1.12	1.23	1.13	1.07	1.11
CHF/$	1.01	1.01	0.98	1.03	1.02	1.03	1.11	1.10	1.08	1.19

* Mondelez International, Inc, is a multinational confectionery and snack food business which was spun off from Kraft Foods in 2011 following the acquisition of Cadbury Schweppes.

Table 4.2: Share prices of Unilever and peer group

	Calendar year-end share prices									
	2014	2015	2016	2017	2018	2019	2020	2021	2022	2023
Unilever	$39.68	$43.57	$41.14	$59.38	$31.48	$57.39	$60.96	$53.30	$50.28	$48.49
Nestlé	$70.87	$76.05	$70.95	$82.54	$87.86	$109.96	$111.32	$130.61	$120.61	$115.96
P&G	$91.09	$79.41	$84.08	$91.88	$91.92	$124.90	$139.14	$163.58	$151.56	$146.54
Mondelez	$36.33	$44.84	$44.33	$42.80	$40.03	$55.08	$58.07	$66.31	$66.65	$72.43
Kraft Heinz Company	$50.21	$51.25	$63.27	$57.96	$33.46	$26.41	$30.14	$32.56	$38.50	$36.56

Figure 4.1: Comparative share prices on 31 December indexed to 2014

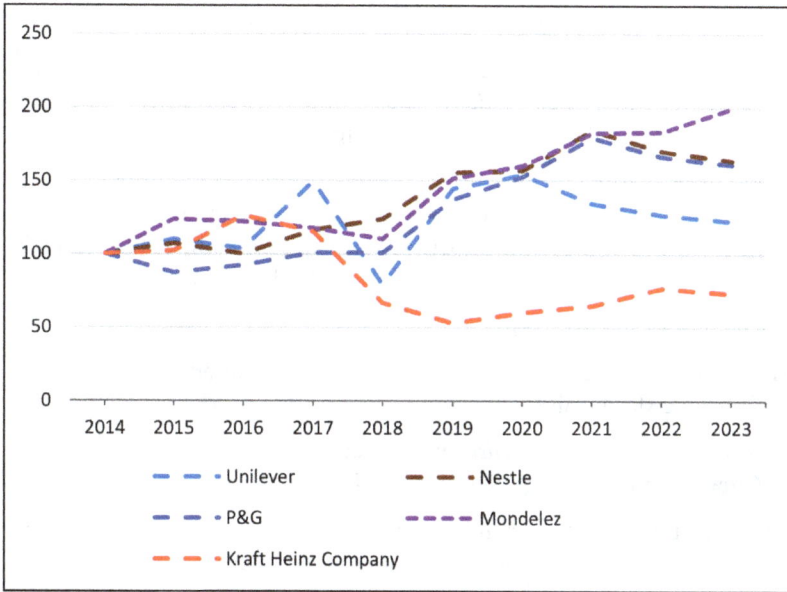

Figure 4.2: Unilever sales segmentation, 2023 (€ billion)

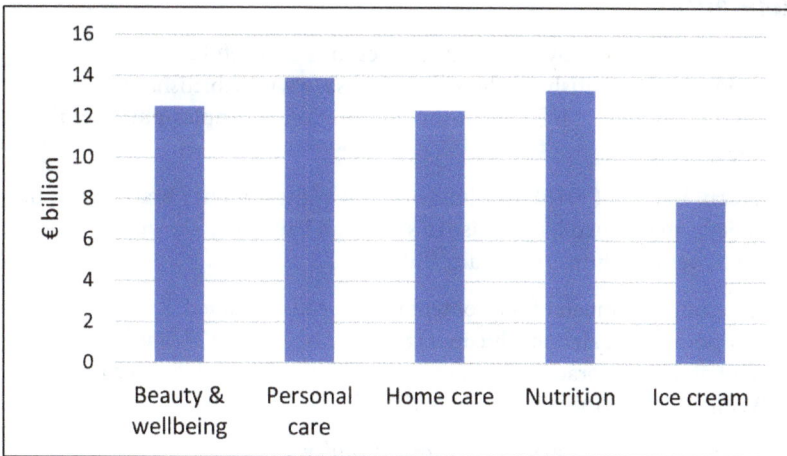

Sources

This case draws on a variety of sources, including two other case studies:

George, William W. and Migdal, Amram (2017, revised 2024) *Battle for the Soul of the Corporation: Unilever and the Kraft Heinz Takeover Bid'*, Harvard Business School case 9-317-127. https://www.hbs.edu/faculty/Pages/item.aspx?num=52733

Salinas, Gabriela and Somasundaram, Jeeva (2024) *'Unilever chief signals rethink on ESG'*, FT Business School teaching case study, 24 May. https://www.ft.com/content/1d685544-abaf-4b32-9da3-6dbb5ed97d3b).

Official histories of Unilever:

Jones, Geoffrey (2005) *Renewing Unilever – Transformation and Tradition.* Oxford: Oxford University Press.

Wilson, Charles (1954) *The History of Unilever – A Study in Economic Growth & Social Change.* Vols 1 and 2. London: Cassell & Co Ltd.

Other material has been drawn from Unilever's annual report and accounts for years 2017 to 2023 and various newspaper articles.

References

[1] The British Academy (2019) 'Principles for Purposeful Business A report by The British Academy', p.8. https://www.thebritishacademy.ac.uk/documents/224/future-of-the-corporation-principles-purposeful-business.pdf

[2] Fearn, Hannah (2016) 'In a final betrayal of the Cadbury brand, Kraft has quietly abandoned its promise to stick with Fairtrade', *The Independent*, 29 November. https://perma.cc/EBY3-97TS

[3] The source of much of the content in the section headed 'Kraft Heinz Corporation' is Harvard Business School case 9-317-127 'Battle for the soul of the corporation: Unilever and the Kraft Heinz Takeover Bid', by William W. George and Amram Migdal.

[4] Wilson, Charles (1954) *The History of Unilever – A Study in Economic Growth & Social Change.* Vols 1 and 2. London: Cassell & Co Ltd.

[5] The Economist (2017) 'The parable of St Paul – Unilever is the world's biggest experiment in corporate do-gooding', *The Economist*, 31 August.

[6] Reuters (2017) 'Unilever rejects $143 bln Kraft offer as bid too low', 17 February. https://www.reuters.com/article/technology/unilever-rejects-143-bln-kraft-offer-as-bid-too-low-idUSKBN15W1FR/

[7] Jope, Alan (2019) 'Marketing has a titanic trust problem', *Unilever News*. 19 June. https://perma.cc/6TVQ-7DWK

[8] Agnew, Harriet and Evans, Judith (2022) 'Terry Smith launches a new attack on Unilever management' *Financial Times*, 20 January. https://www.ft.com/content/210a5297-159c-4d34-8096-933b1d04c4a1

[9] Agnew, Harriet and Evans, Judith (2022)

[10] Agnew, Harriet (2022) 'Unilever has 'lost the plot' by fixating on sustainability, says Terry Smith', *Financial Times*, 12 January. https://www.ft.com/content/7aa44a9a-7fec-4850-8edb-63feee1b837b

[11] Speed, Madeleine (2023) 'Unilever's new chief says corporate purpose can be 'unwelcome distraction'. *Financial Times*, 26 October. https://www.ft.com/content/72ea5061-914a-4bfc-874f-94163bb10c2f

[12] Speed, Madeleine; Levingston, Ivan and Wheatley, Jonathan (2024) 'Unilever to split off ice cream business and cut 7,500 jobs'. *Financial Times*, 19 March. https://www.ft.com/content/c7b44b4a-e4c7-45b4-8831-c07c2172b181

Part 3
Governance, accounting and control

5. Asset allocation and governance at the Imperial Tobacco pension fund in the mid-20th century

Yally Avrahampour

The Imperial Tobacco pension fund case considers a seminal moment in the history of occupational pension fund management in the UK. The case engages with Imperial Tobacco's defined benefit pension fund trustee board at the moment in 1955 when the trustees revisited the proposal by Imperial Tobacco's pension fund manager, George Ross Goobey, to invest the pension fund, one of the largest in the UK, entirely in common stocks, preference stocks and real estate.

This case is concerned with exploring the relationship between the practice of management as an internal set of rules and management as interacting and advocating standards that relate to external rules relating to governance. It highlights the reasons that managers engage with professional standards as part of their management practice. More generally, the case is an opportunity to consider cultural changes in the approach to governance.

Guidance on how to write a case analysis can be found in Chapter 1, 'Business cases: What are they, why do we use them and how should you go about doing a case analysis?'.

A teaching note for this case is available to bona fide educators. To request a copy please email y.avrahampour@lse.ac.uk

Introduction

Sir Percy James 'PJ' Grigg, chair of Imperial Tobacco's Investment Committee, looked across the table at Imperial Tobacco's chief accountant and the board of trustees of the Imperial Tobacco pension fund. It was 1955 and the trustees were considering a change to the investment policy of the pension fund,

---

How to cite this book chapter:

Avrahampour, Yally (2025) 'Asset allocation and governance at the Imperial Tobacco pension fund in the mid-20th century', in: Sallai, Dorottya and Pepper, Alexander (ed) *Navigating the 21st Century Business World: Case Studies in Management*, London: LSE Press, pp. 71–87. https://doi.org/10.31389/lsepress.nbw.e

proposed by George Ross Goobey, Imperial Tobacco's pension manager. Ross Goobey proposed that the trustees approve the investment of the pension fund's assets entirely in common stock, preferred stock and real estate.

The trustees were not surprised to be considering this proposed change, for two reasons. First, they had considered and rejected this proposed change in 1953. The primary reason for the rejection was that Ross Goobey's proposed policy would require them to sell the substantial proportion of the fixed income securities held by the pension fund at a loss. Consequently, in 1953 the trustees permitted Ross Goobey to invest only new contributions to the pension fund into equities. Figure 5.1 shows the asset allocation of the Imperial Tobacco pension fund between 1930 and June 1954.

Second, Ross Goobey, a qualified actuary, was hired at Imperial Tobacco in 1947 and tasked with providing professional investment management and increasing the returns on the investments made by the pension fund, in advance of the quinquennial actuarial valuation taking place in 1949. Ross Goobey was taking over the management of the pension fund from the chief accountant, in part because the actuarial valuation entailed that the management of the pension fund increasingly required investment sophistication. In 1951, Randall Haigh, also an actuary, joined Imperial Tobacco pension fund as Ross Goobey's assistant. Over subsequent years, Ross Goobey, assisted by Haigh, set about engaging the trustees with a view to converting them to his view regarding equity investment. By now the trustees were quite familiar with Ross Goobey's arguments.

Figure 5.1: Imperial Tobacco pension fund distribution of investments at book value (1930–June 1954)

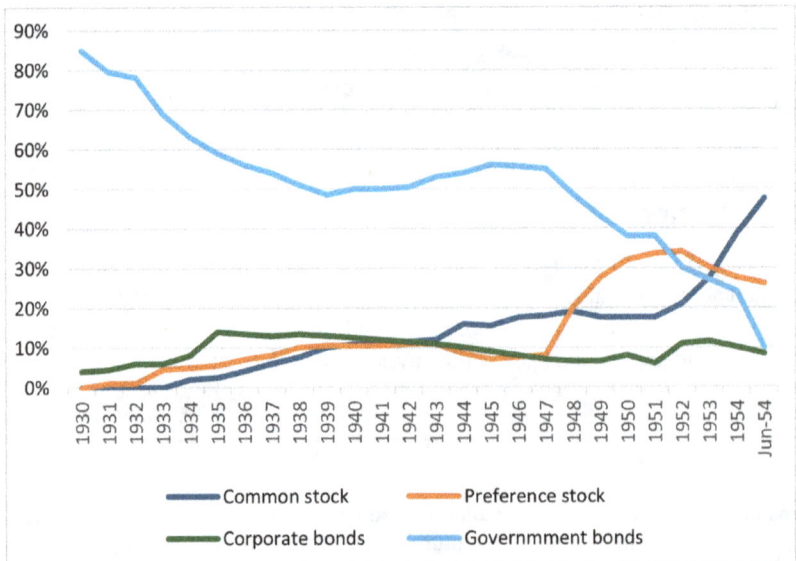

Source: Ross Goobey, G. (1955a)[1]

It was, therefore, time for the trustees to reconsider this proposed change to the pension fund's investment policy, and Grigg wondered whether they would approve it. At the heart of the dilemma faced by the trustees was the fact that, for the past century, UK pension funds, including Imperial Tobacco's, had focused on a safety-first approach, investing predominantly in gilts. In this respect, pension funds were replicating the investment policy of life insurance companies, which also focused on gilts and other high-quality fixed income securities. Of course, large insurance companies and pension funds had already invested a little in equities. It was well known in life insurance circles that, in the 1930s, Professor John Maynard Keynes, serving as the chair of the investment committee of the National Mutual insurance company, advocated that the National Mutual should invest more in equities and real estate. Sam Clayton, manager of the Rowntree pension fund, invested around a third of the assets of this pension fund in common stock in the 1930s and 1940s. However, no occupational pension fund had taken the decision to invest the entirety of its assets in common stock, preferred stock and real estate.

In December 1954, the Imperial Tobacco pension fund had assets of £20 million. This made it one of the largest UK pension funds. If the trustees followed Ross Goobey's recommendation, their decision would challenge conventional investment practice in the pensions and insurance industry and would signal acceptance of the idea that pension funds could dramatically increase the risk of their investment policy.

Grigg also wondered how the trustees would respond to Ross Goobey's growing influence in the actuarial profession and in the pensions industry. In 1953, Ross Goobey was invited to coordinate the investment protection service of the Association of Superannuation and Pension Funds (ASPF), the pension fund industry body. This investment protection service, established by Gordon Hosking in 1950, enabled pension funds to collaborate with the British Insurance Association and Association of Investment Trusts who had established their own investment protection committees in 1932.

Further, as a qualified actuary, Ross Goobey participated in increasingly fractious debates at the Institute of Actuaries regarding the actuarial assessment of the funding level of occupational pension funds, known as the 'actuarial valuation'. A new generation of consulting actuaries were rethinking the traditional approach to the actuarial valuation of pension funds. They sought to expand the scope of the jurisdiction of the actuarial profession towards developing expertise in financial matters.[2] Ross Goobey was supportive of the approach adopted by the new generation.[3]

However, the consulting actuary of Imperial Tobacco's pension fund was Sir John Gunlake, an eminent practitioner and head partner at the leading consulting actuarial partnership, R. Watson & Sons. Gunlake was sceptical about Ross Goobey's proposed investment policy and unsupportive of the modern approach to the actuarial valuation. This scepticism was also evident in his assessment of the funding level of Imperial Tobacco's pension fund. Grigg was well aware that the traditional, conservative approach to actuarial valuation would delay the financial recognition of the gains from riskier assets, and to some extent undermine the financial impact of the changes to the investment policy being proposed by Ross Goobey. Still, Grigg felt optimistic.

Background

Occupational pension funds

In the UK, in addition to the role of the state in providing a social security safety net through the state pension, employers also play a role in providing their employees with income in retirement. Whereas the state pays the pension on a pay-as-you-go basis, from taxation, and is therefore 'unfunded', occupational pension provision is 'funded'. In funded occupational pension systems, the retirement income paid to beneficiaries is paid either from the invested assets of a pension fund or of a life insurance company. Pension funds are established as a trust, an investment vehicle into which the employing organisation, and sometimes the employees, pay monetary contributions. The accumulated contributions are the assets that are invested and ultimately used to pay retirement income to beneficiaries. Alternatively, the sponsoring firm pays the contributions to a life insurance company, which invests the contributions and pays retirement income to the sponsoring firm's beneficiaries.

Pension fund benefit design

There are two primary approaches to the design of the benefits paid as retirement income. In the 'defined contribution' benefit design, the contributions of the sponsoring firm are fixed, and the income paid in retirement to the beneficiary fluctuates in relation to investment performance of the assets. In contrast, in the 'defined benefit' pension benefit design, the beneficiary receives a defined income in retirement. The income paid in retirement is based primarily on salary during employment and length of service to the employer. The employing firm's contributions to the pension fund fluctuate in response to the changes in the value of the assets of the pension fund which are available to pay the income in retirement and the present value of the retirement income that the pension fund has promised to pay to the beneficiaries, namely, its liabilities.

Occupational pension fund governance: pension fund actuarial valuation

The actuarial valuation of a defined benefit pension fund is an assessment of the ability of the pension fund to pay the promised level of retirement income to its beneficiaries. The valuation assesses the funding level of the pension fund, namely whether the pension fund has sufficient assets to pay its liabilities. The liabilities reflect the pension fund's obligation to provide a defined level of income in retirement. The difference between the value of the assets and the value of the liabilities determines whether the funding level of the pension fund is in deficit or surplus. If the assets exceed the liabilities, the pension fund is in surplus. In such an instance, the sponsor may reduce its contributions or even take a 'contribution holiday': a determinate period of time when the employer is permitted to pause its contributions to the pension fund. Alternatively, if liabilities exceed assets and the pension fund is in deficit, the sponsor increases its contributions to cover the deficit. The actuarial valuation of the pension fund's funding level thus also determines the schedule of contributions that the sponsoring firm must pay until its defined benefit pension fund has an adequate level of funding.

In assigning values to assets and liabilities, the actuarial valuation of a defined benefit pension fund makes two types of assumption, collectively known as the 'actuarial basis'. The first are statistical assumptions. These enable the actuary to estimate the magnitude and timing of future pension payments to beneficiaries that arise from the benefit design of the pension fund, the membership's longevity, salary levels and macroeconomic conditions, such as inflation. The second are financial assumptions. These enable the actuary to assign a present value to the estimated future retirement income payments made to the beneficiaries of the pension fund. To do this, the actuarial valuation makes use of discounted income techniques and specifically selects a discount rate. The lower the discount rate selected to assign a present value to future payments, the higher the present value of those payments and the greater are the liabilities. The higher the discount rate, the lower the present value of the estimated future payments and the pension fund's liabilities.

Governance of occupational pension funds: pension fund financial accounting

There are two types of pension fund financial accounting standard. The first relates to the disclosures made in the financial accounts of the sponsoring firm regarding the financial condition of its pension fund. The second relates to the financial accounts of the pension fund itself. Key information relating to defined benefits pension funds in both types of report includes the value of assets and liabilities, whether the funding level is in surplus or deficit, the cost of the pension fund to the sponsor and the annual contributions paid to the pension fund by the sponsoring firm. Accounting reports may use a separate actuarial basis from that of the actuarial valuation or may simply replicate the assumptions and information provided within the actuarial valuation within the financial accounts.

History of investment policy at the Imperial Tobacco pension fund to 1955

The Imperial Tobacco pension fund

The Imperial Tobacco company established a defined benefits pension fund in 1929. Initially, the chief accountant of Imperial Tobacco managed the fund and it guaranteed a minimum annual rate of return of 5 per cent on its assets. If the investment return on the assets fell below this rate, the sponsoring firm was obliged to increase its contributions to match the level the fund would have had if its assets had increased by the guaranteed rate. This policy of providing a guarantee was not uncommon at the time and was a means of providing assurance to the beneficiaries of the pension fund (Imperial Tobacco's current and former employees) that the pension fund was and would remain in good financial health. Consistent with actuarial valuation standards of that time, the discount rate used to assign a present value to the liabilities was also set at 5 per cent. The guaranteed return was achieved by investing in safe securities, such as UK government bonds or corporate bonds yielding 5 per cent or more. Increasingly, however, in the 1930s and 1940s, as interest rates fell, the yield on government securities and corporate securities also declined, and it became increasingly difficult for the pension fund to meet its 5 per cent guarantee by investing in high-quality fixed income securities.

In response to these falling yields, the chief accountant diversified the pension fund into higher-yielding investments, such as corporate bonds, preference shares, real estate and, to a smaller extent, common stocks, which offered attractive yields compared to fixed-income securities. Thus, although

Figure 5.2: Yield on invested assets of the Imperial Tobacco pension fund (1930–June 1954)

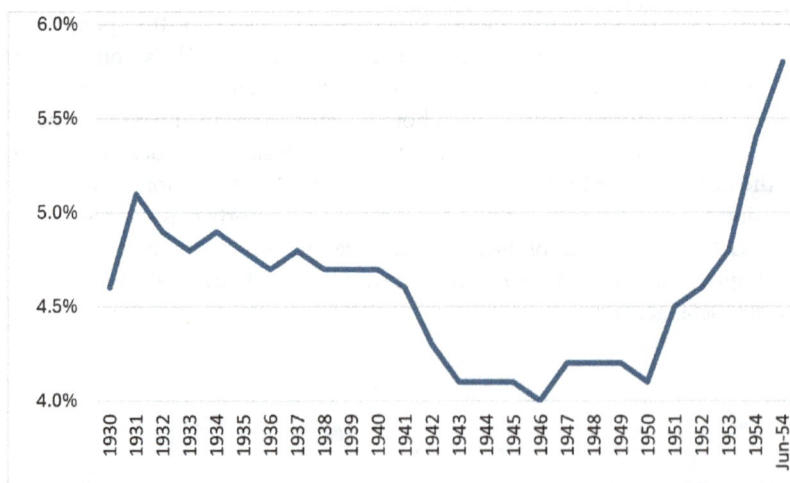

Source: Ross Goobey, G. (1955a)[4]

the Imperial Tobacco pension fund had initially been invested almost entirely in gilts, by 1949 the asset allocation of the pension fund was approximately 50 per cent gilts, 10 per cent corporate fixed income, 20 per cent preference shares and 20 per cent common shares. The changing investment policy of the pension fund was a consequence of the ongoing difficulty of achieving the goal of a 5 per cent yield. Figure 5.2 shows the yield of the pension fund between 1930 and June 1954.

Following the 1949 actuarial valuation, the trustees reduced the guaranteed increase on the assets of the pension fund from 5 per cent to 4 per cent, making it easier to invest in assets with a sufficiently high yield, exceeding the 4 per cent guaranteed rate. However, simultaneously, the discount rate used to assign a present value to the pension fund's liabilities was lowered to 4 per cent. A consequence of the lower discount rate was that the value of the liabilities increased. The increase in the value of the liabilities reduced the funding level of the pension fund and increased the contributions that Gunlake advised Imperial Tobacco company to pay to its pension fund.

Sir Percy James 'PJ' Grigg

Sir Percy James Grigg had a distinguished career in the British Civil Service in India in the inter-war years. Increasingly specialising in issues relating to finance, he was subsequently chair of the board of the Inland Revenue and Secretary of State for War in Churchill's coalition government during the Second World War. Grigg was a non-executive director of Prudential Assurance Company, the National Provincial Bank and the Distillers Company, as well as at Imperial Tobacco. He joined the board of directors of Imperial Tobacco in 1947 after his return to England, having contributed to the establishment of the International Bank for Reconstruction and Development in New York. Grigg was chair of the two-member investment advisory committee to the Imperial Tobacco board of directors. The other member was Imperial Tobacco's chief accountant.

George Ross Goobey

Ross Goobey qualified as an actuary between 1930 and 1941. During this time, he worked at various small insurance companies, specialising in the investment part of the insurance world. In 1934, he moved to the Legal & General Assurance Society. Legal & General's chief actuary, Harold Raynes, had published influential articles on the long-term outperformance of common stocks relative to government bonds, and his influence on Ross Goobey was evident.[5] Ross Goobey referred to Raynes' studies when advocating investment in equities. Ross Goobey's decision to work for a pension fund, rather than a life insurance company or a consulting actuarial partnership, was an unconventional one for an actuary. In doing so, he followed the career path of Gordon Hosking, fellow actuary, pension manager at Courtaulds and author of a textbook on the topic of occupational pension fund management.

Ross Goobey's arguments in favour of an equities only investment policy

Ross Goobey's investment philosophy was based on the income or yield paid by the security. The rationale for investing in common stocks was that the dividend yield paid by them exceeded the rate of interest received from government bonds. To reduce the risk posed by common stocks, Ross Goobey would diversify the portfolio by investing in a large number of shares. The assets of the Imperial Tobacco pension fund were consequently invested in the common stock of over a thousand companies, including large and small, and listed and unlisted companies, as well as in a large number of real estate holdings.

Moreover, Ross Goobey argued that the inflation of the post-war era also justified investment in common stock and real estate. He recognised early on that inflation would remain a feature of the investment environment and understood the effect this would have on increasing liabilities of defined benefit pension funds and falling bond prices. UK government bonds were fixed income or had a coupon that was linked to short-term interest rates. In neither case were these payments linked to an index measuring the rate of inflation. In contrast, the dividends from common stocks could increase as the profits earned by companies increased. This was regarded as a safeguard against the negative effects of inflation on the funding levels of defined benefit pension funds. For example, in an inflationary environment, the value of pension fund liabilities rose as salary levels rose. The Exhibits section provides excerpts from a series of explanatory statements by Ross Goobey in setting out his policy to the trustee board.

Imperial Tobacco Company

The Imperial Tobacco company was formed from the amalgamation of 13 companies in the tobacco sector. During the Second World War, wartime rationing strictly limited sales of tobacco products and Imperial Tobacco reduced costs by eliminating almost all advertising. There was a slow return to normality in the early to mid-1950s. Table 5.1 shows the Imperial Tobacco net profit on return on capital employed in the early to mid-1950s.

Table 5.1: Returns of Imperial Tobacco Co in the early 1950s

Year	% net profit /capital employed
1951	15.0%
1952	14.3%
1953	14.4%
1954	14.0%
1955	13.8%

Source: Alford (2013) p. 418[6]

Engagement with the setting of standards relating to governance

In the pre-war years, actuarial valuations of defined benefit pension funds were conservative and were dominated by the requirements of life insurance companies. Actuarial expertise was considered to be associated with the statistical assumptions relating to longevity. It was accepted that consulting actuaries would use judgement in applying statistical models to estimate the longevity of the members of the pension fund. However, the financial assumptions used to value the pension fund assets and liabilities were not regarded as a legitimate area of actuarial expertise.

Consequently, in first half of the 20th century, the actuarial profession took careful steps to reduce, as far as possible, the potential for consulting actuaries to exercise judgement in relation to the financial assumptions. The assets of the pension fund were valued at historical cost or market price, whichever was lower – a traditional accounting valuation technique. The discount rate used to assign a present value to liabilities was equated to the rate of return that could be expected to be earned on the pension fund's investments. In estimating this expected rate, actuarial valuations sought to avoid relying on the judgement of the consulting actuary. Thus, consulting actuaries derived the expected rate of return of the pension fund in two ways. If the sponsoring firm provided a guarantee regarding the rate of return of the pension fund, the discount rate in the actuarial valuation was equated with the guaranteed rate of return. The rationale was that the sponsor would not set a guarantee that differed from the expected rate of return. If the sponsoring firm did not provide a guarantee, the risk-free government bond rate plus a small percentage was used to assign a present value to the liabilities. In this respect, selection of a discount rate that was based on the risk-free government bond rate also reflected the fact that pension fund investment was primarily oriented towards investment in UK government securities. Both approaches excluded the possibility that actuaries could exercise judgement regarding the future returns of the pension fund.

Consulting actuaries could exercise judgement over the financial assumptions in limited circumstances. For example, if the pension fund invested in equities to achieve higher returns, the consulting actuary would reduce the discount rate. The rationale was that there was the need for safety margins that sought to protect the pension fund in case of decline in the value of its assets.

This conservative approach relating to the actuarial valuation placed increasing pressures on the funding levels of occupational pension funds and culminated in a public expression of dissatisfaction with the UK system of funded occupational pension provision. In 1954, Bedfordshire County Council put forward a parliamentary bill that proposed providing occupational pensions for municipal authorities on an unfunded, pay-as-you-go basis. The bill failed in parliament. Its impact, however, was widespread and while the principle of funding occupational pensions remained widely accepted, the actuarial valuation as the method of implementing the funding approach was subject to increased scrutiny.

Gradually, therefore, the mid-20th century was characterised by actuaries engaging with the financial assumptions for the actuarial valuation. Increased attention was paid to the possible use of judgement by consulting actuaries in relation to the financial assumptions of the actuarial valuation, whereas previously the use of judgement was limited to the making of the statistical assumptions. Actuarial debate was shifting towards valuing both assets and liabilities using discounting techniques, which were the specialism of the actuarial profession. The value of pension fund assets and liabilities would be their present value. Consulting actuaries would select a discount rate for this estimation, based on their estimation of the future returns of the pension fund. The judgement of the consulting actuary regarding the rate of return of the pension fund would suffice to select the appropriate discount rate.

Ross Goobey championed the views of the new generation of consulting actuaries and was critical of the traditional approach to the setting of financial assumptions in actuarial valuations. Notably, Sir John Gunlake, the consulting actuary to the Imperial Tobacco pension fund was on the side of the traditionalists. Furthermore, Gunlake was using conservative assumptions in relation to the Imperial Tobacco pension fund.

Sir John Gunlake

Sir John Gunlake was the senior partner at R. Watson & Sons, the largest actuarial consultancy in the UK. In 1960–1961, Gunlake would become the first consulting actuary to be elected president of the Institute of Actuaries. Previously, all presidents had been life insurance actuaries working in life insurance companies. During the Second World War, Gunlake worked as statistical adviser in the Statistics and Intelligence Division of the Ministry of Shipping and attended the Washington, Quebec, Cairo and Yalta conferences as statistical adviser. He was awarded the CBE in 1947, was a fellow of the Institute of Statistics and was involved in the 1953–1954 Philips Committee, the 'Commission on the Economic and Financial Problems on the Provision for Old Age'.

The setting of pension fund financial accounting standards

In 1942, the Institute of Chartered Accountants in England & Wales (ICAEW) began to promulgate recommendations for its members regarding accounting standards. These accounting recommendations were incorporated into company law in the 1948 Companies Act. In 1953, the ICAEW began to debate the first pension fund financial accounting standard, specifically how sponsoring firms and their pension funds would disclose the value of the assets and liabilities of the pension fund.

The setting of standards relating to corporate governance

In 1953 Ross Goobey joined the ASPF council. The association was established in 1923 but had not dealt with matters relating to the investment of pension funds, focusing instead on lobbying government on matters relating to taxation of pension provision. Ross Goobey's membership on the council brought greater focus by the ASPF on educating its members regarding investment. He gave talks to the membership on investment and administered its investment protection service, the means by which pension funds collectively protected their investments from changes to the terms of those investments in ways that could be detrimental to their value. Cooperation between different pension funds entailed, for example, combining their vote on a particular proposal raised by the company issuing the securities in order to oppose or approve it. Investment protection committees of the British Insurance Association and Association of Investment Trusts had been active in upholding standards relating to corporate governance since 1932. More often than not, investors in a particular committee would contact a company behind the scenes in advance of the proposal being formalised to take pre-emptive action. Since 1953, Ross Goobey and his team had been involved in the determination of the standards relating to investment protection that would be adopted by the ASPF in conducting investment protection for the ASPF's members.

Conclusion: contemporary parallels

The Imperial Tobacco pension fund case considers a seminal moment in the history of occupational pension fund management in the UK. The case engages with Imperial Tobacco's defined benefit pension fund trustee board at the moment in 1955 that the trustees revisited the proposal by Imperial Tobacco's pension fund manager, George Ross Goobey, to invest the pension fund – one of the largest in the UK – entirely in common stocks, preference stocks and real estate. Beyond the interest arising in relation to its unique historical characteristics, this case addresses five theoretical topics relating to management and organisations.

First, the case raises questions regarding the implications of external standards relating to governance for management. The case focuses primarily on the setting of standards relating to governance, such as the recommendations on accounting, standards relating to actuarial valuation and investment protection, rather than the standards relating to management accounting. It therefore seeks to focus attention on the relationship between these external standards relating to governance and management.

Second, the case presents the relationship between external standards of governance and management at a time when the standards under discussion incorporate professional judgement (of consulting actuaries in relation to financial assumptions in the actuarial valuation) to a greater, rather than a lesser, extent. This increased use of professional judgement in relation to financial estimates contrasts with the history from the 1970s to 2025, during which this judgement has gradually been eroded. Furthermore, the literature on the consequences of financial accounting disclosure for organisations has focused on the eras during which the shift has been towards reduction of, rather than increased, professional judgement.

Third, the case describes how, concurrently with implementing the change in investment policy at the Imperial Tobacco pension fund, Ross Goobey sought to increase rather than decrease the degree of reliance on professional judgement in standards relating to the actuarial valuation. It is interesting to note that this intervention took place prior to the development of financial economics in the mid-1960s, of modern portfolio theory and the risk management techniques predicated on improvements in understanding the relationship between risk and return.

Fourth, this case offers a comparison of common approaches to the management of occupational pension funds in the 1930s and in contemporary pension provision, which suggests strong similarities. In 2025, firms sponsor defined contribution rather than defined benefit occupational pension funds. Sponsoring firms with a defined benefit pension fund often seek to close the defined benefit pension fund and transfer it to a life insurance company, or a similar financial entity. The investment policy of defined benefit pension funds is directed in the main to invest in fixed-income securities rather than equities. Further, the standards relating to the selection of the financial assumptions of the actuarial valuation of the pension fund do not permit actuarial judgement. Financial accounting standards offer a high degree of transparency relating to the investments of the pension fund. In short, counter-intuitively, similarities appear to exist between sponsoring firms' occupational pension provision in the 1930s and in 2025.

Fifth, the Imperial Tobacco pension fund case explores the role of chair Sir Percy James Grigg in supporting Ross Goobey. As chair of Imperial Tobacco's Investment Committee, Grigg features in this case as a general manager, who integrates the performance of a specialist manager, Ross Goobey, into the overall financial affairs of Imperial Tobacco. The case raises questions regarding the nature of the agency relationship between Grigg and Ross Goobey. It also raises questions about the nature of management and its relationship to agency by framing the case from Grigg's perspective.

Preparing the case

In preparing the case analysis you might like to consider the following specific questions in particular:

1. Describe the context relating to occupational pension provision prior to the start of the case.

2. What features of the prevailing approach to pension fund management was Ross Goobey seeking to change?
3. Should the trustees of the Imperial Tobacco pension fund have been concerned about Ross Goobey's engagement in the setting of standards relating to the governance of occupational pensions described in the case?
4. Apply the theoretical perspectives outlined in the following two further readings to this case: Rajan & Zingales (1998) and White (1992). Compare and contrast the conclusions that these two perspectives lead you to draw regarding the relationship between Ross Goobey, Sir James Grigg and Sir John Gunlake.
5. What differences and similarities do you observe between the context for pension fund governance and investment in the mid-20th century and in 2025?

Further reading

Avrahampour, Y. (2015) '"Cult of equity": Actuaries and the transformation of pension fund investing, 1948–1960', *Business History Review*, vol. 89, no. 2, pp. 281–304. https://doi.org/10.1017/S0007680515000367

Ross Goobey, A. (1987) *The Money Moguls: The Inside Story of Investment Management*, Cambridge: Woodhead-Faulkner.

Nicholls, A. and Tomkinson, E. (2015) 'Risk and return in social finance', in Nicholls, A., Paton, R. and Emerson, J. (eds) *Social Finance*, Oxford: Oxford University Press, pp. 282–310. https://doi.org/10.1093/acprof:oso/9780198703761.003.0011

Rajan, R. G., and Zingales, L. (1998) 'Power in a theory of the firm', *The Quarterly Journal of Economics*, vol. 113, no. 2, pp. 387–432. https://doi.org/10.1162/003355398555630

White, H. (1992) 'Agency as control in formal networks', in Nohria, N. and Eccles, R. (eds) *Networks and Organizations: Structure, Form and Action*, pp. 92–117. Boston, MA: Harvard Business School Press.

Exhibits: Excerpts relating to Ross Goobey's rationale in advocating for common stock investment to Imperial Tobacco's board trustees

The objectives of pension fund investment policy

Ross Goobey linked the rate of interest used by the actuary to value pension fund liabilities to pension fund investment policy:

> The object of Pension Fund investment is to invest the contributions as they are received at a rate of interest equal to or greater than the rate which the Actuary assumed in his calculations.[7]

Ross Goobey's focus was on creating a portfolio of securities that would generate a yield that was higher than the discount rate assumed by the actuary:

> Our attention need not be focused on the capital side, that is to say, the day-to-day market value of the capital, but can be concentrated on the income, and our chief concern is to ensure that the average annual income is sufficient to produce a yield calculated on the purchase price equal to or greater than the rate assumed by the actuary in his calculations.[8]

The yield of the pension fund portfolio assumes central importance with respect to investment policy:

> In a pension fund the market value position is certainly not the prime consideration. The life blood of a pension fund is the interest earned on the investments, and one is only concerned with the market value insofar as this reflects the improvement in the interest income, which of course it does when a large proportion of ordinary stocks and shares are held.[9]

Ross Goobey's investment strategy was to invest in the asset class that would generate the greatest possible income. The potential for equities to pay increasing dividends led him to consider equities (and property) as the most suitable asset class and as the only appropriate asset class for pension funds. Ross Goobey writes:

> There seems little logic, however, in accepting equities at all for inclusion in investment portfolios without being prepared to agree on a policy of 100%. If one is convinced that they are worth including for the obvious advantages which they possess, then there seems to be no reason why one should not have all of one's investments in the most attractive asset class.[10]

There are several reasons that yield can acquire such a significant role relative to total return, or market value, in a pension fund. These are outlined by Ross Goobey in a comparison of pension funds with insurance companies and include: the long-dated nature of pension fund liabilities, their link with inflation in salary levels, the absence of market-based solvency and accounting requirements, the gross yield on income received by pension funds and the small likelihood of having to liquidate investments.[11]

Ross Goobey focused on the dividend yield, but this was in the context of a successful and continuing business:

> I have been accused of 'being interested only in yield', the implication being that the higher the conventionally quoted yield is the more I am attracted to a stock. This is true to a certain extent, especially when dealing with a Pension Fund, the income of which is free of tax, but I am of course aware that the conventionally quoted yield is based on last year's dividend only, and that the realized yield (and this alone is the yield which we are concerned) depends on the dividends received in the future. Therefore, with each investment that we make there is a mental appraisal of the chances of last years dividend being maintained or increased.[12]

The decision to invest in stocks is not solely based on yield, but also on the ability of the underlying company to cover the dividend yield in the foreseeable future. The selling policy was also oriented around yield so that one would be justified in selling a low-yielding bond in order to purchase one with a higher yield or a share with a higher yield. The development of new and sophisticated ways of analysing companies was perhaps particularly marked in later years.

The objectives of pension fund investment management: integration with corporate organisation

> During 'Daltonian' [low interest rates] eras we should avoid investing as far as possible and the recent policy of anticipation will help in this respect. Although under the terms of the Trust Deed we cannot 'lend money to the Company' we can by anticipation or deferment of the Company's acknowledged liabilities to the Pension Fund regulate to a certain extent the investment of Pension Fund monies ... During periods of cheap money we might well seek refuge in dated Debentures in the hope that when these come to be redeemed we may then be back on higher interest rates for its re-investment or we might even consider exchanging the Debentures into undated securities (Ordinary shares again perhaps) when conditions are suitable.[13]

Ross Goobey concludes a presentation to the trustees as follows:

> The pension fund has become a profitable part of the company's activities, the annual rate of profit of which, including excess interest and the other activities briefly mentioned above, is running well in excess of ½ million pounds per annum.[14]

References

[1] Ross Goobey, G. (1955a) 'The effect of the change in the investment policy of the pension fund', 18 January. Ross Goobey Collection, The London Archives, LMA/4481/01/006.

[2] Puckridge, C. (1948) 'The rate of interest which should be employed in the valuation of a pension fund and the values which should be placed on the existing investments.' *Journal of the Institute of Actuaries*, vol. 74, pp.1–30.

[3] Menzler, F. (1925). 'Proposed Extension of Professional Scope.' *Journal of the Institute of Actuaries*, vol. 55, pp. 88–126.

[4] Ross Goobey, G. (1955a)

[5] Raynes, H. (1928) 'The Place of Ordinary Stocks and Shares (As Distinct From Fixed Interest Bearing Securities) in the Investment of Life Assurance Funds.' *Journal of the Institute of Actuaries*, vol. 59, pp. 21–50; and Raynes, H. (1937) 'Equities and Fixed Interest Stocks during Twenty-Five Years', *Journal of the Institute of Actuaries*, vol. 68, pp. 483–507.

[6] Alford, B. W. E. (2013) *WD & HO Wills and the Development of the UK Tobacco Industry: 1786–1965*. London: Routledge.

[7] Ross Goobey, G. (1955b) 'Note prepared for Sir James Grigg to endeavour to reassure him why it is not unsound to sell a security at a loss', July. Ross Goobey Collection, The London Archives, LMA/4481/01/006.

[8] Ross Goobey, G. (1955b)

[9] Ross Goobey, G. (1955a) p. 2.

[10] Ross Goobey, G. (1989) 'Pension Fund Investment Policy, Review of the Investment Policy of the Pension Fund', in Ellis, C. and Vertin, J. (eds), *Classics: An Investor's Anthology*, London: Longman Higher Education, p.254.

[11] See Ross Goobey, G. (1956) 'Pension Fund Investments', Circular Letter 255: Report of the ASPF Autumn Conference, Brighton, November. London: Association of Superannuation and Pension Funds, National Association of Pension Funds Collection, The London Archives, LMA/4494/A/04, pp. 26–34; also Ross Goobey, G. (1961–1962) 'Pension Fund Investment', *Stock Exchange Journal*, vol. 7, pp. 15–18.

[12] Ross Goobey, G. (1989) p. 256.

[13] Ross Goobey. G. (1953) 'Notes on investment policy for the pension fund', 5 October, Ross Goobey Collection, The London Archives, LMA/4481/01/002, p. 2.

[14] Ross Goobey, G. (1955a) p. 3.

6. The fall of the Maxwell empire

Alexander Pepper

This case uses a number of independent reports on Robert Maxwell's business practices and the flotation of Mirror Group Newspapers (MGN), videos and other secondary material, to examine the rise and fall of the Maxwell empire. It can be used to teach how corporate governance in the UK has developed since 1990, the role of auditors and directors, the significance of pension funds in the capital markets, developments in pensions law, and the strengths and risks of a 'productive narcissist' CEO. 'The fall of the Maxwell empire' is a 'raw case' – an open-ended, multi-perspective study that can feature thousands of pages of relevant material that students must analyse, such as statutory documents, analyst reports, news articles, stock charts and interviews with key players. This format reflects the way managers must access and analyse information to make informed business decisions.

The Maxwell case can be used to teach students about corporate governance, focusing on why good corporate governance is necessary, how the UK corporate governance regime developed in response to the Maxwell debacle, the importance of pension funds, and the role and responsibilities of auditors. It also examines a particular type of business leader and how productive narcissism can become toxic.

Guidance on how to write a case analysis can be found in Chapter 1, 'Business cases: what are they, why do we use them and how should you go about doing a case analysis?'.

A teaching note for this case is available to bona fide educators. To request a copy please email a.a.pepper@lse.ac.uk

How to cite this book chapter:

Pepper, Alexander (2025) 'The fall of the Maxwell empire', in: Sallai, Dorottya and Pepper, Alexander (ed) *Navigating the 21st Century Business World: Case Studies in Management*, London: LSE Press, pp. 89–93. https://doi.org/10.31389/lsepress.nbw.f

Introduction

On 5 November 1991, Robert Maxwell, a media mogul, was pronounced dead after his body was found floating in the Atlantic Ocean. He had last been seen alive on his yacht the *Lady Ghislaine*, and it was assumed that he had fallen overboard – the official ruling was of accidental death by drowning. After his death, Maxwell's publishing empire collapsed as banks called in their loans. At the same time a massive hole was discovered in the pension fund of the Mirror group, money having been diverted fraudulently by Maxwell in an attempt to shore up the finances of his business empire. The Maxwell companies filed for bankruptcy in 1992. Two of Robert Maxwell's children, Ian and Kevin, were subsequently prosecuted for fraud, though many years later both were eventually acquitted.

In 2001, following the conclusion of the legal cases against Ian and Kevin Maxwell, a report into the circumstances surrounding the flotation of the Mirror Group Newspapers was published by the Department of Trade and Industry (DTI). The DTI had commissioned the report in June 1992 and appointed a senior judge and leading accountant to carry out the investigation. The report, which runs to 372 pages and 20 appendices and is contained in two volumes, is very detailed and is the primary source of data for this case study.

Robert Maxwell

Robert Maxwell (or 'RM' as he was widely known) was born in 1923 to Jewish parents in a town called Solotvino, which is now part of Ukraine. At the time of Maxwell's birth Solotvino was in what was then called Czechoslovakia, although the town was later reclaimed by Hungary in 1939. RM escaped to France before the start of the Second World War and subsequently moved to Britain. Most of his family was killed at Auschwitz.

RM became a successful businessman in his adopted homeland, building up an academic publishing group, Pergamon Press, based in Oxford. In 1970, RM lost control of Pergamon in circumstances which led to a DTI investigation. This concluded that Maxwell was 'not fit to run a public company'; nevertheless, he eventually regained control of Pergamon and, in 1981, acquired a majority stake in the British Printing Corporation, a listed company, subsequently renamed Maxwell Communications Corporation (MCC). In 1984, RM achieved a lifetime ambition to become the proprietor of a major British newspaper when Pergamon acquired the Daily Mirror from Reed International.

Mirror Group Newspapers (MGN)

The *Daily Mirror* was launched in 1903 by Alfred Harmsworth, later Viscount Northcliffe, elder brother of Viscount Rothermere, both famous British newspaper proprietors. Shares in the *Daily Mirror* were listed on the London

Stock Exchange in 1953, but the company was subsequently acquired by International Publishing Corporation, which in turn was later acquired by Reed International. In 1984, Reed International, which was planning to dispose of the *Daily Mirror* by floating its shares separately on the London Stock Exchange, sold the newspaper instead to Pergamon. RM immediately installed new management under his direct control as executive chair. Having improved the state of the company's finances by making substantial cost savings, RM instigated an ambitious expansion programme, acquiring the book publishers Macmillan, Inc. in the US in 1988 for $2.6 billion and OAG Inc. for $750m, these acquisitions being funded by $3 billion of bank debt.

RM initially tried to float the Mirror group in the late 1980s to raise money to pay down some of his now substantial bank debt, but was unable to do so, in part because MCC owned the printing presses used to print the *Daily Mirror*. These were eventually transferred to MGN in 1989 at a price of around £300m, which was thought to be significantly in excess of fair value. MGN was subsequently floated on the London Stock Exchange in April 1991. Six months later RM was dead and his business empire was rapidly collapsing.

Maxwell's business empire at the time of the MGN flotation

At the time of the flotation of MGN the Maxwell publishing empire comprised three distinct though interconnected parts: MGN; MCC; and Pergamon and other private companies owned by Maxwell (known as 'the private side'). Half the shares in MGN and MCC were listed separately on the London Stock Exchange. RM also controlled the assets of the Mirror Group Pension Scheme via Bishopsgate Investment Management Limited (BIM).

Auditors

Both public and private companies in the Maxwell group were audited by Coopers & Lybrand Deloitte, now part of PwC.[1] Following the collapse of the Maxwell business empire, the firm was investigated by the accountancy profession's joint disciplinary tribunal.

Further information

Further information about the Maxwell publishing empire and its demise can be obtained from various sources, in particular the following:

The Robert Maxwell Documentaries. 'Maxwell: the Downfall' DVD. This is a BBC *Inside Story* documentary produced by Tom Bower which can be found on YouTube.

A summary of the case which can be found in:
Wearing, R. (2005) *Cases in Corporate Governance*. London: Sage Publications. Chapter 4 'Maxwell'.

The DTI report on the flotation of MGN, which was published after the collapse of the Maxwell empire can be found at:
https://webarchive.nationalarchives.gov.uk/20060213225148/http://www.dti
.gov.uk/cld/mirrorgroup/index.htm

Biographies of Robert Maxwell include:
Bower, T (2008) *Maxwell: The Final Verdict*. HarperCollins. An earlier book, Bower, T. (1992) *Maxwell – The Outsider*. Mandarin Publishers, is an earlier version of the same.

Greenslade, R. (1992) *Maxwell: The Rise and Fall of Robert Maxwell and his Empire*. London: Birch Lane Press.

Preston, J. (2021) *Fall: The Mystery of Robert Maxwell*. New York: Viking.

Preparing the case

The Maxwell case raises many important questions about the personality and behaviours of successful businessmen, the role of auditors, the responsibilities of City of London institutions, family ownership of major stakes in listed companies, and corporate governance generally. You might like to think about the following questions in particular:

1. Identify from the case as many examples as you can of failures in corporate governance. To what extent did these failures contribute to the collapse of the Maxwell business empire? How could they have been avoided? What changes have subsequently been made to the UK Corporate Governance Code?
2. In what ways did corporate governance failures allow the misappropriation of pension fund assets to take place? How could they have been avoided? What changes have subsequently been made to the way that occupational pension schemes are regulated in the UK?
3. Consider the role and responsibilities of directors in public companies, drawing a distinction between executive and non-executive directors. What is meant by the term 'fiduciary duties'? Reflect on the part played by directors of the various companies in the Maxwell case – how well did they perform? What responsibility should directors other than Robert Maxwell and the Maxwell brothers bear for what happened?

4. Consider the role and responsibilities of auditors in public companies. Reflect on the role played by the auditors Coopers & Lybrand Deloitte (C&LD) in the Maxwell case, considering in particular: the purpose of an audit; C&LD's role in the flotation of MGM; C&LD's role as auditors of the Mirror Group Pension Scheme; how C&LD managed conflicts of interest and employed separation of responsibilities between different audit teams; who the auditors reported to at the companies they audited; and whether RM should have been accepted as a client by C&LD.

Further reading

Ellison, R. (1993) 'Pensions law reform after Maxwell: The possible content of new pension regulations following the Maxwell case,' *Journal of Financial Regulation and Compliance*, vol. 1, no. 3, pp. 278–290. https://doi.org /10.1108/eb024776

Stiles, P. and Taylor, B. (1993) 'Maxwell – The failure of corporate governance,' *Corporate Governance*, vol. 1, no. 1, pp. 34–45. https://doi.org/10 .1111/j.1467-8683.1993.tb00008.x

References

[1] When the Deloitte Haskins and Sells global network merged with Touche Ross in 1989 to become Deloitte Touche Tohmatsu, the UK firm decide to merge with Coopers & Lybrand instead.

7. Activist investors: Alliance Trust and Elliott International

Alexander Pepper[1]

This is the story of the decline of Alliance Trust, an investment company established in 1888 in Dundee, Scotland, as a result of the actions of an active investor, Elliott International. The case examines the business model of investment funds, the role of active investors, corporate governance, business ethics and leadership.

Alliance Trust and Elliott International examines the role played in the economy by activist investors – do they provide important discipline in the capital markets or are they just 'barbarians in the board room'? It considers the importance of a company's history and its position in the local economy – is there room for sentiment, or is all that matters hard-nosed financial metrics? It asks, can finance be a force for good?

The case provides an introduction to the investment management industry, especially investment trusts and the closed-end fund puzzle – why do shares in many investment trusts trade at a discount to net asset value and what are the implications of this?

From a skills perspective, the case requires students to carry out a financial analysis, to compare the performance of Alliance Trust with that of comparable closed-end funds in order to assess whether Elliott International's assertions about the fund's underperformance have any validity.

Guidance on how to write a case analysis can be found in Chapter 1, 'Business cases: what are they, why do we use them and how should you go about doing a case analysis?'.

A teaching note for this case is available to bona fide educators. To request a copy please email a.a.pepper@lse.ac.uk

---

How to cite this book chapter:

Pepper, Alexander (2025) 'Activist investors: Alliance Trust and Elliott International, in: Sallai, Dorottya and Pepper, Alexander (ed) *Navigating the 21st Century Business World: Case Studies in Management*, London: LSE Press, pp. 95–110. https://doi.org/10.31389/lsepress.nbw.g

Introduction

Dundee, the fourth largest city in Scotland with a population of over 150,000, is situated in a spectacular setting on the north side of the Firth of Tay, the estuary where one of Scotland's most famous rivers meets the sea. If you approach Dundee from the south by train you cross the (second) Tay rail bridge, made famous by the disaster which occurred on the night of 28 December 1879 during a violent storm when the first Tay rail bridge collapsed as a train passed through the central high girders, killing all aboard. If instead you approach by road, you might cross the spectacular road bridge, over a mile long, built in the 1960s to link Fife and Dundee, thus saving a 40-mile round trip via Perth. Alternatively, you might arrive by road from the west through the Carse of Gowrie, a fertile strip of land stretching for about 24km along the north shore of the Tay between Perth and Dundee, bordered by the Sidlaw hills to the north, a rich agricultural area famous for its strawberries, raspberries and other soft fruit.

Dundee is a post-industrial city, known historically for its three main industries – jute, jam and journalism. Jute, a natural fibre imported from the Far East through Dundee's readily accessible seaport, was the basis of Dundee's textile industry in the 19th century. Journalism is the bailiwick of the DC Thomson group, a long-established local firm still owned and run by the Thomson family, best known for publishing *The Dundee Courier*, the *Beano*, the *Dandy*, the *People's Friend* and the *Scots Magazine*. Jam has historically been manufactured from the soft fruit grown in substantial quantities in the Carse of Gowrie. James Keiller & Son produced Great Britain's first commercial brand of marmalade with imported Seville oranges until the company ceased to exist in 1992.

After a period of post-industrial decline in the 1970s and 1980s, Dundee has partially revived in recent years with the growth of the biotechnology and computer gaming industries, linked to the city's two thriving universities.[2] There has also been a major public investment in the waterfront area, including the opening of V&A (Victoria and Albert) Dundee in September 2018. This is an international design centre linked to London's Victoria and Albert Museum and designed by the renowned Japanese architect Kengo Kuma.

Alliance Trust

Dundee was once the home of a number of listed companies. Now only one remains, Alliance Trust plc, an investment company established in the late 19th century to help local businessmen invest their wealth, historically focusing in particular on investment opportunities in post-Civil War America.[3] Alliance Trust is an investment trust, a closed-end investment fund constituted as a public company and listed on the London Stock Exchange. Between 2008 and 2011, Alliance Trust was briefly a constituent member of the FTSE100 index, although it has subsequently been relegated to the

FTSE 250. Customers include large numbers of individual retail investors as well as other institutional investors. Its main investment focus is now on the global equity markets.

The Alliance Trust was formed in 1888 on the merger of three mortgage and land management companies: The Dundee Investment Company, The Dundee Mortgage and Trust Investment Company and The Oregon and Washington Trust. The trust attracted funds from many prominent Dundee figures – the original investors included merchants, ship owners, textile manufacturers and other business people. After formation, the firm expanded into asset classes beyond mortgages over land in America. For some years after 1918 it shared its premises and costs with another firm called the Western & Hawaiian Investment Company, which was subsequently renamed The Second Alliance Trust. In the 1920s and early 1930s, the two companies continued to focus mainly on mortgages and other fixed-income securities, but it divested its mortgage and land interests during the American great depression so that, by 1938, it was reported that stock and bonds constituted 92.41 per cent of the company's assets. In 1986, a savings division was established to sell pensions and other retail investments.

An investment trust is an unusual form of investment vehicle, similar in nature to a unit trust (UK), OEIC (Europe) and mutual fund (US), but with a number of important differences. Investment trusts have a fixed number of shares, unlike, for example unit trusts, which create and cancel units as people invest or remove their funds. In strict legal terms, investment trusts take the form of companies with shares, rather than being English law trusts. Investment trusts which satisfy certain conditions set out in section 842 of the UK Income and Corporation Taxes Act 1988 are exempt from UK tax on capital gains, thus avoiding two levels of capital gains tax which would otherwise be payable by investors. The tax rules are complex and have to be followed very carefully by the investment managers. Dividend income and bond interest are also effectively exempt from UK tax, so investment trusts typically only suffer overseas taxes on their investment income and gains.

A common and peculiar feature of investment trusts is that the net asset value of underlying assets is often greater than the market capitalisation of the trust's own shares, known in the investment industry as the 'discount'. The discount has been the source of much debate and academic research over the years and plays a major part in the Alliance Trust story. Some other specific features of investment trusts are that they are closed-ended. Compared to an open-end fund, a closed-end fund has a fixed number of shares and has a relatively stable capital base; managers' investment decisions are therefore not usually affected when investors buy or sell the investment trust's shares. They are capable of gearing – unlike many other kinds of investment fund, investment trusts can use debt finance to leverage their capital. Income retention is possible – in any year investment trusts can retain 15 per cent of their income for reinvestment, unlike open-end funds which must distribute all their income. And they have significant shareholder rights – shareholders of an investment trust have full shareholder voting rights, which are generally more extensive than the rights of investors in other kinds of fund.

Alliance Trust's shares have historically been widely distributed; in December 2014 70 per cent of its shares were held by over 50,000 retail and institutional investors. Major shareholders at 31 December 2014 included DC Thomson & Co Ltd (5.51 per cent) and Elliott International (5.07 per cent). Alliance Trust's board comprised the chair, Karen Forseke, a very experienced investment professional, the chief executive, Katherine Garrett-Cox (of whom more below), the chief financial officer and five non-executive directors. The board was responsible for setting the long-term objectives of the company, for approving its strategy and business plans, for ensuring that a framework of prudent controls was in place and that risks were managed effectively. However, somewhat unusually in the context of the modern investment industry, prior to 2016 the company was a self-managed investment fund – all investment management was carried out in-house by an investment team employed by a wholly owned investment management subsidiary, Alliance Trust Investments Ltd.

Opportunities and challenges

The late 1990s and early 2000s were challenging years for Alliance Trust. Substantial changes took place in the ways in which people saved and invested money after the 'Big Bang' – the deregulation of the London financial markets in 1986 – and as a result of the Thatcher government's privatisation programme. A raft of reports and recommendations, starting with the Cadbury report in in 1992, made corporate governance stricter and more highly regulated. The Cadbury report was followed by Greenbury (1995), Hampel (1998), Turnbull (1999), and the Smith and Higgs reports (both 2003). The new rules were enshrined in the Combined Code of Corporate Governance, which has itself been regularly revised. In addition, there were substantial modifications to the UK Companies Acts, together with major changes to the regulatory framework with the creation of the Securities and Investments Board in 1985 and its successor body, the Financial Service Authority, in 2001.

These were also challenging times for the financial markets. The period known by some economists as the 'long boom' and the 'great moderation' – a time of economic growth and reduction in the volatility of business cycle fluctuations in developed economies – came to an end with the bursting of the dot-com bubble between 2000 and 2002 and the global financial crash in 2008. The formal merger of The Alliance Trust and The Second Alliance Trust took place at the start of 2006, and the combined company was renamed simply 'Alliance Trust'. In the Exhibits section at the end of this case, Table 7.1 provides details of Alliance Trust's financial performance in the nine-year period to 31 December 2014 following the merger of the two companies. For comparison, Table 7.2 provides financial information relating to a number of other investment trusts with comparable investment strategies. Table 7.3 provides information on a number of stock indices.

Katherine Garrett-Cox

Katherine Garrett-Cox joined Alliance Trust as a chief investment officer in 2007. She had previously had very substantial experience in the investment management industry. From 1993 to 2000 she had been investment director and head of American equities at Hill Samuel Asset Management, a position she had been appointed to at just 26 years of age after working her way up from being a portfolio manager. It was during this period that Garrett-Cox was labelled 'Katherine the Great', due to her 'no prisoners' approach and 'hunger for success'. She joined Aberdeen Asset Management PLC as a chief investment officer in 2000 before moving on to Morley Fund Management in 2003. Aviva, Morley's parent company, had £166bn under management and Garrett-Cox became one of the most well-known, well-paid women in London. Her departure from Aviva for a position at Alliance Trust caused some surprise and was seen as a step down by some. However, she had been overlooked for promotion to CEO at Aviva, and with a Scottish husband and large family (she is a mother of four), others interpreted this as a wish for a quieter lifestyle. However, in 2008 she succeeded Alan Harden as Alliance Trust's CEO, less than two years after her appointment as chief investment officer. Her responsibilities included investment policy and asset allocation, as well as executive oversight of the company. During a five-year period when the trust was seen to be underperforming, Garrett-Cox`s compensation doubled. Figure 7.1 (in the Exhibits section at the end of this case) compares her remuneration with that of the CEO of Witan, an investment trust with an in-house investment management capability. Table 7.4 shows single-figure total remuneration of the directors of Alliance Trust for the years ended 31 December 2013 and 2014. Table 7.5 shows average CEO pay in the FTSE 100 and FTSE 250 for 2008–2014.

Activist investors target Alliance Trust

Activist investors, who are often hedge funds, operate by buying shares in a company – normally a small equity stake rather than a controlling one – with a view to forcing the board of directors to execute a short-term turnaround in the company's financial performance. They use various tools and techniques to influence other shareholders and put pressure on the target company's board. These include pushing for changes in corporate governance systems, altering the company's business strategy and seeking changes in its capital structure. PR experts will often be engaged to help influence the media to support the activist investor's strategy. A favourite tactic is to encourage target firms to use cash reserves to increase dividend payments or to buy back shares. Activism often results in putting a company 'in play', making it a potential takeover target. The target company's share price may rise simply on announcement of the activist fund's involvement, as other investors believe that the company may become a takeover target and sense an opportunity for selling their shares at a premium. Activist hedge funds therefore develop expertise at identifying undervalued companies and their exit strategy often involves a share sale on a merger or acquisition.

Laxey Partners

In 2010, Laxey Partners, an activist investor holding 1.3 per cent of Alliance Trust, began making demands for share buy-backs to reduce the discount at which Alliance Trust's shares were trading, at the same time pointing out Alliance Trust's underperformance relative to comparable companies. Alliance Trust has historically eschewed share buy-backs, arguing that they could make higher returns by reinvesting surplus cash. Laxey Partners argued that Alliance Trust should establish a programme of regular share buy-backs. Other trusts, such as Witan, have such mechanisms in place to do this automatically as soon as their discount hits 10 per cent. Further criticisms levelled by Laxey Partners included the block voting system, which Alliance did amend in April 2011 ahead of the AGM to a one share, one vote system. It also started buying back shares on a selective basis in the months leading up to the AGM and announced that buy-backs would now be 'part of Alliance's DNA'.

Specific proposals advanced by Laxey Partners were rejected at the AGM in May 2011; however, a significant minority vote of 33.5 per cent in favour of Laxey's proposals showed significant discontent with the management of Alliance Trust. Following the 2001 AGM, Laxey Partners kept up its pressure on Alliance Trust's management. They expressed discontent with the level of operating costs, challenged the level of remuneration of Katherine Garrett-Cox, and asked questions about secret dealing with other institutional investors. Despite further buy-backs, Alliance Trust's shares continued to trade at a discount of 16.6 per cent in November 2011. At the 2012 AGM, Laxey Partners demanded that Alliance Trust's investment management should be outsourced, arguing that the asset management team was too large for the size of the fund. Karin Forseke, appointed as chair of Alliance Trust in 2012, defended in-house management as being more cost-effective in the long term. Laxey's proposal at the AGM was again resisted, with only around 21 per cent of shareholders voting in support. At this point Laxey Partners withdrew from the battle, announcing that it was 'extraordinarily unlikely' that they would bring further proposals to a general meeting. However, this was not to be the end of the challenge by activist investors.

Elliott International[4]

Elliott International is an associate of Elliott Management Corporation, an American investment management firm which is the world's largest activist hedge fund. Elliott Management Corporation and its various associates was established by Paul Singer, described by *The New York Times* as 'one of the most revered hedge fund managers on Wall Street'. Gordon Singer, Paul Singer's son, runs Elliott's London office. Paul Singer originally made a name for himself with high-profile campaigns against the Argentinian government and companies ranging from Hyundai in South Korea to ThyssenKrupp in Germany. Alliance Trust was its first major intervention in the UK, though it has subsequently acquired Waterstone's the bookshop chain, and more recently targeted Saga's insurance and travel business.

In February 2014, Elliott International disclosed that it had acquired a stake in Alliance Trust, subsequently increasing this to become the single largest shareholder with a 12 per cent shareholding and triggering a great deal of media activity speculating on the reason for Elliott's increased stake. In March 2015, Elliott issued a press release expressing their discontent with Alliance Trust's investment performance, the costs associated with in-house investment management, and a criticism of its two loss-making subsidiaries. Much of Elliott's dissatisfaction was based on what they perceived to be a lack of communication between Alliance Trust and its shareholders about its business strategy, financial performance and the composition of its board of directors, especially when new directors were appointed. They also publicly challenged the pay level of Alliance Trust's CEO, Katherine Garrett-Cox. To address these concerns Elliott nominated three additional non-executive members for appointment to the board at the AGM in April. An acrimonious dispute ensued. Elliott International publicly argued that its nomination of new board members was part of an attempt to improve Alliance's financial performance and corporate governance. Alliance Trust's board responded that Elliott only had its sights on short-term profit, contrasting this with the company's long-term investment perspective and strategy of 'investing for generations'.

In an open letter to Alliance Trust investors published before the AGM in 2014, Elliott quoted a former director at Alliance Trust, Tim Ingram, who stated:

> It is an uncomfortable fact that the latest annual accounts show that the remuneration of the Alliance Trust Chief Executive over the five years of such dismal performance has totalled over £6 million. The chief executive of an investment trust with good third-party managers and without these loss-making subsidiaries could not possibly justify such a remuneration level, and this would, therefore, save additional money for us shareholders. ... I will be voting my shares in favour of the three new directors joining the board, and would

suggest that any other shareholder seeking better returns does likewise. The overall performance of Alliance Trust in the medium term has been dismal…[5]

Elliott redoubled its criticism of Alliance Trust, saying that administrative costs had doubled from 2007 to 2014, comparing in-house management cost unfavourably with those of similar-sized investment trusts. The Alliance board responded by claiming that their fixed cost represented good value as the percentage of costs over net assets was expected to decrease in time with a projected increase in the size of the fund. One long-term retail investor argued:

> I would welcome the fund cutting costs but am unlikely to support Elliott's initiative, as I fear that the hedge fund might steer the trust away from its conservative profile. People like this come in for the short term, and I'm a long-term investor. I'm very happy with the fund. It's stable and they keep their gearing low.[6]

In March 2014, six weeks before the AGM and after what they regarded as being an unsatisfactory meeting with Garrett-Cox and Forseke, Elliott decided to go on the offensive. They announced that they would be putting forward three nominees for the Alliance board, to be voted on at the annual shareholders' meeting on 29 April. The nominees were Peter Chambers, former chief executive of Legal & General Asset Management, Anthony Brooke, formerly of SG Warburg and Rory Macnamara, a former director of Morgan Grenfell. In this way they hoped to be able to influence Alliance's future strategy.

Preparing the case

In preparing the case analysis you might like to consider four specific questions in particular:

1. To what extent were Laxey Partners and Elliott International correct in saying that Alliance Trust's financial performance was unsatisfactory?
2. How do Alliance Trust's corporate governance practices prior to 2015 compare with UK best practice?
3. Is Garrett-Cox overpaid and, if so, why does it matter?
4. Consider the role played by activist investors in the financial ecosystem – are they a force for good, or do they prioritise short-term financial gains over other important factors?

Further reading

Munn, C. (2013) 'Growth and instability: 1996–2012', *Investing for Generations: A History of Alliance Trust*, Dundee: Dundee University Press, Chapter 10.

Walker, O. (2016) 'Who are activist investors' and 'What activists want and how they get it', *Barbarians in the Boardroom – Activist Investors and The Battle for Control of the World's Most Powerful Companies,* London: FT Publishing International, Chapters 1 and 2.

Exhibits

The data for all exhibits comes from company accounts.

Table 7.1: Alliance Trust financial performance 2006–2014*

Year#	2006	2007	2008	2009	2010	2011	2012	2013	2014
Assets at y/e (£m)									
Total assets	2,844	2,894	2,211	2,704	3,268	2,676	2,702	3,478	3,415
Loans	(12)	(195)	(88)	(191)	(373)	(276)	(211)	(592)	(396)
Net assets	2,832	2,699	2,123	2,513	2,895	2,400	2,491	2,886	3,019
Net asset value (p)									
NAV per share §	421.5	402.3	316.8	377.7	439	405.8	444.9	516.5	544.8
Share price (p)									
Closing price	365.5	338.0	268.0	313.0	364.0	342.8	375.3	450.1	478.9
Earnings									
Profit after tax (m)	£52.5	£61.5	£69.5	£61.1	£63.8	£61.9	£55.6	£60.6	£68.8
Earnings per share (£)	8.66	9.17	10.37	9.14	9.67	9.87	9.74	10.83	12.38
Dividend per share (£)	7.575	7.90	8.00	8.15	8.395	9.00	9.27	9.55	9.83
Special dividend	-	-	0.50	-	-	-	0.36	1.28	2.55
Expenses									
Total expenses (£m)	£10.1	£15.0	£16.8	£16.0	£17.0	£16.0	£18.7	£21.5	£20.8
Ratio exc. comp	0.36%	0.42%	0.60%	0.64%	0.53%	0.56%	0.67%	0.75%	0.60%
Total expense ratio	0.38%	0.45%	0.67%	0.69%	0.60%	0.60%	0.71%	0.80%	0.64%

Notes: * Prior to 31 January 2007 there were two companies, The Alliance Trust and The Second Alliance Trust; # In 2010 Alliance Trust's accounting year-end changed from 31 Jan to 31 Dec. Figures for 2011 have been annualised as appropriate; § Debt is calculated at fair value from 2014.

Table 7.2: Comparative performance 2006–2014

	2006	2007	2008	2009	2010	2011	2012	2013	2014
Total assets (£m)									
Foreign & Colonial Investment Trust	£2,587	£2,694	£2,003	£2,069	£2,425	£2,214	£2,401	£2,657	£2,838
Scottish Mortgage Investment Trust	£1,985	£2,045	£2,276	£1,398	£2,154	£2,502	£2,378	£2,593	£2,986
Witan Investment Trust	£1,383	£1,371	£1,024	£1,139	£1,261	£1,125	£1,243	£1,501	£1,605
Dividend yield									
Foreign & Colonial Investment Trust	1.9%	1.8%	2.8%	2.4%	2.2%	2.5%	2.7%	2.4%	2.2%
Scottish Mortgage Investment Trust	1.6%	1.8%	1.7%	2.9%	1.9%	1.6%	1.8%	1.7%	1.4%
Witan Investment Trust	2.0%	2.1%	2.9%	2.4%	2.1%	2.7%	2.6%	2.2%	2.0%
Total shareholder return									
Foreign & Colonial Investment Trust	11.1%	12.6%	-36.7%	18.5%	14.3%	-4.9%	12.6%	17.6%	12.5%
Scottish Mortgage Investment Trust	37.8%	5.5%	11.4%	-67.1%	43.9%	19.5%	-3.0%	15.6%	22.6%
Witan Investment Trust	10.9%	7.1%	-33.4%	23.4%	16.0%	-12.1%	13.2%	27.0%	13.3%
Discount									
Foreign & Colonial Investment Trust	11.4%	12.3%	13.0%	12.2%	11.8%	11.7%	11.0%	11.3%	8.1%
Scottish Mortgage Investment Trust	10.7%	10.7%	7.9%	8.1%	12.1%	9.1%	7.9%	4.1%	-0.4%
Witan Investment Trust	10.6%	11.0%	12.3%	10.5%	10.7%	10.7%	11.6%	6.8%	-0.6%
Gearing									
Foreign & Colonial Investment Trust	15.8%	15.8%	15.8%	15.8%	15.8%	15.8%	14.3%	8.0%	8.9%
Scottish Mortgage Investment Trust	11.7%	13.5%	19.3%	22.7%	14.6%	14.8%	15.4%	14.5%	13.0%
Witan Investment Trust	2.5%	11.1%	14.2%	10.3%	9.4%	11.6%	11.0%	8.5%	10.2%
Share price (p)									
Foreign & Colonial Investment Trust	284.5	318.8	228.5	272.1	309.6	288.5	320.5	378.0	421.2
Scottish Mortgage Investment Trust	104.3	108.4	120	70.6	121.8	148.4	141.6	164.5	208.8
Witan Investment Trust	454.5	478.5	351	444.6	516.5	450.0	503.0	669.0	753.5

Table 7.3: Stock indices 2006–2014 (taking 2006 as 100)

Year	2006	2007	2008	2009	2010	2011	2012	2013	2014
FTSE All-World Index	100	107	105	84	124	135	134	157	168
MSCI ACWI	100	106	61	78	85	79	89	111	114
RPI	100	105	109	108	113	119	123	128	131

FTSE All-World index series is a stock market index that covers over 3100 companies in 47 countries, starting in 1986. It is calculated and published by the FTSE Group, a wholly owned subsidiary of the London Stock Exchange which originated as a joint venture between the *Financial Times* and the London Stock Exchange.

The MSCI ACWI (MSCI All Country World Index) is a market capitalisation weighted index designed to provide a broad measure of equity-market performance throughout the world. The MSCI ACWI is maintained by Morgan Stanley Capital International (MSCI) and is comprised of stocks from 23 developed countries and 24 emerging markets.

The RPI (Retail Price Index) is one of the two main measures of consumer inflation produced by the United Kingdom's Office for National Statistics.

Figure 7.1: CEO remuneration – Alliance Trust and Witan Investment Trust: 2008–2014

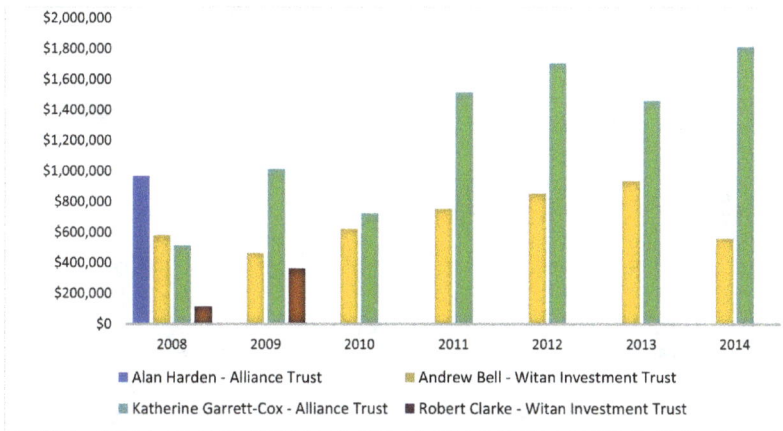

- Alan Harden - Alliance Trust
- Andrew Bell - Witan Investment Trust
- Katherine Garrett-Cox - Alliance Trust
- Robert Clarke - Witan Investment Trust

Source: BoardEx (figures in US$)

Notes: Investment management at both Foreign & Colonial Investment Trust and Scottish Mortgage Investment Trust is outsourced, to FCIB and Baillie Gifford respectively; neither investment trust has any full-time employees of its own. Witan Investment Trust is effectively a fund-of-funds, investing solely in other collective investment vehicles through a panel of independent investment managers. It employs a CEO who is responsible for investment performance, business development, shareholder relations, investment trust industry matters and administration. The CEO also manages a small direct holdings portfolio and is supported by a small management team.

Table 7.4: Alliance Trust – single figure total remuneration 2013–2014

Notes: * Taxable benefits include the value of accommodation allowance, medical and life assurance. Car allowance was consolidated into salary in 2014; § Annual bonus includes the AESOP award. The Chief Executive Officer deferred 100% of her annual bonus into shares and the Chief Financial Officer deferred 50% of his annual bonus into share. ± This is a cash payment instead of a pension contribution.

	Salary/Fees		Taxable benefits*		Annual bonus §		Long-term awards		Pension ±		Total	
	2014	2013	2014	2013	2014	2013	2014	2013	2014	2013	2014	2013
	£000	£000	£000	£000	£000	£000	£000	£000	£000	£000	£000	£000
Executive Director												
Katherine Garrett-Cox	450	425	20	43	576	369	184	436	112	106	1,342	1,379
Alan Trotter	245	225	1	16	216	122	102	229	49	45	613	637
Non-Executive Director												–
Karin Forseke	120	120	–	–	–	–	–	–	–	–	120	120
John Hylands	49	49	–	–	–	–	–	–	–	–	49	49
Alastair Kerr	50	50	–	–	–	–	–	–	–	–	50	50
Susan Noble	48	47	–	–	–	–	–	–	–	–	48	47
Win Robbins	41	36	–	–	–	–	–	–	–	–	41	36
Gregor Stewart	3	–	–	–	–	–	–	–	–	–	3	–

Table 7.5: Average CEO remuneration 2008–2014

CEO Pay	2008	2009	2010	2011	2012	2013	2014
FTSE 100 lead executives	£3,271,129	£3,393,953	£3,983,493	£4,096,295	£4,059,334	£4,284,000	£4,155,480
FTSE 250 lead executives	£1,232,000	£1,267,080	£1,695,013	£1,623,937	£1,669,250	£1,697,111	£1,646,198
Ave US / £ ccy rate for year	1.855443	1.565394	1.545893	1.604123	1.584877	1.564768	1.647701

Source: IDS Directors' Pay Reports

References

[1] This case was prepared by Professor Alexander Pepper with the help of Lukas Cejnar, Kazuma Fushimi, Ruihan Gao, Alina Jaeger and Marco Ramsbacher.

[2] See in particular Tomlinson, J., and Whatley, C. (eds) (2011) *Jute No More – Transforming Dundee*. Dundee: Dundee University Press.

[3] See Munn, C. (2013) *Investing for Generations: A History of Alliance Trust*. Dundee: Dundee University Press.

[4] Walker, O. (2016) *Barbarians in the Boardroom – Activist Investors and the Battle for Control of the World's Most Powerful Companies*, London: FT Publishing International, Chapter 10.

[5] Quoted by Gavin Lumsden in *Citywire* on 30 March 2015. https://perma .cc/8KA2-C6PW

[6] Dew, Laura (2015) 'Elliott publishes Alliance Trust correspondence as the war of words escalates', 16 March *Investment Week*.

8. The failure of the Royal Bank of Scotland

Alexander Pepper

This case tells the story of how a major corporate acquisition, coinciding with the 2008–2009 global financial crisis, brought about the near bankruptcy of the Royal Bank of Scotland (RBS). Referring to newspaper articles and other secondary material, it considers how subprime mortgages were securitised and sold throughout the global financial industry, creating systemic risk and leading to large losses when the American housing market went into recession, and how an ill-conceived acquisition came about because of overweening ambition, with catastrophic consequences.

'The failure of the Royal Bank of Scotland' is a 'raw case' – an open-ended, multi-perspective study that can feature thousands of pages of relevant material that students must analyse, such as statutory documents, analyst reports, news articles, stock charts and interviews with key players. This format reflects the way managers must access and analyse information to make informed business decisions.

The RBS case can be used to teach students about the global financial crisis, business strategy (mergers and acquisitions), leadership, governance and business ethics.

Guidance on how to write a case analysis can be found in Chapter 1, 'Business cases: what are they, why do we use them and how should you go about doing a case analysis?'.

A teaching note for this case is available to bona fide educators. To request a copy please email a.a.pepper@lse.ac.uk

How to cite this book chapter:

Pepper, Alexander (2025) 'The failure of the Royal Bank of Scotland', in: Sallai, Dorottya and Pepper, Alexander (ed) *Navigating the 21st Century Business World: Case Studies in Management*, London: LSE Press, pp. 111–118. https://doi.org/10.31389/lsepress.nbw.h

Introduction

In October 1999 Peter Burt, chief executive of Bank of Scotland (not to be confused with the *Royal* Bank of Scotland) launched an audacious bid for the National Westminster bank ('NatWest'). Bank of Scotland was a small retail bank headquartered in Edinburgh, Scotland. NatWest was a much larger commercial bank, based in London. Not to be outdone by their local rivals, the Royal Bank of Scotland (RBS), led by Sir George Mathewson, decided to launch a competitive bid for NatWest. RBS was ultimately the successful acquirer.[1]

The success of any business acquisition is typically heavily dependent on the achievement of cost savings. The post-acquisition integration of RBS and NatWest is often regarded as a model of its kind. It was led by Fred Goodwin, Matthewson's deputy at RBS. Goodwin was a tough taskmaster, relentless in his pursuit of efficiency, and known to his colleagues as 'Fred the Shred'. As one director of RBS put it: 'Fred was very good at delivery. He did the integration planning. His rigorous nagging saw the deal through. We truly delivered £3bn of synergies.'[2]

By 2007, RBS, now under the leadership of *Sir* Fred Goodwin (who had been knighted by the Queen in her 2004 Birthday Honours List for his services to the banking industry) was one of the largest banks in the world. It had become a universal bank, incorporating an investment banking division, Global Banking & Markets (GB&M) which accounted for almost half the group's total risk-weighted assets – £195bn out of a total of £482bn.

In October 2007, history appeared to repeat itself. In March, RBS's great rival, Barclays, led by John Varley, announced that it was in merger discussions with a Dutch bank, ABN Amro. Sir Fred had previously considered bidding for ABN Amro, in particular because of his interest in its US subsidiary, La Salle Bank, but the RBS board had been reluctant to pursue such a large and complex transaction. The Barclays announcement caused them to rethink. Spurred into action, in April 2007, RBS announced that it was leading a consortium of banks, including the Belgian bank Fortis and Spanish bank Santander, which was making a cash offer for ABN Amro valued at around $16bn.

ABN Amro's strong preference was to merge with Barclays, and in an attempt to thwart the RBS bid it sold its US subsidiary, La Salle Bank, to Bank of America. The board of RBS was determined to outbid Barclays and decided to proceed with the takeover at an unchanged offer price. A copy of RBS's press release justifying this decision is reproduced in the Exhibits section.

The Barclays bid for ABN Amro was an all-share offer, as opposed to the RBS-led consortium's all-cash offer. During August 2007, as the first signs of trouble in global financial markets began to emerge, Barclays' share price fell, reducing the value of its bid. By October, it had become clear that the RBS-led consortium would be the new owners of ABN Amro.

The global financial crisis

The global financial crisis (or 'GFC') provides the background to the RBS case. The roots of this crisis lay in the sale of 'subprime' mortgages by a number of US banks.

RBS got into trouble for a number of reasons, but in particular because of its exposure to the subprime mortgage markets, which was exacerbated by the acquisition of ABN Amro. A subprime mortgage is a type of mortgage that is normally issued by a lending institution to borrowers with low credit ratings. As a result of the borrower's lower credit rating, a conventional mortgage is not offered because the lender views the borrower as having a larger-than-average risk of defaulting on the loan. Lending institutions often charge interest on subprime mortgages at a rate that is higher than a conventional mortgage in order to compensate for carrying more risk.

The banks initiating subprime mortgages, especially in the US, bundled them into securities, which were then sold on to other banks and investment companies. The securities (known as 'collateralised debt obligations' or 'CDOs') were stratified into tranches with different risk profiles (rated AAA, AA, A, BBB – all 'investment grade' – and BB, B, CCC, CC, C, D – all 'speculative' grade). The whole system was predicated on the assumption that house prices were bound to continue to rise, and worked well while they were rising, as repossessions of property on any forgone mortgages could be used to cover interest costs. However, when house prices started to fall in the US in 2007–2008, the value of CDOs crashed, leaving huge parts of the banking system facing massive losses. Banks around the world with substantial investment in CDOs found their capital bases significantly depleted, bringing their financial sustainability into question.

The bailout

Over the summer of 2007 as the battle raged for ABN Amro very strange things were happening in the credit markets. Back in February, HSBC had been the first bank to openly signal the problems it was having in the US subprime market and had fired the head of its US mortgage business as losses hit $10.5bn. For Johnny Cameron,[3] the HSBC announcement was his first indication of the problems in the US subprime market that would end up costing the bank several billion dollars. Calling up Jay Levine, the Chief Executive of RBS Greenwich, Cameron was assured that the bank's US investment banking arm was on top of the problem. 'We're ahead of the game,' Levine told Cameron, adding that RBS Greenwich, which ran with little oversight from London, had already sold down much of its portfolio of the most risky parts of subprime collateralised debt obligations. Crucially, though, the bank retained its holding of the triple-A tranches, which were thought to be a safe investment.[4]

After the consortium's completion of the purchase of ABN Amro, it quickly became apparent to analysts that the RBS board had made a major strategic error. Goodwin had been warned about ABN Amro's exposure to subprime mortgages. RBS itself, through GB&M, was heavily invested in CDOs. Fortis Bank was itself in financial difficulty and would eventually receive an emergency bailout from the governments of Belgium and the Netherlands before being broken up.

In October 2008, in order to prevent the collapse of RBS and the expected consequential systemic failure of the UK banking system, the UK government was forced to inject £45.5bn into RBS, becoming its major shareholder. Fred Goodwin was sacked and his knighthood subsequently annulled. Stephen Hester, chief executive of British Land and a non-executive director of RBS, was asked to take over as RBS's new chief executive, with a brief to sort out the catastrophic legacy of his predecessor.

Further information

This case study draws on an article in *The Telegraph* newspaper by Harry Wilson and Philip Aldrick, published on 5 March 2011 under the headline: 'Royal Bank of Scotland: The Full Story of How the 'World's Biggest Bank' went bust'. This can be found at https://www.telegraph.co.uk/finance/newsbysector /banksandfinance/8363417/Royal-Bank-of-Scotland-investigation-the-full -story-of-how-the-worlds-biggest-bank-went-bust.html. Information about the case can be found in many other newspaper articles, with the caveat that it is always wise to check facts for accuracy and to take care when assessing journalists' opinions.

A BBC documentary entitled 'The Bank That Almost Broke Britain' was broadcast in September 2018. This can be found on YouTube at: https:// www.youtube.com/watch?v=W_ZWGuQ07Q8

You should also draw on other material, including the following:

Financial Services Authority Board (2011) 'The failure of the Royal Bank of Scotland', December. https://perma.cc/QZH6-ST5W

Fraser, I. (2014) *Shredded – Inside RBS, The Bank that Broke Britain*. Edinburgh: Birlinn Ltd.

Martin, I. (2013) *Making it Happen: Fred Goodwin, RBS and the Men who Blew up the British Economy*. London: Simon & Schuster.

Preparing the case

In preparing the case analysis, and as you read the RBS case and reflect upon what happened, you might like to consider the following specific questions in particular:

1. Was it appropriate for brokers to sell mortgages to customers, some of whom they knew would struggle to make the interest payments, because the banks believed that they could cover their risks by repossessions?
2. Was RBS right to proceed with the acquisition of ABN Amro? What is the relevance of the expedited sale of La Salle Bank to Bank of America to this question?
3. Sir Tom McKillop, who became chair of RBS in 2006, had no prior experience in the banking industry. Did he act responsibly when agreeing to take on a role which, arguably, he was not competent to perform?
4. What caused RBS's corporate governance arrangements to fail so spectacularly?
5. What character traits exhibited by Fred Goodwin made him at first a very successful leader, but ultimately brought about his fall from grace? Could his demise have been predicted?
6. What ethical responsibilities do Sir Tom McKillop and Fred Godwin bear for the collapse of RBS?
7. Does high bankers' pay involve ethical as well as economic and business considerations?

Exhibits

Press release:

The Royal Bank of Scotland Group plc 16 July 2007

RBS's Acquisition of ABN AMRO Businesses[5]

Following the ruling of the Dutch Supreme Court regarding the sale of LaSalle, RBS, Fortis and Santander have today announced revised terms for their proposed offer for ABN AMRO as set out in the Banks' Press Release.

RBS's announcement of 29 May 2007 set out the rationale for its participation in the proposed offer to acquire ABN AMRO. That announcement remains unchanged except in relation to LaSalle.

RBS intends to continue with the acquisition of the Global Whole-sale Businesses and International Retail Businesses of ABN AMRO ("the ABN AMRO Businesses"). Instead of acquiring LaSalle, RBS will acquire cash from the sale of LaSalle and, in the absence of LaSalle, the synergies anticipated in North America have been revised.

The consideration for the ABN AMRO Businesses net of the sale of LaSalle will be €16 billion, of which €5 billion will be financed by equity.

RBS believes that this transaction will provide enhanced growth prospects and attractive financial returns. As a result of the transaction, RBS expects to deliver cost savings amounting to €1,237 million (or €1,319 million, including its share of central cost savings) and net revenue benefits amounting to €481 million, by the end of 2010.

On RBS's forecasts for business growth and transaction benefits, the internal rate of return on the acquisition of the ABN AMRO Businesses will be 15.5% post-tax, well above the Group's hurdle rate of 12% post-tax. The acquisition is expected to deliver a post-tax return on investment[1] of 13.2% in 2010, and to increase Group adjusted earnings per share[2] by 2.0% in 2009 and by 7.0% in 2010.

Sir Fred Goodwin, Group Chief Executive, said:

"The acquisition of the ABN AMRO Businesses remains compelling from a financial point of view, as evidenced by the fact that it produces essentially the same earnings enhancement for the Group, despite the smaller size of the transaction. From a strategic perspective, whilst we would have preferred to acquire LaSalle as well, the businesses we are acquiring open up many new markets and growth opportunities, enabling us to significantly accelerate our strategic development."

(1) Return on investment defined as profit after tax plus post-tax transaction benefits over consideration plus post-tax integration costs

(2) Adjusted for purchased intangibles amortisation and integration costs

Important Information

In connection with the proposed Offer, RBS expects to file with the SEC a Registration Statement on Form F-4, which will constitute a prospectus, and the Banks expect to file with the SEC a Tender Offer

Statement on Schedule TO and other relevant materials. INVESTORS ARE URGED TO READ ANY DOCUMENTS REGARDING THE PROPOSED OFFER IF AND WHEN THEY BECOME AVAILABLE, BECAUSE THEY WILL CONTAIN IMPORTANT INFORMATION. Investors will be able to obtain a copy of such documents, without charge, at the SEC's website (http://www.sec.gov) once such documents are filed with the SEC. Copies of such documents may also be obtained from RBS and the other Banks, without charge, once they are filed with the SEC.

This communication shall not constitute an offer to sell or the solicitation of an offer to buy any securities, nor shall there be any sale of securities in any jurisdiction in which such offer, solicitation or sale would be unlawful prior to registration or qualification under the securities laws of any such jurisdiction. This press release is not an offer of securities for sale into the United States. No offering of securities shall be made in the United States except pursuant to registration under the US Securities Act of 1933, as amended, or an exemption therefrom.

Forward-Looking Statements

This announcement includes certain "forward-looking statements". These statements are based on the current expectations of RBS and are naturally subject to uncertainty and changes in certain circumstances. Forward-looking statements include any statements related to the benefits or synergies resulting from a transaction with ABN AMRO and, without limitation, statements typically containing words such as "intends", "expects", "anticipates", "targets", "plans", "estimates" and words of similar import. By their nature, forward-looking statements involve risk and uncertainty because they relate to events and depend on circumstances that will occur in the future. There are a number of factors that could cause actual results and developments to differ materially from those expressed or implied by such forward-looking statements. These factors include, but are not limited to, the presence of a competitive offer for ABN AMRO, satisfaction of any pre-conditions or conditions to the proposed Offer, including the receipt of required regulatory and anti-trust approvals, the successful completion of the Offer or any subsequent compulsory acquisition procedure, the anticipated benefits of the proposed Offer (including anticipated synergies) not being realized, the separation and integration of ABN AMRO and its assets and the integration of such businesses and assets by RBS being materially delayed or more costly or difficult than expected, as well as additional factors, such as changes in economic conditions, changes in the regulatory environment, fluctuations in interest and exchange rates, the outcome of litigation and government actions. Other unknown or unpredictable factors could cause actual results to differ materially from those in the forward-looking statements. RBS does not undertake any obligation to update publicly or revise forward-looking statements, whether as a result of new information, future events or otherwise, except to the extent legally required.

Merrill Lynch International, which is authorised and regulated in the United Kingdom by the Financial Services Authority, is acting as financial adviser to Fortis, RBS and Santander and as underwriter for Fortis, RBS and Santander, and is acting for no one else in connection with the proposed Offer, and will not be responsible to anyone other than Fortis, RBS and Santander for providing the protections afforded to customers of Merrill Lynch International nor for providing advice to any other person in relation to the proposed Offer.

The Royal Bank of Scotland plc, which is authorised and regulated in the United Kingdom by the FSA, is also acting as financial adviser to RBS and is acting for no one else in connection with the proposed Offer, and will not be responsible to anyone other than RBS for providing the protections afforded to customers of The Royal Bank of Scotland plc nor for providing advice to any other person in relation to the proposed Offer.

Any Offer made in or into the United States will only be made by the Banks and/or RFS Holdings directly or by a dealer-manager that is registered with the SEC.

References

[1] Bank of Scotland subsequently merged with Halifax plc to become HBOS. Like RBS, HBOS got into difficulty during the global financial crisis and had to be rescued by Lloyds Bank plc. HBOS is now a wholly owned subsidiary of Lloyds Banking Group.

[2] Wilson, H., and Aldrick, P. (2011) 'Royal Bank of Scotland: The Full Story of How the World's Biggest Bank went bust', *The Telegraph*, 5 March. https://www.telegraph.co.uk/finance/newsbysector/banksandfinance/8363417/Royal-Bank-of-Scotland-investigation-the-full-story-of-how-the-worlds-biggest-bank-went-bust.html

[3] Johnny Cameron was the head of RBS's GB&M division. After the failure of RBS, Cameron was reprimanded by the Financial Services Authority and barred from working full-time or holding a position of significant influence in the financial sector.

[4] Wilson, H. and Aldrick, P. (2011)

[5] Press release reproduced with permission from NatWest Group, plc. Text available from https://perma.cc/A2PU-YJ73

Part 4
Economics, politics and the business environment

9. China National Petroleum Corporation in Sudan

Roger Fon

This case examines the internationalisation strategy of China National Petroleum Corporation (CPNC) in Africa, a state-owned Chinese oil company. It describes the unique competitive advantages of Chinese state-owned multinational enterprises (SOMNEs), and how the Chinese government plays a crucial role in the internationalisation strategy of Chinese SOMNEs. The case of CNPC's investments in the Sudan provides material for tackling a scope of questions relating to the international strategic decisions of multinationals from emerging markets. The case delves into the following issues:

- host country – the challenges of operating in the least developed countries such as Sudan

- home country effects – the role played by the Chinese government in influencing the investment location choices of Chinese SOMNEs

- the difficulties in investing in extractive sectors where international investment opportunities are restricted because of geographic constraints

- how the internationalisation strategy of Chinese SOMNEs like CNPC differs from their counterparts from developed economies

- the distinctive resources and capabilities of CNPC

- the limitations of the classic theory of the multinational enterprise (MNE) in explaining the foreign investment activities of Chinese SOMNEs.

For guidance on how to write a case analysis please refer to Chapter 1, 'Business cases: what are they, why do we use them and how should you go about doing a case analysis?'.

A teaching note for this case is available to bona fide educators. To request a copy please email roger.fon@northumbria.ac.uk

How to cite this book chapter:

Fon, Roger (2025) 'China National Petroleum Corporation in Sudan', in: Sallai, Dorottya and Pepper, Alexander (ed) *Navigating the 21st Century Business World: Case Studies in Management*, London: LSE Press, pp. 121–133. https://doi.org/10.31389/lsepress.nbw.i

Introduction

The need to ensure access and control of international petroleum reserves is imperative for China to satisfy the demand of its growing economy. Apart from merely purchasing crude oil on the international market, Chinese SOMNEs now seek access to and control of oil fields around the globe. Sudan was the seminal testing ground for China's global pursuit of energy resources in an adventure where the investing company and its home government acted as one.

In December 1996, Canadian oil company Arakis sold most of its interest in the Greater Nile Petroleum Operating Company (GNPOC). In its evaluation of the bids made by international oil companies, the Khartoum government had three main priorities: keeping the favourable terms of the Arakis contract to the government; ensuring adequate finances to develop the oil resources; and the construction of an oil export pipeline in a rapid fashion. After satisfying all key conditions of the Khartoum government – and offering to build an oil refinery, CNPC became the leading player in the GNPOC in 1997.[1] At the time, this investment represented the largest overseas oil project ever carried out by a Chinese company.

Unlike their Chinese counterparts, the companies from the west represented at the table found it difficult to compete as their business logics are primarily guided by the financial rewards of a business agreement. This highlights the softer budget constraints large Chinese SOMNEs face in comparison to their counterparts from the west.

A few years later, CNPC's position in the Sudanese oil industry became even more entrenched when in 2001 it bought a majority stake in the Petrodar Operating Company (PDOC) in Blocks 3 and 7 of Upper Nile State. These investments in Sudan form part of an overarching regional strategy of Chinese SOMNEs, setting the tone for subsequent entry into more oil- and gas-producing African countries like Angola, Algeria and Nigeria. In this strategy, the Chinese government plays an influential role in the location and direction of corporate strategic behaviour.

The influence of the Chinese government is largely owing to its unquestionable ownership and control of CNPC. Moreover, the close diplomatic relations between the Chinese government and the Khartoum government were a catalyst for the legitimacy of CNPC in Sudan – and significantly leveraged its position vis-à-vis its western competitors. Such close ties between the home- and host-country governments can potentially influence the strategic behaviour of SOMNEs.

Investing in emerging and least-developed countries can be risky because of relatively weak institutional frameworks. Firms operating in developing economies, including most African economies, tend to face a high degree of institutional, economic and political uncertainty. In Sudan, the existence of underdeveloped institutional frameworks is compounded by the fact that the country is mired in civil conflict. For MNEs, the capacity to navigate opaque political constraints and cumbersome regulations is pivotal.

It is under such an atmosphere that western MNEs – with relatively high expectations of corporate responsibility – were forced to abandon the Sudanese oil sector because of human rights pressures from western governments and non-governmental organisations (NGOs). How did the unique corporate character of CNPC help its strategic entry and operation in Sudan? To what extent did the role of the home government influence the strategic location of CNPC in Sudan? In what ways did CNPC's experience in Sudan alter the competitiveness and future global strategy of the company?

The company

CNPC began its operations as the Ministry of Petroleum Industry in 1978. The company signed its first offshore oil project with foreign oil companies in 1980 and onshore oil cooperation projects in 1985. The Ministry of Petroleum Industry was dissolved, and CPNC was established in 1988. In 1989, exploration and production activities started in the Tarim Basin in northwest China.

CNPC's international operations began in the 1990s. In 1993, CNPC won a contract to explore crude oil in Peru after winning the bid for the Talara oil project. This project marked the first foreign investment activity in oil exploration and production. The investment in Peru was closely followed by the signing of an oil contract with the Sudanese government in 1997. CPNC was incorporated in 1998.

A separate company, PetroChina, was created in 2000 with CNPC as its parent company. PetroChina was listed on the Shangai Stock Exchange (SSE) in 2007. In 2011, the company's global projects produced the equivalent of 100 million tons of crude oil for the first time.

Civil war and oil in Sudan

The Anglo-Egyptian treaty of 1899 recognised Sudan as an Egyptian possession – administered by Britain on behalf of the King of Egypt. The former Anglo-Egyptian colony gained independence on 1 January 1956[2] and, almost immediately, fell into a civil conflict. The failure of the Arab-led government in the north to fulfil its promises to the south of the country to create a federal structure, compounded by continuous economic and political marginalisation of the south, resulted in a mutiny by the army in the south, sparking the First Civil War which lasted 17 years (1955–1972).[3] Thus, the First Civil War was primarily a war of secession. March 1972 marked the end of the First Civil War following the signing of the Addis Ababa Agreement.[4] This agreement provided 11 years of relative peace in the country.

However, tensions still existed after the Addis Ababa agreement, as regional marginalisation persisted. This led to the outbreak of the Second Civil War in 1983, when a group of rebels in the south fighting under the banner of Sudan's People's Liberation Army (SPLA) fought an ever-distrustful Khartoum government. Although other reasons exist for the outbreak of the Second Civil

War, such as poverty and religious and ethnic tensions, the major cause was consistent regional marginalisation by the Khartoum government and the exploitation of social divisions in the south. For instance, the dissolution of the Southern Regional Assembly and the alteration of the southern borders was a major bone of contention. From a religious standpoint, the forceful establishment of sharia law in the predominantly Christian south proved problematic. The sentiment that the Khartoum government neglected the south contributed to a growing rebellion in the Darfur region, triggering a full-fledged civil conflict.

The Second Civil War also had a significant economic dimension, following the discovery of oil along the traditional north-south border. It is hardly surprising that the discovery of oil coincided with the outbreak of the Second Civil War. Following the development of oil – predominantly in the south – the Khartoum government, led by President Jaafar Mohammad al-Nimeiri, altered the southern boundaries to ensure the northern part of the country would have access to future oil earnings. This ensured the economic impact of oil on the Second Civil War was far greater as oil production by large MNEs increased considerably. Thus, the economic dimension of the war (mainly about 'who' controls the oil fields) was also important. Consequently, oil development led to high-level military decisions to gain control of oil-producing regions, thereby escalating the civil conflict – later empowering the Khartoum government's brutal military campaign.

In summary, the discovery and development of oil escalated the north-south Second Civil War in Sudan as it represented an economic reward for the Khartoum government that had aggravating consequences for the conflict. Government advances to capture territory in oil-producing regions and protect extraction activities were interrupted by disruptive activities by the SPLA, leading to a substantial rise in the economic logic of the civil conflict.

Oil development in Sudan

The first MNE to explore and develop Sudan's oil sector was the American energy company Chevron. Chevron's exploration activities laid the ground for future oil MNEs in Sudan by showing how the inherent character of the MNE would have to navigate extreme institutional conditions if oil resources were to be developed and extracted. Chevron was granted the right by President Nimeiri to explore Sudan's onshore oil potential two years after the signing of the Addis Ababa agreement in 1972.

The perception of Chevron as an ally of the repressive government in Khartoum made the company a target. In 1984, its facilities were attacked by the rebel group Anyanya II, killing three workers and resulting in Chevron suspending operations to bring Sudanese crude to the market. The insecurity in the south became too risky for Chevron. However, Chevron's operations in similarly risky environments in the oil region of Cabinda in Angola made the Khartoum government sceptical of its suspension of production – and it threatened to terminate the company's contracts if it did not resume operations. As a major private oil company seeking considerable profit margins, Chevron viewed the legacy of civil war, political uncertainty and unstable economic environment in Sudan as highly unattractive for business.

More importantly, the relationship between the Khartoum government and the United States was an uneasy one, which did not help Chevron's already weak bargaining position. Washington became worried about the establishment of sharia law in Sudan, and its welcoming attitude towards terrorist groups such as elements of Al Qaeda. This led the United States to impose sanctions and to place Sudan on the list of countries sponsoring terrorism. This, coupled with pressure from the Khartoum government for Chevron to restart production or face being expelled from Sudan altogether, led to the complete deterioration in relations between Washington and Khartoum and sealed the company's fate in Sudan. The MNE finally pulled out of Sudan in 1992.

Chevron's withdrawal and the deterioration of relations between Washington and Khartoum meant that US oil companies were barred from operating in Sudan. Other major oil MNEs like Royal Dutch Shell, British Petroleum and Total had avoided engaging in oil exploration in Sudan because of the continuing civil conflict. The lack of available options in the early 1990s placed the Khartoum government in an awkward financial position. Although the improvement of its worsening finances was significant, Khartoum was also obsessed with keeping control and finding a partner that did not interfere or question its war practices in the south.

The experience and financial strength of Chevron were replaced by a far less experienced private Sudanese company, ConCorp, that purchased concessions from Chevron at Unity and Heglig, Blocks 1, 2 and 4 for a bargain price of $US23 million. However, they lacked experience, and so sold its concessions to State Petroleum Corporation, which was eventually taken over by Arakis – a Canadian company – in 1994. Like most of the companies that operated after the withdrawal of Chevron, Arakis lacked the necessary capital, experience and technology to explore Sudanese crude successfully.

Arakis' financial difficulties led to its takeover by a Canadian counterpart, Talisman, which provided the finances needed to exploit Sudan's oil. As oil production grew, so also did oil revenues rise for the Khartoum government, which allowed them to upgrade their military capabilities through arms purchases from China.[5] Increased arms for the Sudanese army led to further destruction of villages in the south. In the case of Talisman, its shareholders were determined not to be associated with the human rights abuses perpetrated by the Khartoum government.

In the west, MNEs operating in the Sudanese oil industry were viewed as accomplices in the deaths of thousands of civilians. These pressures had significant reputational damage for Talisman. However, it was the threat by the US government to delist Talisman from raising capital on the New York Stock Exchange (NYSE) that eventually forced the company to stop its operations in Sudan. The threat of barring Talisman from raising capital in US financial markets was part of the Sudan Peace Act passed by the US Congress, alongside humanitarian support in the country.

Extreme institutional conditions and human rights pressures, therefore, had adverse effects on the western MNEs. In the end, the disinvestment outcomes of western MNEs did not weaken the Khartoum government. On the contrary, the government's financial lifeline would remain largely unchanged. Increasing demand for energy resources from China protected the Khartoum government from the effects of criticisms by western governments. China's most urgent energy demands meant CNPC would eventually dominate the oil industry in Sudan and South Sudan as western MNEs pulled out. Besides the escalating demand for energy resources, the role played by the Chinese government in outward foreign direct investment (OFDI) contributed to CNPC's high propensity for risk and consequent domination of the oil industry in Sudan.

The role of the Chinese government in outward foreign direct investment

Since the advent of the 'go global' policy at the beginning of the millennium, Chinese OFDI abroad has grown at a fast rate, making China the second-largest outward investor in 2018.[6] This high growth in Chinese capital abroad is due to the role of the Chinese government in influencing the corporate strategy of its SOMNEs.

China is home to a very high number of SOMNEs. The Chinese government's policies and influence can impact the investment location strategy of Chinese SOMNEs through ownership and control. The direct ties to and dependence on the Chinese government can lead to a high-risk propensity by Chinese SOMNEs when engaging in value-added activities across national borders – especially in locations with weak institutional frameworks.[7]

Compared to their private counterparts, Chinese SOMNEs are the largest group of investors in greenfield foreign direct investment (FDI) projects in terms of capital expenditure.[8] There is a tendency for them to invest in highly risky environments because they face only soft budget constraints given the policy objectives of the Chinese government. This means capital is available to these firms at below-market rates, with Chinese SOMNEs receiving financial support in conditions of losses, thus eliminating the possibility of bankruptcy. Higher levels of capital availability help offset the higher transaction costs that usually accompany investments in African countries with extreme institutional conditions.

Second, their direct ties to and dependence on the Chinese government mean Chinese SOMNEs engage in FDI abroad for non-market objectives of the Chinese government.[9] Geopolitical and nationalist objectives of the Chinese government are important factors driving the investment location strategy of Chinese SOMNEs, irrespective of the institutional conditions of the host location.[10] Chinese SOMNEs in the extractive sectors make investments in highly risky environments largely to secure energy resources for the home country. Furthermore, the Chinese government's selection of countries along the Belt and Road Initiative is carried out irrespective of the institutional conditions of chosen locations, thus influencing the internationalisation strategy of Chinese SOMNEs carrying out investments in these locations.

Third, direct ties to the Chinese government mean that Chinese SOMNEs also benefit from government policies that provide certain advantages that can impact their internationalisation strategy. Official government visits by Chinese leaders to African countries – a phenomenon that has steadily increased since President Jiang Zeming's seminal tour of Africa in 1995 – benefit the operations of Chinese SOMNEs. The Chinese government has also steadily increased the number of African countries that maintain good diplomatic relations with Beijing.

Good home- and host-country diplomatic relations provide an advantage for Chinese SOMNEs as their close ties to the Chinese government provide them with better access to diplomatic networks than their peers in the private sector.[11] This is particularly advantageous for Chinese SOMNEs in conditions of a high risk of expropriation of assets or expulsion by the host-country government.

The strategic entry of CNPC into Sudan following the exodus of MNEs from developed economies was greatly influenced by the unique role played by the Chinese government in the internationalisation strategy of Chinese SOMNEs. However, a key foreign policy principle of the Chinese government that ensured CNPC won market share and eventually dominated the oil industry in Sudan is the policy of non-interference.

The Chinese policy of non-interference

China's engagement with Africa since the first Afro-Asian conference in Bandung, Indonesia, in 1955 is centred on Beijing's policy of non-interference in what it considers the sovereign affairs of African governments.[12] This policy implies that decisions on government-sponsored FDI projects carried out by Chinese state-owned enterprises in African countries are made without considering the quality of institutions in African countries.

The policy of non-interference is also employed in the allocation of Chinese loans to African countries, which has been on the rise since the turn of the millennium. Loan allocation decisions are made without consideration of the political institutions of recipient (borrower) countries.[13] The growth in Chinese loans to Africa in the pre-pandemic years is shown in Figure 9.1.

Applying this policy to Chinese FDI, the Chinese government uses loans to facilitate the entry and operations of Chinese SOMNEs in African countries to compensate for the 'latecomer status' of Chinese SOMNEs vis-à-vis their counterparts from the west. Notably, Chinese aid to African countries tends to be strategically integrated with FDI projects with most loans provided by the China Export-Import Bank.

Figure 9.1: Chinese loans to Africa (2000–2020)

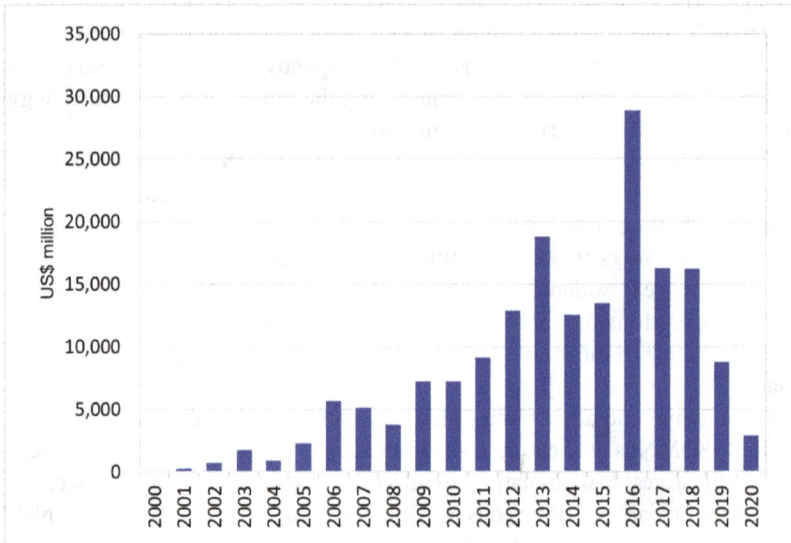

Source: data from Chinese Loans to Africa Database, Boston University, Global Development Policy Centre

The Chinese government's policy of non-interference is in sharp contrast to the conditionality approach of western donors and Bretton Woods institutions like the World Bank and the IMF.[14] Consequently, western observers claim the Chinese policy of non-interference helps to prop up rogue political regimes and provides a rationale for Beijing to pursue its economic interests by providing aid and encouraging investments in African countries with governments with poor human rights records.

The strategic entry of CNPC into the Sudan

In the early 2000s, the withdrawal of western MNEs from Sudan's oil industry, starting with Chevron, provided a fitting opportunity for China. CNPC gradually took over Sudan's oil industry. The Chinese government's ownership and control of CNPC are clearly reflected in the firm's information to its shareholders.[15] This control was exemplified by the support granted to CNPC by the China Export-Import Bank – a state-run bank – to cover its initial oil exploration.

Considering the close ties between the Chinese government and CNPC, the Chinese state provided the financial leeway for CNPC to win oilfields in Sudan by tabling significant bids. The Chinese government has developed a close diplomatic relationship with Sudan. The relationship is also deeply economic, mainly through Beijing's provision of soft loans and grants throughout the years. From a political standpoint, China supported the Khartoum government in the UN Security Council against political and economic sanctions. In combination, deep economic and political relations between the Chinese government and the Khartoum government ensured that CNPC dominated Sudan's oil industry in the two largest oil-producing consortiums, PDOC and GNPOC in Sudan before the partition of the country in 2011. In 2000, CNPC contributed to the construction of oil infrastructure, pipelines and a large refinery near the capital Khartoum.

Like the western oil MNEs before it, CNPC had to deal with the violence and the overall insecurity of armed conflict in Sudan to access its oilfields. A case in point was the kidnapping of CNPC employees, coupled with an attack on a drilling rig by the SPLA that inhibited CNPC's activities and oil development.[16] However, despite these high levels of insecurity, government-appointed executives of CNPC, who were motivated to explore and acquire energy resources for the home market, persevered. The difficult relationship between the Khartoum government and Washington added to CNPC's woes. In line with the Sudan Peace Act, Washington limited CNPC's access to capital offerings on the US financial markets when the company decided to list shares on the NYSE in 1999 through an initial public offering. However, failure to include capital market restrictions in the Sudan Peace Act eventually allowed CNPC to gain access to US financial markets.

Although the insecurity in Sudan and initial difficulties in accessing US financial markets slowed down CNPC's international expansion, the pressures of human rights had a minimal impact on operations in the country. On the contrary, the only significant impact human rights pressures from the west had on CNPC was in helping the company avoid competition from major western oil MNEs. Indeed, accusations of human rights directed towards CNPC were met with no response, which reflects CNPC's protected position as a state-owned MNE.

The influence of Sudan on the internationalisation strategy of CNPC

Sudan was one of the first major international investments for CNPC and it had a significant impact on the company's global strategy. Sudan accounted for over 40 per cent of CNPC's overseas oil production between 2003 and 2007. However, CNPC's operations in Sudan went beyond economic rewards.

CNPC's operations in Sudan played a significant role in improving the firm's global competitiveness. Sudan provided CNPC with an opportunity to improve supervision over its subsidiaries across the different crude oil activities – ranging from the upstream activities of oilfield development to the pipeline and downstream activities of oil refining. These opportunities helped CNPC adopt an overarching strategy that exploits CNPC's strengths as an oil and construction company.

Sudan also provided a venue for CNPC to realise its comparative advantage by offering host countries oil development and infrastructure-building capabilities at a low cost. This competitive advantage was imperative to CNPC in its later acquisitions of oil fields in Niger and Chad. CNPC also improved its competitiveness by developing its technical and managerial staff in Sudan. The company benefited from its collaboration with its international partners, which included Malaysia's Petronas and the Canadian oil company Talisman, thus helping CNPC build an international labour force to manage other international activities in the future.

CNPC's operations in Sudan meant it gained valuable experience in bidding for international contracts and preparing agreements for sharing production. For some of CNPC's oil development and construction companies, Sudan was their first significant international experience. For example, the China Petroleum Engineering and Construction Company (CPECC), its main construction service company, carried out its first significant construction of oil infrastructure for Sudan's oil pipeline and refinery.[17] In addition to providing valuable experience, Sudan also augmented the organisational capabilities of the assortment of CNPC's oil and construction companies.

CNPC's experience with extreme institutional conditions in Sudan was also an important factor in altering its global strategy by diversifying its global investment portfolio towards less high-risk locations. Diversification does not mean CNPC has stopped investing in countries immersed in civil conflict, which allows the company to avoid competition from traditional oil companies from the west. However, it has ensured the company was less exposed to uncertainty in conflict-affected locations by investing in more politically stable countries. For instance, in 2012, CNPC purchased a large share in the Canadian oil firm Encana for US$2.2 billion.[18] Similarly, the China National Offshore Oil Corporation (CNOOC) made the largest investment by any Chinese oil company by acquiring the Canadian oil company, Nexen for US$15.1 billion.[19] Such acquisitions by Chinese National Oil Companies (NOCs) acted as a 'springboard' in helping them to close the technological gap with major oil companies from developed economies.

Preparing the case

In preparing the case, you might like to consider four specific questions:

1. *Firms' resources and capabilities.* How would you describe CNPC's core resources and capabilities in China? Are these transferable across national borders? Think about transferability to developed and developing economies.

2. *Host-country institutions.* Why were multinationals from developed countries unable to maintain their operations in Sudan and what were the main challenges in operating there?

3. *Role of home government.* In what ways did the Chinese government influence the entry of CNPC into Sudan?

4. *Post-Sudan.* What has been CNPC's internationalisation strategy to date? How did its investments in Sudan influence its future internationalisation strategy?

Further reading

Cuervo-Cazurra, Alvaro and Genc, Mehmet (2008) 'Transforming disadvantages into advantages: Developing-country MNEs in the least developed countries,' *Journal of International Business Studies*, vol. 39, pp. 957–979. https://doi.org/10.1057/palgrave.jibs.8400390

Cuervo-Cazurra, Alvaro; Inkpen, Andrew; Musacchio, Aldo and Ramaswamy, Kannan (2014) 'Governments as owners: State-owned multinational companies,' *Journal of International Business Studies*, vol. 45, pp. 919–942. https://doi.org/10.1057/jibs.2014.43

Fon, Roger and Alon, Ilan (2022) 'Governance, foreign aid and Chinese foreign direct investment,' *Thunderbird International Business Review*, vol. 64, no. 2, pp. 179–201. https://doi.org/10.1002/tie.22257

Fon, R. M; Filippaios, F; Stoian, C. and Lee, S. H. (2021) 'Does foreign direct investment promote institutional development in Africa?', *International Business Review*, vol. 30, no. 4. https://doi.org/10.1016/j.ibusrev.2021 .101835

Palepu, K. G. and Khanna, T. (1998) 'Institutional voids and policy challenges in emerging markets,' *The Brown Journal of World Affairs*, vol. 5, p. 71. https://bjwa.brown.edu/5-1/institutional-voids-and-policy-challenges-in-emerging-markets/

Ramamurti, Ravi (2001) 'The obsolescing "bargaining model"? MNC-host developing country relations revisited', *Journal of International Business Studies*, vol. 32, pp. 23–39. https://doi.org/10.1057/palgrave.jibs.8490936

References

[1] Patey, L. A. (2007) 'State rules: Oil companies and armed conflict in Sudan', *Third World Quarterly*, vol. 28, no. 5, pp. 997–1016. https://doi .org/10.1080/01436590701371728

[2] Collins, R. O. (2008) *A History Of Modern Sudan*, Cambridge: Cambridge University Press, pp. 6–9.

[3] Johnson, D.H. (2011) *The Root Causes Of Sudan's Civil Wars: Peace Or Truce*. Martlesham: Boydell & Brewer Ltd.

4 Kasfir, N. (1977) 'Southern Sudanese politics since the Addis Ababa Agreement', *African Affairs*, vol. 76, no. 303, pp.143–166. https://www.jstor.org/stable/721529

5 Alden, C. (2005) 'China in Africa', *Survival*, vol. 47, no. 3, pp. 147–164. https://doi.org/10.1080/00396330500248086

6 UNCTAD (2019) 'World Investment Report: Special Economic Zones', United Nations. https://perma.cc/C669-JYQR

7 Pan, Y.; Teng, L.; Supapol, A.B.; Lu, X.; Huang, D. and Wang, Z. (2014) 'Firms' FDI ownership: The influence of government ownership and legislative connections', *Journal of International Business Studies*, vol. 45, no. 8. pp 1029–1043. https://link.springer.com/article/10.1057/jibs.2014.27

8 FDI Markets (2023) https://www.fdimarkets.com/

9 Bass, E. and Chakrabarty, S. (2014) 'Resource security: Competition for global resources, strategic intent, and governments as owners', *Journal of International Business Studies*, vol. 45, no. 8, pp 961–979. https://link.springer.com/article/10.1057/jibs.2014.28

10 Shi, W.; Hoskisson, R. E. and Zhang, Y. A. (2016) 'A Geopolitical Perspective into the Opposition to Globalizing State-Owned Enterprises in Target States', *Global Strategy Journal*, vol. 6, no. 1, pp. 13–30. https://doi.org/10.1002/gsj.1105

11 Li, J.; Meyer, K.E.; Zhang, H. and Ding, Y. (2018) 'Diplomatic and corporate networks: Bridges to foreign locations', *Journal of International Business Studies*, vol. 49, no. 6, pp. 659–683. https://link.springer.com/article/10.1057/s41267-017-0098-4

12 Holslag, J. (2011) 'China and the coups: Coping with political instability in Africa', *African Affairs*, vol. 110, no. 440, pp. 367–386. https://doi.org/10.1093/afraf/adr022

13 Tan-Mullins, M.; Mohan, G. and Power, M. (2010) 'Redefining "Aid" in the China–Africa Context', *Development and Change*, vol. 41, no. 5, pp. 857–81. https://doi.org/10.1111/j.1467-7660.2010.01662.x

14 Hernandez, D., (2017) 'Are "new" donors challenging World Bank conditionality?', *World Development*, vol. 96, pp 529–549. https://doi.org/10.1016/j.worlddev.2017.03.035

15 CNPC (2018) Annual Report, p. 10.

16 Patey, L., (2017) 'Learning in Africa: China's overseas oil investments in Sudan and South Sudan', *Journal of Contemporary China*, vol. 26, no. 107, pp. 756–768. https://doi.org/10.1080/10670564.2017.1305489

[17] Johnson, Ian (1999) 'China takes a long view in overseas oil projects', *The Wall Street Journal*, 16 December. https://www.wsj.com/articles/SB945285475375546693

[18] Hook, Leslie (2012) 'PetroChina in $2.2bn Canada gas deal', *Financial Times*, 14 December. https://www.ft.com/content/eb4e91e0-45cf-11e2-b7ba-00144feabdc0

[19] Rampton, Roberta and Hagget, Scott (2013) 'CNOOC–Nexen deal wins US approval its last hurdle', *Reuters*, 12 February. https://www.reuters.com/article/us-nexen-cnooc/cnooc-nexen-deal-wins-u-s-approval-its-last-hurdle-idUSBRE91B0SU20130212.

10. TRQ and Rio Tinto: the Oyu Tolgoi copper mine and the obsolescing bargain in Mongolia

Christine Côté, Saul Estrin, Daniel Shapiro and Ellie Cumpsty[1]

Oyu Tolgoi is one of the largest known copper and gold deposits in the world. Based in the Mongolian section of the Gobi Desert, the mine is being developed by Oyu Tolgoi LLC (OT LLC) and is jointly owned by the government of Mongolia (GOM) and the Canadian company, Turquoise Hill Resources (TRQ), in which Rio Tinto has a 50.8 per cent ownership stake. Copper demand and prices are rising and reached an all-time high in May 2013. However, despite the strong incentives to finish the project, there have been numerous disruptions and hold ups, with issues including poor project management, technical challenges, disagreements between the government and investors and attempts by the GOM to renegotiate the terms of the original investment agreement. The key questions to consider in this case study include:

- Is it possible to re-write a new investment contract in these circumstances to solve the current disagreements?

- Why have the agreements negotiated to date failed to overcome the problem of the obsolescing bargain and what lessons can be learned for future contracts?

- What actions must be taken by both sides to ensure renegotiations are not necessary in the future? Is this outcome even possible? Or would TRQ/Rio Tinto's optimal strategy be to sell the mine to a competitor and exit the project?

How to cite this book chapter:

Côté, Christine, Estrin, Saul, Shapiro, Daniel and Cumpsty, Ellie (2025) 'TRQ and Rio Tinto: the Oyu Tolgoi copper mine and the obsolescing bargain in Mongolia', in: Sallai, Dorottya and Pepper, Alexander (ed) *Navigating the 21st Century Business World: Case Studies in Management*, London: LSE Press, pp. 135–157. https://doi.org/10.31389/lsepress.nbw.j

Guidance on how to write a case analysis can be found in Chapter 1, 'Business cases: what are they, why do we use them and how should you go about doing a case analysis?'.

A teaching note for this case is available to bona fide educators. To request a copy please email c.cote@lse.ac.uk.

Oyu Tolgoi was one of the largest known copper and gold deposits in the world.[2] Based in the Mongolian section of the Gobi Desert, 50 miles north of the Chinese border, the Oyu Tolgoi mine has held the potential to be the fourth largest copper mine in the world and contribute a third to Mongolia's GDP.[3] The mine has been developed by Oyu Tolgoi LLC (OT LLC) and has been jointly owned by the GOM and the Canadian company, Turquoise Hill Resources (TRQ). As seen in Figure 10.1, TRQ has held a 66 per cent stake in OT LLC and the GOM has owned the remaining 34 per cent. Although Rio Tinto does not have a direct stake in OT LLC, they have managed the project and have had a 50.8 per cent (majority) stake in TRQ.[4] The GOM have been funding their share of the costs through loans from TRQ, which must be paid back prior to the government receiving any royalties from the project.

Copper demand and prices have been rising and reached an all-time high in May 2021.[5] Therefore, production from OT LLC has the potential to greatly benefit its shareholders. However, despite the strong incentives to finish the project, there have been numerous disruptions and hold ups. Indeed, the mine has been besieged with problems since the signing of the 2009 Oyu Tolgoi Investment Agreement (OTIA) between the GOM, Ivanhoe Mines (later renamed TRQ) and Rio Tinto. Despite cost overruns occurring regularly in the mining business, there was a lack of clarity around the impact of cost overruns when the agreement was created. Over time, this and the general tendency known as the 'obsolescing bargain' has motivated the GOM to seek to renegotiate the OTIA with TRQ and Rio Tinto.

The mine construction project consisted of Phase 1, an open-pit mine, and Phase 2, an underground mine. Both phases were subject to signed investment contracts, but disputes still arose throughout construction. Phase 1 was completed in 2013. However, Phase 2 has remained incomplete despite an initial forecasted completion date of 2016.[6] The delays reflected a number of issues, such as poor project management of the mining operations by Rio Tinto and technical challenges which have led to a host of disagreements between the government and investors, linked to the GOM's desire to realise their expected return on the project as outlined in the original investment agreement signed in 2009.

In 2021, the GOM, TRQ, and Rio Tinto agreed to renegotiate the Underground Development Plan (UDP) after allegations from the GOM that the agreement lacked legitimacy as it was not approved by the Mongolian parliament in 2015.[7] The GOM have been seeking to exchange their stake in the project for more stable, regular cash flows. This was the second time the GOM has successfully pushed TRQ and Rio Tinto to renegotiate the terms of its previous agreements, as seen in Figure 10.2. Furthermore, this and previous conflicts have had an impact on the TRQ share price, which has underperformed comparable benchmark firms in the sector. The key dilemma facing TRQ and Rio Tinto senior management was how to proceed in the face of these challenges. Was it possible to re-write a new investment contract to solve the current disagreements between TRQ/Rio Tinto and the GOM? Why have the agreements negotiated to date failed to overcome the problem of the obsolescing bargain and what lessons can be learned for future contracts? What actions must be taken by both sides to ensure renegotiations are not necessary in the future? Was this outcome even possible? Or would TRQ/Rio Tinto's optimal strategy be to sell the mine to a competitor and exit the project?

The global copper industry

The demand for copper has risen over 250 per cent since the 1960s,[8] as developing countries undergo urbanisation by building modern infrastructure, including supplying citizens with electricity and water. This has been particularly driven by China, who has been the world's biggest importer of copper, consuming around half of the world's supply.[9] China has also been a global leader in the development of and transition to renewable energy, and has become the world's largest producer of solar panels, wind turbines, batteries and electric vehicles (EVs). All of this has contributed towards China's strong demand for copper.[10]

Copper has been the most used metal in renewable energy technologies as it has been a relatively cheap, malleable and efficient conductor of electricity and heat.[11] Battery storage and charging technologies use copper,[12] which is why EVs require approximately four times more copper than the average car. Copper demand from EVs is expected to reach 1.2 million tonnes by 2025. This places upwards pressure on copper prices, which have been expected to rise 60 per cent by 2025.[13]

Moreover, the supply of copper has been depleting, which will also push copper prices higher. An upwards trend in copper prices has already been observed, with a 21 per cent price increase since January 2021.[14] The global copper market was predicted to have a 521,000-tonne shortfall in 2021.[15] Unless explorations discover more sites with a high-quality copper ore grade, this trend is set to continue. Some of the shortfall could be reduced by recycling copper – more than 50 per cent of the European Union's (EU) copper has been sourced from recycling.[16] But while recycled copper can mitigate the shortfall, mining operations would still be necessary to meet future demand and prevent soaring prices.

Copper has been supplied from a few regions, which has made the supply chain susceptible to disruptions, underlying copper's price volatility, exacerbated by the Covid-19 pandemic. Chile and Peru have produced 40 per cent of global copper supplies.[17] However, falling ore grades have been threatening future production in these countries and have forced mining giants to search for copper resources further afield. The average copper grade declined approximately 25 per cent between 2006 and 2016.[18] Oyu Tolgoi has a copper grade of 1.52 per cent, which is more than double the 2020 average global copper ore grade for copper mines.[19] At maximum capacity, Oyu Tolgoi would be expected to produce 480,000 tonnes of copper between 2028 and 2036.[20]

The top five largest copper mines in 2028 are predicted to be:

1. Escondida (Chile)
2. Grasberg (Indonesia)
3. Collahuasi (Chile)
4. Oyu Tolgoi (Mongolia)
5. Kamoa-Kakula (Democratic Republic of Congo)

The underground development of Oyu Tolgoi will ramp up copper production, transforming Oyu Tolgoi from the 26th largest copper mine in 2021, to the 4th largest copper mine by 2028, once Oyu Tolgoi reaches its full production.[21]

Mongolia's history and extractive sector

Mongolia is a landlocked country located in the East Asia and Pacific region, sitting between Russia and China, with a cold dry climate. The Gobi Desert covers the south of the country. It is one of the least densely populated countries in the world,[22] with a population of 3.2 million people and a GDP per capita of US$4007.30, above India, Indonesia, the Philippines and just below South Africa, Peru and Brazil.[23] Mongolia's borders contain some of the largest mineral reserves in the world,[24] estimated to be valued between US$1 trillion and $3 trillion.[25]

The Mongolian people were mostly subsistence herders in the early 20th century, looking after animals belonging to nobility, government officials or Buddhist monastery estates.[26] After the Soviet-supported revolution in 1921, which fought for independence from China, the Mongolian People's Party (MPP) came to power.[27] Mongolia's new ties to the Soviet Union led to a communist regime and a centrally planned economy.[28] Mongolia became a satellite state to the USSR and their economy benefited from subsidies estimated to total approximately 37 per cent of GDP.[29]

When the USSR collapsed, Russia suffered a financial crisis, causing a decline in Russian foreign trade and influence. This impacted Mongolia because the Soviet Union was previously their largest trade partner. This external shock reduced economic support and forced Mongolia to seek alternative allies. The democratic revolution in 1990 saw Mongolia distance itself from Russia, and the World Bank stepped in with the Economic Rehabilitation Project, aimed at supporting Mongolia's transition.[30] During Mongolia's rapid transition to a market-based economy, living standards dropped significantly, as over a third of inhabitants recessed into poverty.[31] The transition saw an initial decline in Mongolia's GDP, as the country experienced a transformational recession, only returning to their pre-transition GDP in 2001.[32]

Prior to the democratic revolution in 1990, Mongolia's economy consisted primarily of agricultural industries. However, this changed after the transition, when a new foreign investment law was passed in 1993, allowing foreign enterprises to invest in Mongolia more easily in a simplified, two-step process.[33] Bilateral Investment Treaties (BITs) were also signed, with the intention of encouraging FDI. Between 1991 and 2001, Mongolia signed the majority of their 43 BITs, primarily with European countries.[34] This encouraged foreign enterprises to invest in Mongolia and granted access to their rich mining resources.[35] Since then, Mongolia's economy has been transformed into an economy oriented towards extractive industries, such as mining, which now account for over half of Mongolia's GDP.[36] Mongolia's dependence on extractive industries heightens their economy's volatility, rendering them vulnerable to mineral price fluctuations.[37]

Since 1990, China has become Mongolia's largest trade partner.[38] Mongolia has exported primarily coal and copper ore to China, which accounted for 55 per cent of total exports to China in 2000.[39] Mongolia's economic dependence on China has grown, increasing at an annualised rate of 19.4 per cent between 1995 and 2019.[40] China was Mongolia's primary customer for copper ore, dominating nearly 100 per cent of copper exports. Despite their economic dependence on China, Mongolian people have remained wary of Chinese investment because of past tensions in their relationship.[41]

Unemployment rates have fluctuated, generally with an upwards trend, since 1990.[42] Despite the extractive industry contributing the majority of Mongolia's GDP, it has not been the country's biggest employer. The livestock sector has employed 40 per cent of Mongolians, though it only generates 20 per cent of GDP.[43] The economy has therefore not diversified, relying heavily on the extractive industry, which could be challenging for the government, leading them to have to negotiate between sectors of high employment versus sectors contributing more towards GDP. There have been conflicts between the mining and herding sectors,[44] highlighting how the GOM may need to manage conflicts and support different sectors, despite the more significant contribution the extractive industry makes to Mongolia's GDP.

In 2011, the commodities boom made Mongolia the fastest growing economy in the world. However, when prices declined towards the end of 2012, the country was damaged more as a consequence of its debt-fuelled spending in the peak of the cycle.[45] Government debt had dramatically increased since 2011, when public debt was below 40 per cent of GDP, to 2016 when it reached 100 per cent of GDP.[46] The country was relying on the recovery of commodity prices to reduce this debt, highlighting how vulnerable the Mongolian economy has been because of its lack of diversity.

Overall, Mongolia has proven to be a suitable location for FDI. A number of key indicators reflect this attractiveness, though challenges have remained with respect to the weak institutional environment and levels of perceived corruption. Mongolia has ranked reasonably well in the World Bank 'Doing Business' measure, coming in at number 81 out of 190 countries, ahead of such emerging markets as Brazil and South Africa. This reflects the attractiveness of the country's regulatory environment and how it is conducive to starting and operating a business. The Fragile State Indicator (FSI) has ranked Mongolia 132nd out of 179,[47] comparing it favourably with other extractive economies such as Chile and Peru. Finally, there was some work that needed to be done with respect to issues of corruption. Transparency International's Corruption Perceptions Index, which ranks countries according to perceived levels of public sector corruption, indicated that in 2020 Mongolia ranked 111 out of 180 countries. While this data has shown the promise of Mongolia as a good location for FDI, in reality there have been many challenges for TRQ and Rio Tinto in their Oyu Tolgoi JV.

TRQ history and governance

Exploration between 2000 and 2009 established Oyu Tolgoi as the world's largest undeveloped copper-gold mine.[48] Once fully operational in 2030, the mine is expected be the fourth largest copper mine in the world.[49] Ivanhoe Mines had controlling ownership of the Oyu Tolgoi project after buying out BHP in 2002, and then Rio Tinto joined Ivanhoe Mines as a strategic partner, investing US$1.5 billion in 2006.[50]

After nearly six years of negotiation with the GOM, Ivanhoe Mines, with its subsidiary Oyu Tolgoi LLC, and strategic partner Rio Tinto, signed the OTIA in 2009 to govern the JV arrangement and to provide stabilisation and mitigate the risk to the project.[51]

Key features of the agreement are:[52]

- 30 years of stable tax for the construction and operation of the project, with the option to extend for a further 20 years.[53]
- Elimination of the Windfall Profits tax.
- Erdenes MGL LLC, a Mongolian state-owned company, acquired a 34 per cent stake in the Oyu Tolgoi project, with Ivanhoe Mines maintaining the majority 66 per cent stake. Erdenes MGL LLC has the option to increase its 34 per cent interest to 50 per cent in 30 years.
- The Erdenes' share of capital investment (the 'Government Debt') will accrue interest and must be paid back prior to receiving any royalties. Erdenes has the right to contribute any required funding but is not obliged to do so.

- A management fee of 3 per cent will be charged before production, and 6 per cent thereafter.
- Four years after commercial production starts, the Oyu Tolgoi project is required to source power from within Mongolia.
- Recourse to international arbitration should disputes arise under this agreement.

The OTIA was attractive to the GOM when they signed it in 2009 because they believed having a stake in the project would grant them more control over the mine and provide them with a reliable stream of income. However, they failed to predict the consequence of cost overruns on their future royalties, overestimating their return from the Oyu Tolgoi project.

In 2010, the revised Heads of Agreement established that Rio Tinto would manage the core operations of the mine,[54] thereby receiving the 3–6 per cent management fee for the project. Rio Tinto then acquired a majority stake in Ivanhoe Mines, who changed their name to Turquoise Hill Resources (TRQ), which was an element of the memorandum of agreement (2012).[55]

Oyu Tolgoi LLC has had a board of nine people, with three nominees from Rio Tinto, TRQ and the government respectively.[56] Rio Tinto has, however, effectively controlled the Oyu Tolgoi board through a variety of rights and mechanisms.

The Oyu Tolgoi investment opportunity for TRQ and the GOM

Investing in the Oyu Tolgoi mine has posed a balance between risks and rewards for TRQ (and Rio Tinto) and the GOM.

Benefits for the GOM

Based on a report commissioned by Ivanhoe Mines Mongolia Inc. and published in August 2005, the Oyu Tolgoi project would have the following impacts on the economy of Mongolia between 2002 and 2043:[57]

- 34.3 per cent average increase in real GDP
- 10.3 per cent average increase in employment
- 11.5 per cent average increase in real per capita disposable income
- US$7.9 billion cumulative increase in government operating balance, excluding debt payments
- US$54 billion cumulative increase in exports.

Risks to the GOM

Undiversified customer base

Most of TRQ's copper has gone to China, which is 80km away from the Oyu Tolgoi mine.[58] The lack of a diverse customer base has posed a risk to Mongolia because if Chinese demand for copper slows, which it recently has, then this could disrupt the mine's profits.[59] However, this risk was somewhat mitigated by the long-term expectation for copper demand to rise due to renewable technologies.[60]

Dependency on the extractive sector

Oyu Tolgoi was the largest foreign investment project in Mongolia, and it may increase the GOM's dependency on the extractive sector. This can make the Mongolian economy more vulnerable towards commodity shocks.

Discouragement of other foreign investors

If the government was perceived as unreliable and challenges the project's progress, other future foreign investors may be deterred.

Negative public perception of the extraction of Mongolia's natural resources

Mongolia is a democracy, and so public opinion of the government's actions can influence the career prospects of politicians. If the Oyu Tolgoi project was not positively received by Mongolians, increased pressure could be placed on the government to improve the returns in the eyes of the Mongolian people. This pressure has been recurrent because of elections every four years.

Benefits for TRQ/ Rio Tinto

- Potential to produce 3 per cent of global copper production at peak production, while demand has risen.
- Access to the Oyu Tolgoi metal deposits of estimated:[61]
  - 40,500,000 tonnes of copper [62]
  - 1437.5 tonnes of gold.

The value of the copper deposit alone was estimated to be over US$386 billion if sold at the current price of US$9542.35 per tonne. The real value of the deposit could be much higher if copper prices continue to rise.

Risks to TRQ/ Rio Tinto

Large capital investment

The mine became operational in 2013 and up to that point an investment of US$6 billion was made with US$700 million paid in taxes to the government.[63] Phase 2, the underground development, was expected to cost a further US$5.3 billion, but costs have overrun and the updated estimated cost was US$6.75 billion. Further delays could accumulate higher unknown costs.

Political risk

Because the investment represents such a high portion of Mongolia's GDP, it has put the project in the spotlight, and the outcome of the mine could have a substantial impact on the government's access to capital and the living standards of Mongolian people. This could result in the Oyu Tolgoi mine being used as a political tool to gain voters. Mongolia is a democracy, so if the voters want an improved deal, this could exert pressure on the government. The democratic nature of Mongolia may harm the government's ability to plan long term, as it has presidential and local government elections every four years,[64] so planning beyond their four-year term may not benefit them in the next election. Therefore, a project like Oyu Tolgoi, which would take years to reach optimal production, may create political challenges for TRQ where the government may overvalue the present impact relative to the future return.

Institutional risk

Mongolian people have not always strictly obeyed laws. This is apparent on the roads of Ulaanbaatar, which can be chaotic.[65] However, this trait has not been restricted to ignoring traffic lights, as there have been high-level politicians involved in corruption scandals, which has weakened trust in the political system.[66] A lack of government regulation and the high commercial value of natural resources has led to transparency concerns.[67]

The obsolescing bargain

The obsolescing bargain represents the greatest risk to TRQ and Rio Tinto in the context of this project. The idea of the obsolescing bargain has been one of the oldest ideas in international business literature.[68] Applied primarily to natural resources, it holds that host governments would seek to attract MNEs to develop their resources and would offer attractive incentives for them to do so. The bargaining advantage at that stage would rest with the MNE. However, once the investment was made, and costs were sunk, exit would become difficult so the host government might try to renegotiate the initial terms, including raising taxes and royalties, and possible expropriation. This is the obsolescing bargain.

More specifically the Harvard economist, Raymond Vernon, argues that several factors cause governments to reconsider bargains over time:[69]

- Initially, accumulating the technology and skilled human capital to achieve the project may seem financially risky and overwhelmingly complex. However, once the project is successful, maintenance of the project is less challenging.
- Initially, foreign provision of technology, knowledge and skilled human capital seems indispensable. However, once local suppliers and workers close the skills gap, more inputs can be domestically supplied. Therefore, foreign company's self-sufficient structure could be resented over time by the domestic government.
- Initially, the government gratefully receives additional income from the venture, but as it starts to depend on the income over time, the government feels threatened by the power the foreign investor gains from this.
- At first the foreign venture is welcomed, but national opinion changes, especially if an opposition party replaces the previous government. Even without a change in power, criticism of favouritism towards foreign companies could influence the government.
- Initially, the foreign investors may have made a small investment, but over time this investment typically expands, and they find it increasingly difficult to abandon the venture.

Given this problem, it was not surprising that various institutional and firm responses became common. This became known as two-tier bargaining,[70] whose purpose was to reduce the possibility of an obsolescing bargain. In the first tier, home and host countries negotiated agreements that protected home-country companies, generally known as International Investment Agreements (IIAs) or BITs. In the second tier, MNEs negotiated specific entry conditions with the host government, including ownership conditions (such as joint ventures) and individual project investment agreements. It was argued that these contractual solutions mitigated the obsolescing bargain problem.[71] The Oyu Tolgoi JV in Mongolia reflected these two-tier bargaining efforts aimed at avoiding the problem of the obsolescing bargain. The Canadian-Mongolia BIT and the OTIA between TRQ and GOM have been cases in point.

The Oyu Tolgoi mine dispute

The Oyu Tolgoi mine was the biggest foreign investment project in Mongolian history,[72] and it was thought to be the largest undeveloped deposit of its type in the world, with approximately 40,500,000 tonnes of copper and 1,437.5 tonnes of gold within the site.[73] Once the mine reaches full production capacity, it will be expected to contribute a third of Mongolia's total GDP and employ 3000 Mongolian people. The dispute between the GOM and OT LLC has been mainly caused by the asymmetric impact of cost overruns on the GOM and TRQ/Rio Tinto. When costs overrun, the date the GOM would expect to receive royalties would be delayed because there are larger loans to repay to TRQ/Rio Tinto. On the other hand, Rio Tinto would continue to receive management fees between 3 per cent and 6 per cent and accrue 6.5 per cent interest on loans to the GOM,[74] thereby causing an asymmetric cost impact for different stakeholders.

There have been cost overruns for both Phase 1 and 2 of the Oyu Tolgoi project.

Phase 1 (2009–2013)

A feasibility study in 2010 updated the expected cost of the first phase of construction – the open-pit mine – from $4.6 billion to $5.7 billion. As seen in Figure 10.2, in October 2011, MPs within the GOM announced their intention to renegotiate the OTIA to increase their stake from 34 per cent to 51 per cent.[75] This was instigated as cost increases estimated at around US$2 billion delayed by decades the start date for the government's expected dividends.[76,77] Because of the geographical complexity of the project, the actual cost was $6.6 billion.[78] This higher cost meant that the GOM were not expected to start receiving dividends from the project until 2033, rather than the anticipated 2019. In response, the GOM attempted to renegotiate some of the terms outlined in the OTIA, leading to delays and further cost increases.[79]

A copper price bust led to the GOM introducing the Strategic Entities Foreign Investment Law (SEFIL) in June 2012.[80] This was an attempt by the GOM to renegotiate the OTIA. The Mongolian president, President Elbegdorj, questioned the OTIA in a speech and raised the question about the need for its revision and Rio Tinto's accounts were briefly frozen. Rio Tinto and TRQ rejected this proposal, but the GOM continued to challenge Rio Tinto by delaying signing off the Phase 2 financing plan. This provided some bargaining power for the government to examine problematic areas of Phase 1, such as cost overruns, Rio Tinto's management fee and taxes.

Production from Phase 1, the open-pit mine, began in mid-2013.[81]

Phase 2 (2015–present)

In 2013, Rio Tinto postponed Phase 2 developments for the underground mine until the outstanding renegotiation attempts from the GOM were resolved.[82] After two years of further negotiations, and a three-year delay to construction, the UDP was signed in 2015, signalling a breakthrough for Oyu Tolgoi.

The renegotiated terms of the UDP decreased Rio Tinto's management fee from 6 per cent to 3 per cent, cancelled a regular payment to Rio Tinto, settled the tax dispute and confirmed the Phase 2 financing plan.[83] This agreement was estimated to have transferred 2 per cent of the total project value to Mongolia, and this allowed Phase 2 construction to commence, with the first underground blast in August 2016. Despite the challenges caused by cost overruns in Phase 1, further cost overruns in Phase 2 were not accounted for in the renegotiations of the UDP.

When the UDP was signed, the construction of the underground mine (Phase 2) was expected to cost US$5.3 billion and reach sustainable production by the first quarter of 2021.[84] Unfortunately, due to complications causing further delays and higher costs, the updated expected completion date was October 2022 at the earliest with an inflated budget of US$7.1 billion.[85] This pushed the date Mongolia expected to receive royalty payments back to 2051, a delay of 32 years.[86] This long delay was particularly troubling for the democratic GOM, who prefer to see benefits from projects before their four-year term is over to aid re-election.

In 2017, the Canada-Mongolia investment agreement came into force to attempt to mitigate disruptions for Canadian MNEs operating in Mongolia.[87] Mongolia also introduced new banking regulations which required MNEs to use domestic banks, however Rio Tinto filed a complaint to the IMF which delayed the first bailout payment to Mongolia and forced the government into a U-turn on their banking regulation.[88]

A second tax audit demanded US$155 million from Oyu Tolgoi LLC due to unpaid taxes which OT LLC disputed.[89] A payment of US$4.8 million was made, however the remainder is still outstanding and being dealt with through arbitration under the OTIA. These tax audits have been perceived as attempts by the GOM to reclaim some value from the Oyu Tolgoi mine since their expected future royalties have diminished.

Phase 2 cost overruns had pushed total expected cost up to US$7.1 billion and potential delays up to 2.5 years, heightening tensions between Rio Tinto as the mine operator, the GOM and TRQ.[90] Rio Tinto blamed delays on technical issues and the geographic complexity of the project in 2019. Due to the cost overruns and delays preventing the government receiving royalties until a new updated estimated date of 2051 and the project incurring US$22 billion of debt for Mongolia, OT LLC agreed to appoint an independent committee of experts.[91] The committee was appointed by the GOM and TRQ to determine the cause of the cost overruns. This independent committee of experts announced in August 2021 that weak geography has not been the cause of the project's delays but rather poor project management, which contradicted Rio Tinto's claims from 2019.[92]

Misaligned incentives to minimise delays have gone some way to explaining the clashes between the two sides and eroded trust which may now be challenging to rebuild.[93] The same year, the GOM's desire to increase their stake shifted to an aspiration to trade their stake for a higher royalty.[94] This reflected the realisation that unless changes were made, their stake in the project would not provide reliable income for the GOM. The GOM hoped to scrap the UDP and renegotiate the terms.

Complicating matters further, in 2020, TRQ took Rio Tinto to arbitration over the company's obligation to secure funding, highlighting the conflict between the two firms.[95] Different opinions on how to fund the additional costs of Phase 2 were resolved in April 2021, when an updated funding plan was agreed.[96] The GOM used this as an opportunity to push again for a renegotiated UDP.

The decision point – Phase 3

Cost overruns had fuelled the GOM's fears that they would receive no dividends before the copper reserves were depleted.[97] Consequently, the GOM threatened to void the UDP agreement unless Rio Tinto and TRQ renegotiated the terms. In March 2021, TRQ/Rio Tinto and the GOM agreed to cancel the UDP from 2015 and form a new contract for the underground development of the Oyu Tolgoi mine. A new negotiation period had begun.

Preparing the case

In preparing the case analysis you might like to consider the following questions in particular:

1. Was it possible to re-write a new investment contract to solve the current disagreements between TRQ/ Rio Tinto and the GOM? Why have the agreements negotiated to date failed to overcome the problem of the obsolescing bargain and what lessons can be learned for future contracts?
2. What actions must be taken by both sides to ensure further renegotiations are not necessary in the future?
3. Was a successful renegotiation even possible? Or would TRQ and Rio Tinto's optimal strategy be to sell the mine to a competitor and exit the project.

Exhibits

Figure 10.1: Governance structure of Oyu Tolgoi LLC[98]

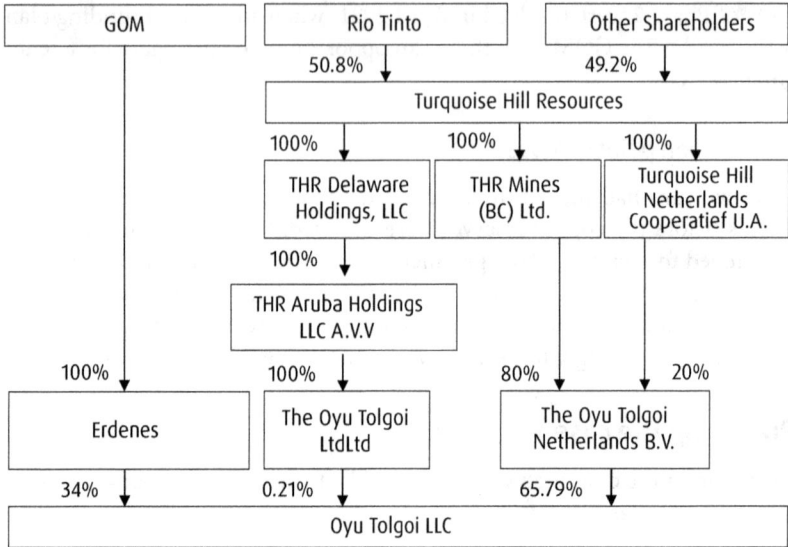

Figure 10.2: A timeline of the Oyu Tolgoi Copper Mine deal

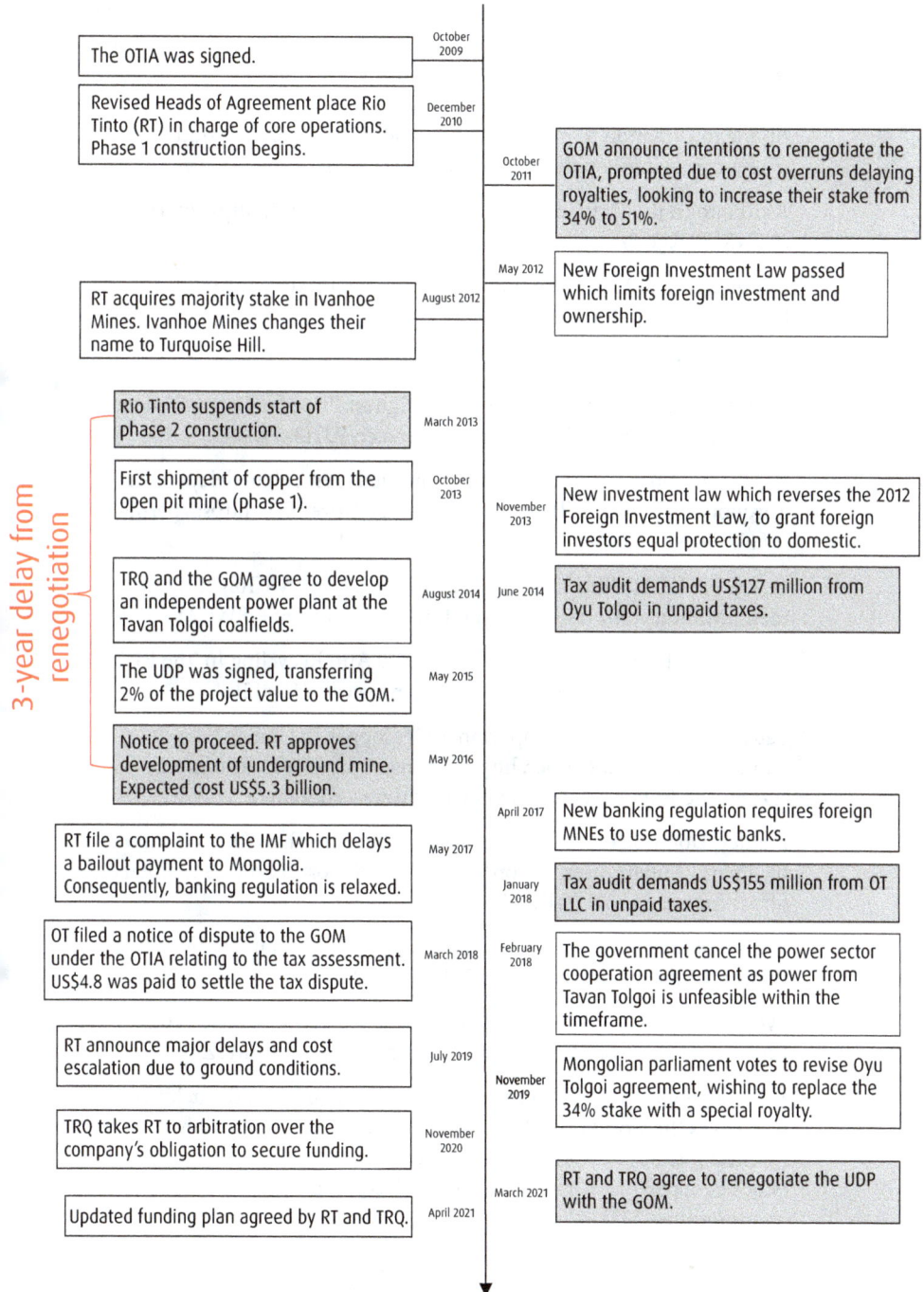

3-year delay from renegotiation

October 2009	The OTIA was signed.
December 2010	Revised Heads of Agreement place Rio Tinto (RT) in charge of core operations. Phase 1 construction begins.
October 2011	GOM announce intentions to renegotiate the OTIA, prompted due to cost overruns delaying royalties, looking to increase their stake from 34% to 51%.
May 2012	New Foreign Investment Law passed which limits foreign investment and ownership.
August 2012	RT acquires majority stake in Ivanhoe Mines. Ivanhoe Mines changes their name to Turquoise Hill.
March 2013	Rio Tinto suspends start of phase 2 construction.
October 2013	First shipment of copper from the open pit mine (phase 1).
November 2013	New investment law which reverses the 2012 Foreign Investment Law, to grant foreign investors equal protection to domestic.
June 2014	Tax audit demands US$127 million from Oyu Tolgoi in unpaid taxes.
August 2014	TRQ and the GOM agree to develop an independent power plant at the Tavan Tolgoi coalfields.
May 2015	The UDP was signed, transferring 2% of the project value to the GOM.
May 2016	Notice to proceed. RT approves development of underground mine. Expected cost US$5.3 billion.
April 2017	New banking regulation requires foreign MNEs to use domestic banks.
May 2017	RT file a complaint to the IMF which delays a bailout payment to Mongolia. Consequently, banking regulation is relaxed.
January 2018	Tax audit demands US$155 million from OT LLC in unpaid taxes.
February 2018	The government cancel the power sector cooperation agreement as power from Tavan Tolgoi is unfeasible within the timeframe.
March 2018	OT filed a notice of dispute to the GOM under the OTIA relating to the tax assessment. US$4.8 was paid to settle the tax dispute.
July 2019	RT announce major delays and cost escalation due to ground conditions.
November 2019	Mongolian parliament votes to revise Oyu Tolgoi agreement, wishing to replace the 34% stake with a special royalty.
November 2020	TRQ takes RT to arbitration over the company's obligation to secure funding.
March 2021	RT and TRQ agree to renegotiate the UDP with the GOM.
April 2021	Updated funding plan agreed by RT and TRQ.

References

[1] Saul Estrin, Christine Côté, Daniel Shapiro, and Eleanor Cumpsty wrote this solely to provide material for class discussions. The authors do not intend to illustrate either effective or ineffective handling of a management situation. The authors may have disguised certain names or identifying information to protect confidentiality. An earlier version of this case was previously published by the Case Centre.

[2] Rio Tinto (n.d.) 'Oyu Tolgoi', accessed 20 March, 2022. https://perma.cc/6TNX-TDUY

[3] Turquoise Hill (2016) 'The future of Oyu Tolgoi is underground', 30 June. https://perma.cc/35FH-K9GL

[4] Rio Tinto (n.d.).

[5] Pistilli, Melissa (2021) 'What Was the Highest Price for Copper?'. Investing News Network, 17 June. https://perma.cc/P3H3-99L8

[6] Canadian Mining Journal (2013) 'Continued Oyu Tolgoi delays force Turquoise Hill into $2.4B rights offering', 18 November. https://perma.cc/9LSU-D2MZ

[7] Lewis, Jeff (2021) 'Rio Tinto Willing To Negotiate Oyu Tolgoi Agreement', Mining.com, 19 February. https://perma.cc/86SP-8WCM

[8] Christofyllidis, Symeon (2020) 'Circularity And Recycling In The EU', Copper Alliance, 9 November. https://perma.cc/JYJ4-4J2R

[9] Patel, Sachin (2020) 'The Importance Of Copper In China's Economy', CME Group, 10 September. https://sponsor.marketwatch.com/cme-group/the-importance-of-copper-in-chinas-economy/.

[10] Dudley, Dominic (2019) 'China Is Set To Become The World's Renewable Energy Superpower, According To New Report', Forbes, 11 January. https://perma.cc/C3DY-FWV7

[11] Holmes, Frank (2021) 'The Race For Copper, The Metal Of The Future', Forbes, 1 June. https://perma.cc/9LKT-NR2P

[12] Lynch, Jon (2021) 'Copper's Role In Growing Electric Vehicle Production', Open Markets, 19 April. https://perma.cc/Y2TM-3M2Z

[13] Kiderlin, Sophie (2121) 'Copper is "the new oil" and could reach $15,000 by 2025 as the world transitions to clean energy, Goldman Sachs says', Markets Insider, 14 April. https://markets.businessinsider.com/news/stocks/copper-price-outlook-demand-rise-goldman-sachs-sustainability-commodities-2021-4

14 Tan, Weihzen (2021) 'Copper supply shortfall could linger as green initiatives spur demand, analyst says', CNBC, 17 June. https://perma.cc/S867-7XKL

15 Visual Capitalist (2021) 'Visualizing The Copper Intensity Of Renewable Energy', 20 May. https://www.visualcapitalist.com/copper-intensity-of-renewable-energy/

16 Copper Alliance (2022) 'Copper Demand And Long-Term Availability', International Copper Association. https://perma.cc/5VZS-8RSH

17 Holmes, Frank (2021)

18 Calvo, Guiomar; Mudd, Gavin; Valero, Alicia and Valero, Antonio (2016) 'Decreasing Ore Grades In Global Metallic Mining: A Theoretical Issue Or A Global Reality?', Resources, vol. 5, no. 4. https://doi.org/10.3390/resources5040036

19 Pistilli, Melissa (2021)'Types of Copper Deposits in the World,' Investing News Network, 1 September. https://perma.cc/JQ94-RVAY

20 Rio Tinto (n.d.).

21 Rio Tinto (n.d.).

22 Austin, Rod (2019) '"An example to all": the Mongolian herders who took on a corporate behemoth – and won', The Guardian, 8 April. , https://perma.cc/55HL-798N

23 World Bank (2022) 'GDP per capita, PPP (current international $) – Mongolia', accessed 20 March. https://perma.cc/4YZK-R3BU

24 Melville, Chris; Odkhuru, Erdenedalai and Woolley, Anthony (2015) 'Overview of the Mongolian Legal System and Laws', Globalex, nyulawglobal.org, September. https://perma.cc/JY8P-J8WH

25 Li, Bin Grace; Gupta, Pranav and Yu, Jiangyan (2017) 'From natural resource boom to sustainable economic growth: lessons from Mongolia', International Economics, vol. 151, pp. 7–25. https://doi.org/10.1016/j.inteco.2017.03.001

26 Harris, Chauncy; Saunders, Alan J. K. and Lattimore, Owen (2021a) 'Mongolia – Settlement patterns', Encyclopedia Britannica. https://perma.cc/G3XQ-S27B

27 Ayan Travel (2022) 'People's Revolution (1921) and building socialism', accessed 20 March. https://perma.cc/276Y-S7X6

28 Kwong, Emily (2019) 'Mongolia's Long Road To Mining Wealth', npr, 31 July. https://perma.cc/J6C2-GMPT

[29] Sneath, David (2015) 'Russia's Borders: Mongolia looks to its old Big Brother to counterbalance China', The Conversation, 26 January. https://perma.cc/3PUA-8XQ3

[30] Anderson, James (2016) 'Mongolia and the World Bank – 25 Years on the Path Toward Prosperity', The World Bank, 15 February. https://perma.cc/L85Z-QR5S

[31] Lander, Jennifer (2014) 'A critical reflection on Oyu Tolgoi and the risk of a Resource Trap in Mongolia: Troubling the "Resource Nationalism" Frame', Journal Of Law, Social Justice And Global Development, no. 2, doi:10.31273/LGD.2018.2101. https://warwick.ac.uk/fac/soc/law/elj/lgd/2013_2/2013_2_lander/lander_lgd_2013_2_pub02_2014-.pdf?ContensisTextOnly=true

[32] Cheng, Kevin C. (2003) 'Growth and Recovery in Mongolia During Transition', IMF Working Papers, vol. 2003, no. 217. doi:10.5089/9781451875133.001. https://www.imf.org/external/pubs/ft/wp/2003/wp03217.pdf

[33] Aldrich, Michael and Melville, Chris (2013) 'Mongolia revises its regulatory framework for foreign and domestic investment', Lexology, 16 September. https://perma.cc/Q52E-CZRP

[34] Knottnerus, Roeline and Olivet, Cecilia (2016) 'Mongolia's experience with investment treaties and arbitration cases', Transnational Institute. https://www.tni.org/files/publication-downloads/mongolia_paper.pdf

[35] EITI (2019) 'Mongolia', Extractive Industries Transparency Initiative. https://perma.cc/8AYT-Y2TM

[36] Office of the United States Trade Representative (2022), 'Mongolia', accessed 20 March. https://ustr.gov/countries-regions/china-mongolia-taiwan/mongolia

[37] Werker, Addisu and Werker, Eric (2020) 'Are natural resources a curse, a blessing, or a double-edged sword?', Brookings, 16 July. https://perma.cc/4TTT-95FL

[38] The Observatory of Economic Complexity (n.d) 'Mongolia (MNG) Exports, Imports, And Trade Partners', OEC, accessed 6 April. https://perma.cc/T7CQ-BM5M

[39] The Observatory of Economic Complexity (n.d.)

[40] The Observatory of Economic Complexity (n.d.)

[41] Gopalan, Nisha (2012) 'Mongolia Wary of Chinese Investment', The Wall Street Journal, 30 April. https://www.wsj.com/articles/BL-DLB-37922

McLaughlin, Timothy (2020) 'When You Live Next to an Autocracy', *The Atlantic*. https://perma.cc/LSQ5-FXA6

[42] Trading Economics (2022) 'Mongolia Unemployment Rate – 2021 Data – 2022 Forecast – 1990–2020 Historical', accessed 20 March. https://tradingeconomics.com/mongolia/unemployment-rate

[43] World Bank (2009) 'Mongolia – Livestock Sector Study – Volume I – Synthesis Report'. https://documents.worldbank.org/en/publication/documents-reports/documentdetail/299141468323712124/mongolia-livestock-sector-study-volume-i-synthesis-report

[44] Mayaud, Jerome and Sternberg, Troy (2019) 'Mongolian mining boom threatens traditional herding', The Conversation. https://perma.cc/BRC4-QHHB

[45] Hornby, Lucy (2016) 'Mongolia: Living from loan to loan', *Financial Times*. https://www.ft.com/content/4055d944-78cd-11e6-a0c6-39e2633162d5

[46] Li, Bin Grace; Gupta, Pranav and Yu, Jiangyan (2017)

[47] Fragile States Index (2022) 'Comparative Analysis', accessed 20 March. https://fragilestatesindex.org/comparative-analysis/

[48] US Securities and Exchange Commission (2010) 'Ivanhoe Mines Ltd: Management's Discussion And Analysis Of Financial Condition And Results Of Operations', 31 March 31. https://www.sec.gov/Archives/edgar/data/1158041/000095012310031156/o59368exv3.htm

[49] Reuters (2020) 'Rio Tinto confirms $6.75 billion cost for Mongolia Mine, production to start late 2022', 16 December. https://www.reuters.com/article/rio-tinto-oyu-tolgoi-idUSKBN28Q2CG

[50] US Securities and Exchange Commission (2006) 'Ivanhoe Mines Shareholders Overwhelmingly Approve Strategic Partnership Terms With Rio Tinto To Develop Oyu Tolgoi Mining Complex In Mongolia', 30 November 30. https://www.sec.gov/Archives/edgar/data/1158041/000094523406000973/o34012e6vk.htm

[51] Ivanhoe Mines Ltd. (2009) 'Material Change Report', 6 October. https://perma.cc/YFN6-44GW

[52] Ivanhoe Mines Ltd. (2009)

[53] In 2012, Mongolia terminated several tax treaties with countries, such as, the Netherlands, Luxembourg, Kuwait, and the United Arab Emirates. This was due to suspicions of providing MNEs with tax havens and restricting the government's sovereign right to regulate. Despite the double tax treaty being terminated with the Netherlands, this did not impact OT LLC because of their stability agreement within the OTIA

which entitles OT LLC to the same tax conditions available on the day the agreement was signed in 2009.

[54] AMC Consultants Pty Ltd. (2012) 'Oyu Tolgoi Project IDOP Technical Report', 29 March. https://perma.cc/FCL7-U4Y9

Law Insider (2010) 'Heads Of Agreement Between Ivanhoe Mines Ltd. And Rio Tinto International Holdings Limited', 8 December. https://www.lawinsider.com/contracts/7mAG2R9rGrp

[55] Ivanhoe Mines (2012) 'Ivanhoe Mines and Rio Tinto sign omnibus agreement to ensure funding through to commercial production and additional expansion at Oyu Tolgoi copper-gold-silver project', 18 April. https://perma.cc/Y4HZ-TDJ5

GlobeNewswire (2012) 'Ivanhoe Mines Changes Name to Turquoise Hill Resources', 8 August 8. https://perma.cc/4MP3-8EV8

[56] Hume, Neil (2020a) 'Mongolia raises heat on Rio Tinto over vast Oyu Tolgoi copper mine', *Financial Times*, 25 November. https://www.ft.com/content/b01e18f1-a229-4c68-b279-8aa991867297

[57] Ivanhoe Mines (2005) 'Integrated Development Plan: Executive Summary', August. https://perma.cc/NAE2-MU8W

[58] Els, Frik (2012) 'Oyu Tolgoi: All that's left is for China to flip the switch', mining.com, 9 October. https://perma.cc/VP7R-VWYN

[59] Burton, Marl (2021) 'Copper prices slip as Chinese demand ebbs', *Arkansas Democrat Gazette*, 20 June. https://perma.cc/9F45-4SLL

[60] Saefong, Myra (2021) 'Why China Can't Stop the Rally in Copper', Barron's, 17 June. https://www.barrons.com/articles/copper-prices-51623884044

[61] RioTinto (2022) 'Oyu Tolgoi', Web Archive – Rio Tinto, accessed 20 March. https://web.archive.org/web/20131023035324/http://www.riotinto.com/ourbusiness/oyu-tolgoi-4025.aspx

[62] UNCTAD (2013) 'Investment Policy Review Mongolia', June 2013. https://unctad.org/system/files/official-document/diaepcb2013d3_en.pdf

[63] UNCTAD (2013)

[64] Harris, Chauncy; Saunders, Alan J. K. and Lattimore, Owen (2021b) 'Mongolia – government and society', *Encyclopedia Britannica*. https://perma.cc/C93Y-Z4HQ

[65] White, Brent (2011) 'Gridlocked: the uneven road to rule-of-law reform in Mongolia', *East Asia Forum*, 18 June. https://www.eastasiaforum.org/2011/06/18/gridlocked-the-uneven-road-to-rule-of-law-reform-in-mongolia/

[66] OECD (2019) 'Anti-Corruption Reforms In Mongolia', *Fourth Round Of Monitoring Mongolia*, 16 November. https://www.oecd.org/corruption /acn/OECD-ACN-Mongolia-4th-Round-Monitoring-Report-2019-ENG .pdf

[67] Chene, Marie (2012) 'Corruption in natural resource management in Mongolia', Transparency International. https://perma.cc/4MWP-VE64

[68] Vernon, Raymond (1971) *Sovereignty at Bay: The Multinational Spread of U.S. Enterprises.* New York: Basic Books.

[69] Musacchio, Aldo and Schefer, Jonathan (2011) *Sherritt Goes to Cuba (A): Political Risk in Unchartered Territory.* Boston, MA: Harvard Business School Publishing.

[70] Ramamurtim, R. (2001). 'The obsolescing "bargaining model"? MNC-host developing country relations revisited'. *Journal of International Business Studies*, vol. 32, no. 1, pp. 23–39. https://doi.org/10.1057 /palgrave.jibs.8490936

[71] Eden, L.; Lenway, S., and Schuler, D. (2005). 'From the obsolescing bargain to the political bargaining model', In Grosse R. (ed.) *International Business and Government Relations in the 21st Century*, Cambridge: Cambridge University Press, pp. 251–272.

[72] Shafaie, Amir (2015) 'Rio Tinto, Mongolia, and the Art of Negotiating Amidst Price Volatility', *Natural Resource Governance Institute*, 24 June. https://perma.cc/5SED-42ZJ

[73] UNCTAD (2013) 'Investment Policy Review Mongolia', June. https:// unctad.org/system/files/official-document/diaepcb2013d3_en.pdf

[74] Ker, Peter (2019) 'Mongolia floats royalty solution for Rio Tinto tensions', *Financial Review*, 2019, https://www.afr.com/companies/mining /mongolia-floats-royalty-solution-for-rio-tinto-tensions-20191212 -p53j8f

[75] UNCTAD (2013)

[76] Jamasmie, Cecilia (2013) 'Rio Tinto not shipping copper from Oyu Tolgoi any time soon: report', mining.com, 13 June. https://perma.cc/9E69 -RM5K

[77] Shafaie, Amir (2015)

[78] Stanway, David (2013) 'Mongolia to grill Rio over Oyu Tolgoi costs-govt source', *Reuters*, 6 February. https://www.reuters.com/article/riotinto -mongolia-oyutolgoi-idUSL4N0B60XW20130206

[79] ' London Mining Network (2021) '2021 – Rising costs force renegotiation of Oyu Tolgoi'. https://perma.cc/Z4H2-KG7U

Dairtan, Anand (2019) 'Rio Tinto faces having to renegotiate terms of Mongolian copper project', *Reuters*, 21 November. https://www.reuters.com/article/us-mining-riotinto-mongolia-idUSKBN1XV278

[80] Lander, Jennifer (2014)

[81] Els, Frik (2016) 'Mongolia wants Rio to speed up Oyu Tolgoi expansion', mining.com, 30 August. https://perma.cc/PNB8-UL9U

[82] Donville, Christopher; Baer, Todd and Humber, Yuiry (2013) 'Rio Said to Consider Halt At Biggest Mongolia Copper Mine', *Bloomberg*, 31 January. https://www.bloomberg.com/news/articles/2013-01-30/rio-said-to-consider-halt-at-biggest-mongolia-copper-mine

[83] Shafaie, Amir (2015)

[84] Hume, Neil (2020b) 'Rio eyes production from Mongolia copper project in 2022', *Financial Times*, 16 December. https://www.ft.com/content/5ac622fd-653a-4c8b-959b-321bb03259b7

[85] Hume, Neil (2020a)

[86] Yakub, Mehanaz (2021) 'Rio Tinto and Mongolian Government to replace Oyu Tolgoi mine plan', *CIM Magazine*, 11 January 11. https://perma.cc/P78U-ENM3

[87] Scharaw, Bajar (2017) 'Guest Post: Agreement between Canada and Mongolia for the Promotion and Protection of Investments – a Glance at Its Nature, Significance And Features', *Mongolia Focus*, 10 December. https://perma.cc/5VZS-XX92

[88] Reuters (2017) 'IMF delays Mongolia bailout due to banking requirements for foreign firms', 2 May. https://www.reuters.com/article/mongolia-economy-idUSL4N1I41PL

[89] Reuters (2020),'Rio Tinto seeks international arbitration on tax dispute with Mongolia', 20 February. https://www.reuters.com/article/us-rio-tinto-mongolia-arbitration-idUSKBN20E2Y7

[90] Gosden, Emily (2020) 'Rio Tinto Confirms $1.5Bn Cost Overrun At Oyu Tolgoi Mine In Gobi Desert', *The Times*, 17 December. https://www.thetimes.co.uk/article/rio-tinto-confirms-1-5bn-cost-overrun-at-oyu-tolgoi-mine-in-gobi-desert-zmt0gjm6g

Jamasmie, Cecilia (2020) 'Turquoise Hill takes Rio Tinto to arbitration over Mongolia mine funding', mining.com, 5 November. https://perma.cc/PG5E-T99M

Hume, Neil (2019) 'Mongolia parliament seeks 'improved contracts' for Rio Tinto mine', *Financial Times*, 21 November. https://www.ft.com/content/e55cc25a-0c62-11ea-b2d6-9bf4d1957a67

[91] Yakub, Mehanaz (2021)

Hume, Neil (2021) 'Rio Tinto accused of concealing real reasons for Mongolia mine delay', *Financial Times*, 25 March. https://www.ft.com /content/9a23a0c4-5285-4b42-939c-f992a1c18336

[92] Hume, Neil (2021) 'Review casts doubt over Rio Tinto explanation of Oyu Tolgoi problems', *Financial Times*, 9 August. https://www.ft.com /content/443e889e-9b91-475c-b41f-28e519b93683

[93] Unurzul, M. (2021) 'Independent review on the cost overruns and schedule delays of the Oyu Tolgoi underground expansion', *Mongolian National News Agency*, 28 April. https://perma.cc/GWH7-JMXR

[94] Hume, Neil (2019)

[95] Jamasmie, Cecilia (2020)

[96] Rio Tinto (2021) 'Rio Tinto reaches agreement with Turquoise Hill Resources on financing plan for Oyu Tolgoi', 9 April. https://perma.cc /3MZ2-9C78

Reuters (2021) 'Rio Tinto, Turquoise Hill reach deal on Oyu Tolgoi expansion', 9 April. https://www.reuters.com/article/us-rio-tinto-oyu -tolgoi-turquoise-hill/rio-tinto-turquoise-hill-reach-deal-on-oyu-tolgoi -expansion-idUSKBN2BW0P5

[97] Jamasmie, Cecilia (2021) 'Rio Tinto, Mongolia agree to replace Oyu Tolgoi expansion plan', mining.com, 2 March. https://perma.cc/C6LZ-842N

[98] Open Oil (2016) 'Oyu Tolgoi Financial Model: Narrative Report', September.

11. Activist investors versus Big Oil: how should ExxonMobil and British Petroleum respond?

Rebecca Campbell, Alfred Jasansky and Janna Wirth

Typically, activist investors use their power to challenge 'inefficient' management to focus on shareholder returns. But what happens when activist investors push firms to act in more socially oriented ways? This case study contrasts two activist campaigns targeting Big Oil. In one, Arjuna Capital targeted Exxon (pushing it to adopt more ambitious climate targets). In the other, Bluebell Capital targeted British Petroleum (BP) (demanding it to water down its climate goals and exploit current high oil prices).

The case addresses an enduring debate – what is the purpose of the firm? Is it to generate profits for shareholders within the confines of the law (Milton Friedman's famous proposition)? Or does it have obligations to wider society? The issues explored in this case include:

- How should the management of Big Oil companies balance demands from activist investors who are pushing for socially oriented change, and those focused on profit maximisation?

- Is it management's responsibility to maximise shareholder returns in the short term or should they pursue a long-term transition towards a low-carbon business model (at the expense of current shareholders)?

- How can companies and activist investors use legal remedies in pursuit of their positions?

- Do capital markets in their current form allow for a change in the business model of carbon-intensive industries?

How to cite this book chapter:

Campbell, Rebecca, Jasansky, Alfred and Wirth, Janna (2025) 'Activist investors versus Big Oil: how should ExxonMobil and British Petroleum respond?', in: Sallai, Dorottya and Pepper, Alexander (ed) *Navigating the 21st Century Business World: Case Studies in Management*, London: LSE Press, pp. 159–176. https://doi.org/10.31389/lsepress.nbw.k

Guidance on how to write a case analysis can be found in Chapter 1, 'Business cases: what are they, why do we use them and how should you go about doing a case analysis?'.

A teaching note for this case is available to bona fide educators. To request a copy please email r.m.campbell@lse.ac.uk

Introduction

2022 was a record year in the oil and gas industry. Russia's invasion of Ukraine saw oil prices peak to in excess of $100 a barrel. The Big Oil companies Exxon-Mobil (Exxon), Chevron, Shell, BP, TotalEnergies and Equinor made a total of $219 billion in profits in 2022 – more than double the previous year's profits – and distributed more than $110 billion in dividends and share repurchases to its investors. At the same time, global greenhouse gas emissions reached an all-time high in 2022 and the energy sector is responsible for about three-quarters of these emissions.[1] Among all energy sources, oil is the second-largest source of both greenhouse gas (GHG) emissions and pollution-related deaths, surpassed only by coal (see Figure 11.1). As climate experts continue to warn about the potential consequences of global warming, the oil industry is a key focus of most energy transition discussions.

Shareholders of Big Oil companies are divided in their reaction to these trends. While some activist investors demanded an increase in investment into oil and gas to profit from the favourable macroeconomic environment, others proposed a shift towards more climate-conscious investments, such as renewable energy and hydrogen. How should the management of Big Oil companies respond? Is it the responsibility of management to maximise shareholder returns in the short term or should they pursue a long-term transition towards a low-carbon business model at the expense of current shareholders? Do the public markets in their current form possess the patience to support a change in the business model of carbon-intensive energy industries?

Oil markets

Oil prices are determined by global supply and demand, and economic growth is the primary driver of crude oil prices. Contrary to initial expectations, the oil market quickly picked up from its post-Covid slump in 2021 and is projected to continuously grow until 2028. Following the outbreak of war in Ukraine, prices of oil and gas surged in 2022. Oil companies such as BP, Shell, Exxon and Chevron realised record profits and many announced share buybacks. In 2023, total oil demand, measured in million barrels per day (mbd), stood at 102 mbd and is now expected to grow until 2028, peaking at 106 mbd, a higher demand outlook than some experts and executives expected before the Covid-19 pandemic and the war in Ukraine.

Figure 11.1: Global GHG emissions of the oil industry

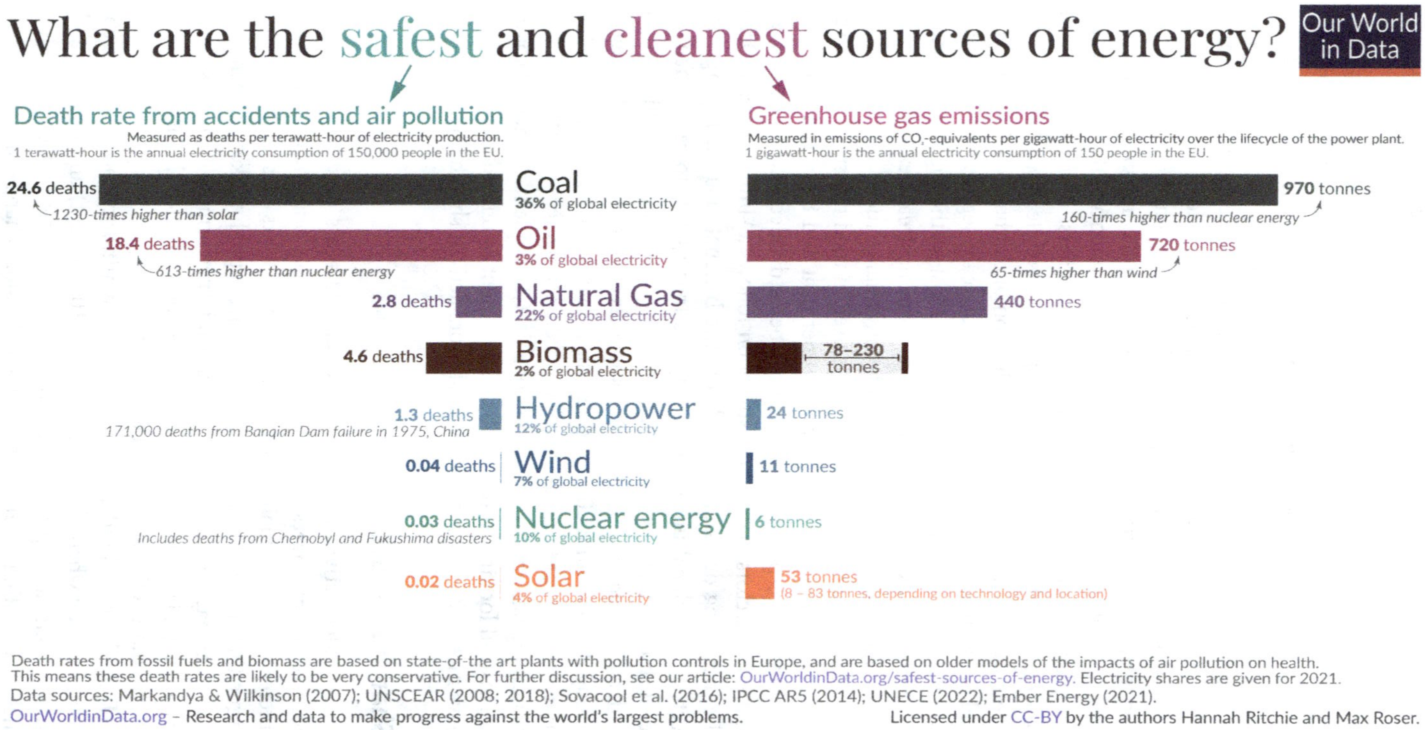

What are the safest and cleanest sources of energy?

Our World in Data

Death rate from accidents and air pollution
Measured as deaths per terawatt-hour of electricity production.
1 terawatt-hour is the annual electricity consumption of 150,000 people in the EU.

Coal 36% of global electricity — 24.6 deaths
↳ 1230-times higher than solar

Oil 3% of global electricity — 18.4 deaths
↳ 613-times higher than nuclear energy

Natural Gas 22% of global electricity — 2.8 deaths

Biomass 2% of global electricity — 4.6 deaths

Hydropower 12% of global electricity — 1.3 deaths
171,000 deaths from Banqiao Dam failure in 1975, China

Wind 7% of global electricity — 0.04 deaths

Nuclear energy 10% of global electricity — 0.03 deaths
Includes deaths from Chernobyl and Fukushima disasters

Solar 4% of global electricity — 0.02 deaths

Greenhouse gas emissions
Measured in emissions of CO₂-equivalents per gigawatt-hour of electricity over the lifecycle of the power plant.
1 gigawatt-hour is the annual electricity consumption of 150 people in the EU.

Coal — 970 tonnes
↳ 160-times higher than nuclear energy

Oil — 720 tonnes
↳ 65-times higher than wind

Natural Gas — 440 tonnes

Biomass — 78-230 tonnes

Hydropower — 24 tonnes

Wind — 11 tonnes

Nuclear energy — 6 tonnes

Solar — 53 tonnes
(8 – 83 tonnes, depending on technology and location)

Death rates from fossil fuels and biomass are based on state-of-the art plants with pollution controls in Europe, and are based on older models of the impacts of air pollution on health.
This means these death rates are likely to be very conservative. For further discussion, see our article: OurWorldInData.org/safest-sources-of-energy. Electricity shares are given for 2021.
Data sources: Markandya & Wilkinson (2007); UNSCEAR (2008; 2018); Sovacool et al. (2016); IPCC AR5 (2014); UNECE (2022); Ember Energy (2021).
OurWorldinData.org – Research and data to make progress against the world's largest problems.   Licensed under CC-BY by the authors Hannah Ritchie and Max Roser.

Source: Ritchie, H. (2020) 'What are the safest and cleanest sources of energy?', OurWorldInData.org, https://ourworldindata.org/safest-sources-of-energy
licensed under CC-BY by the authors Hannah Ritchie and Max Roser

Oil is a key input to various end-products, such as food, transportation and construction, playing a fundamental role in the day-to-day lives of consumers and businesses worldwide. First, drilling operations extract crude oil and natural gas. Once transported into oil refineries, the crude oil is refined into products with both industrial and end-consumer uses. These products include diesel, gasoline, kerosene, jet fuel, asphalt, lubricants and chemical reagents used in pesticides, plastics and pharmaceuticals. Oil markets are structured along these supply chain stages and divided into upstream, midstream and downstream segments. Upstream production includes exploration, drilling and extraction of crude oil. The oil companies dominating this space are national oil companies like Saudi Aramco and the so-called 'Big Oil' companies including BP, Exxon, Shell and others. Midstream activities are concerned with oil storage and transportation while downstream production refers to oil refining, product distribution and other activities closer to the end consumer. Large players in the downstream segment include Marathon Petroleum Corporation and Phillips 66. Most of the Big Oil companies are integrated across segments, operating from upstream exploration and production to downstream spheres with convenience fuels.

In the EU, about half of crude oil is used in road transport, 13 per cent for industrial non-energy use, around 9 per cent and 8 per cent for water and air transport respectively, with the rest being divided into residential, energy, and other sectors.[2] Global consumption follows a similar pattern. Driven by the increasing demand for crude oil, the International Energy Agency projected 2023 global upstream oil and gas investments to reach their highest level since 2015, growing an estimated 11 per cent to $528 billion, compared with $474 billion in 2022.[3] Some companies are eager to take advantage of the strong demand until 2028 by increasing investment in oil and gas. However, from 2028 onwards, oil demand is expected to decrease due to increased efficiency, regulation and rising sales of EVs. Consequently, other oil companies are instead looking to reduce their investment in oil and gas. Both strategies have met with considerable backlash from activist shareholders.

Shareholder activism

Shareholder activism is not new. Over 400 years ago, angry shareholders accused the managers of the Dutch East India Company of neglecting their interests. But it remains controversial. Supporters of shareholder activism argue that it is a vital part of a functioning capital market, challenging inefficient management and shaking up underperforming firms. Its detractors argue that it is a way for (some) shareholders to enrich themselves and that it fosters destructive short-term decisions.

Typically, shareholder activists purchase a minority equity stake in a public company (anywhere from 1 per cent to 10 per cent) and demand a change in the company's governance, strategy or operations. Common demands include divesting from an unprofitable division, changes in capital structure, increased dividend payments, replacing a CEO, cost-cutting or demanding a share buy-back. The activists usually pursue this through proxy battles, publicity campaigns, negotiations with the management or shareholder resolutions. Shareholder resolutions are non-binding proposals to the board, presented to all shareholders and voted on during the company's annual general meeting. Some of the most well-known activist investors are Carl Icahn, Daniel Loeb from Third Point, Bill Ackman from Pershing Square and Nelson Peltz from Train Partners.

Increasingly, shareholder activism has been used as a tool to push beyond financial shareholder returns towards socially oriented goals. The shareholder activism landscape is thus shifting away from purely profit-focused campaigns, and Big Oil companies can face very different activist demands. While Exxon was confronted with a shareholder resolution demanding more ambitious climate targets, BP's climate strategy was deemed too ambitious by a different activist group, who wanted BP to abandon its climate goals and instead exploit the high oil prices and demand.

Case A: Exxon and Arjuna Capital

Darren W. Woods had served as the chief executive officer of Exxon since 2017 and had faced several activist shareholder campaigns, some of which successfully initiated change and, in the case of Engine No.1, had even resulted in board seats. However, the activist campaign launched by Arjuna Capital in 2022 would mark a dramatic shift. Arjuna Capital had repeatedly submitted proposals demanding that Exxon step up its medium-term emission reductions. Exxon was getting increasingly frustrated by what they saw as a misuse of the system by professional activists who had publicly stated that they did not care about shareholder value. In February 2024, Exxon filed a lawsuit against Arjuna Capital. The lawsuit was dismissed but sparked a public backlash and it quickly turned into a broader debate about shareholder rights. Woods was now wondering, was the litigation against one of their own shareholders a step too far? Should he give in to his critics or convince his board to continue to fight Arjuna Capital and refile the case? If his responsibility was to maximise profits for his shareholders, how should he react if short- and long-term profitability seemed to be in conflict? What if not all shareholders agreed on what their interests are? To whom was he ultimately responsible?

The company: Exxon

Exxon is an American oil and gas company and the largest descendant of Rockefeller's Standard Oil company, which was broken up in 1911. Exxon operates in four key segments: upstream, energy products, chemical products and speciality products. The upstream segment explores, drills and supplies crude oil and gas from all over the world, generating $23.6 billion in profits and 3738 thousand barrels per day in 2023. The energy products segment is an integrated business operating in refining, transportation, trading and end-consumer supply of oil and petroleum products through its Esso, Exxon, and Mobil branded petrol (gas) stations. This segment yielded $12 billion in net income in 2023. The chemicals and speciality products divisions generated in total around $4.8 billion in net income in 2023. Low-carbon solutions were included in the corporate overhead costs as they were not mature enough to be included in a standalone division.

In 2011, Exxon was the largest company in the world. But it was to face a difficult decade. Lower crude oil prices on global markets, increased pressure to transition away from hydrocarbons, and fears that reaching 'peak oil' would soon decrease production, all hit its share price. In 2014 Exxon's share price was $103 per share, declining to around $70 per share in 2019. In March 2020, the market plummeted over fears about Covid-19 lockdowns, and the global pandemic sent Exxon's share price to a record low of $33 per share. As lockdowns were introduced, the demand for oil dried up, turning the price of oil negative for a brief time in April 2020 when sellers paid buyers to get oil off their hands. With the price of oil at historic lows, regulatory pressures to decrease carbon emissions and the increasing appeal of asset-light technological companies, asset-heavy oil companies like Exxon were seen as unattractive investments. Yet by 2023, the market had rebounded. Exxon's share price climbed to a high of $120 and the company reported $335 billion in revenues and $36 billion in net income for FY23. Exxon was once again one of the largest companies in the world.

An early warning: Engine No. 1's Exxon campaign

Arjuna Capital was not Exxon's first brush with environmental, social and governance (ESG)-focused activism. In May 2021, with a mere 0.02 per cent stake in Exxon, the small activist fund Engine No. 1 launched a campaign titled 'Reenergize Exxon', demanding change. On the website reenergize-exxon.com, the activist fund stated:

> Over the last 10 years, ExxonMobil's total shareholder return, including dividends, has been negative (15) per cent, versus +271 per cent for the S&P 500. Exxon's deteriorating financial strength has caused the market to question the reliability of its dividend in recent years. Last year for the first time in decades ExxonMobil failed to increase its dividend, and its CEO said, 'The beauty of the dividend is that it is flexible.[4]

Engine No. 1 had four key demands:

1. Refresh the board with independent directors with transformative energy experience.

2. Impose greater capital allocation discipline.
3. Implement a strategic plan for sustainable value creation, including an investment into clean energy which would help the company diversify.
4. Overhaul management compensation, especially the salary of CEO Darren Woods who took $75 million in the previous four years despite underperformance.

Despite their small stake (too small to require disclosure), the activists convinced large Exxon shareholders such as BlackRock and Vanguard to grant Engine No. 1 three board seats – a truly remarkable feat for an activist this size taking on a $400 billion company. However, not long after this campaign, Exxon faced another activist shareholder concerned with its climate strategy – Arjuna Capital.

The activist: Arjuna Capital

The activist fund Arjuna Capital was founded in 2013 by Natasha Lamb and Furnum Brown with the mission to provide investors with competitive financial returns and promote a healthier, more sustainable and more just economy. Its mission statement specifies:

As an investment firm focused on sustainability, we understand that social justice, environmental responsibility, and economic vitality are all 'bottom line' issues. We are convinced that investing in a more equitable, environmentally responsible economy is simply smarter long-term investing to secure your wealth and the prosperity of future generations.[5]

To achieve this, Arjuna Capital typically purchased small stakes in companies and introduced shareholder resolutions, demanding additional disclosures from the management and proposing alternative strategies. Between 2013 and 2016, Arjuna Capital asked Occidental Petroleum three times to 'review the Company's policies, actions and plans to measure, disclose, mitigate, and set quantitative reduction targets for methane emissions and flaring resulting from all operations under the company's financial or operational control'.[6] In 2019, it pressed Chevron and Exxon to '[describe] how the Company could adapt its business model to align with a decarbonising economy'.[7] In 2020, it pressed Comcast to assess 'the effectiveness of the company's workplace sexual harassment policies, including the results of a comprehensive, independent audit/investigation, analysis of policies and practices, and commitments to create a safe, inclusive work environment'.[8] In 2022, it sent proposals to Twitter to nominate a human rights expert to its board, to Wells Fargo and Alphabet to report on their board diversity, and dozens of resolutions trying to persuade various companies to report on differential pay by gender and race.

An unprecedented fight: Exxon and Arjuna Capital

In 2022, Arjuna Capital, in cooperation with the climate non-profit 'Follow This', filed an official motion for Exxon to disclose 'how the company could alter its business model to yield profits within the limits of a 1.5-degree Celsius global temperature rise by substantially reducing its dependence on fossil fuels'.[9] In the same year, Arjuna Capital also asked Exxon to reduce their Scope 3 emissions. This motion received 27 per cent of the shareholder votes and was therefore rejected. It filed the same motion a year later and received 10 per cent of the votes (see Exhibit 1).

On 21 January 2024, however, Exxon took an unexpected step. The company filed a lawsuit against Arjuna Capital, arguing that professional activists were abusing the proposal process (see Exhibit 2). In a statement on their website, Exxon justified the lawsuit as follows:

> Repeatedly submitting proposals that investors overwhelmingly reject is not in the interests of investors or a working shareholder proposal system. We have a responsibility to call attention to the misuse of proposals by professional activist groups who have publicly stated they do not care about growing shareholder value while they pursue their own agendas. We hope to continue the dialogue on these issues.'[10]

Under the US Securities and Exchange Commission ('SEC'), public companies can request to omit shareholder proposals from presentation and voting during the annual general meeting. Potential grounds to request this exclusion include 'micromanaging' the board by interfering with the ordinary business operations, substantially duplicating another shareholder proposal or resubmission of earlier proposals.

While Exxon claimed that it valued the rights of shareholders to submit proposals, it criticised an increasing 'abuse of the shareholder-access system'.[11] Exxon claimed that from 2022 onwards, the SEC increasingly rejected companies' requests for omission of shareholder proposals and created 'a system that's not serving the best interests of investors' where their rights 'are increasingly being infringed by activists masquerading as shareholders'.[12] To set a precedent and push the SEC to change its decision-making on shareholder proposals, Exxon upheld its lawsuit even after Arjuna Capital withdrew its shareholder proposal. However, the lawsuit sparked a backlash from some of the biggest investors. Nicolai Tangen, CEO of the $1.6 trillion Norway Wealth Fund, which owns a $6.2 billion stake in Exxon, said 'It's a worrisome development. We think it's very aggressive and we are concerned about the implications for shareholders rights'.[13] CalPERS, the $484 billion pension fund with a $1 billion stake in Exxon, expressed their concern in a letter and voted against all of Exxon's board nominations. In the letter, CalPERS said 'If ExxonMobil succeeds in silencing voices and upending the rules of shareholder democracy, what other subjects will the leaders of any company make off limits?'[14]

The response: Darren Woods weighs his options

On 17 June 2024, the responsible US District Court Judge dismissed Exxon's lawsuit, stating that Arjuna Capital had already withdrawn its proposal and pledged to not submit similar resolutions in future, thus Exxon's claim was no longer valid. Since the case was dismissed without prejudice, however, Exxon can decide to continue its mission and refile charges.

As Darren Woods was reading the statements from important investors such as CalPERS, he was thinking about whether the lawsuit against Arjuna Capital might have been too aggressive. Yet, he was concerned about how activist investors might influence his business in the future, should Exxon not continue with its lawsuit. He felt unsettled about the whole situation. How was he supposed to balance the conflicting views of the shareholders? Up until now, the share price of Exxon seemed to have done relatively well; however, was this a long-term strategy?

Case B: BP and Bluebell Capital

BP found itself in a battle with very different activist shareholders. While Exxon was being pressed to step up its commitment to climate change, BP was confronted with demands that it drop its climate targets and focus on its rather lacklustre financial performance.

Murray Auchincloss had replaced Bernard Looney as CEO of BP in 2023 and soon found himself in a tough position. He was expected to deliver an ambitious decarbonisation strategy while under scrutiny from Bluebell Capital, an activist shareholder, who was vocal in its demand for greater returns to shareholders. In May 2024, BP had announced earnings that had missed analysts' expectations. 'We remain committed to our strategy', he told the analysts, 'we just have to be pragmatic. We need to deliver the returns we promised to the market, otherwise, we won't move projects forward.'[15] Would it really be possible to remain committed to their decarbonisation strategy and still maintain healthy shareholder returns?

The company: BP

BP is a British FTSE 100 company, founded in 1909 and with more than 80 thousand employees. In 2023, it recorded revenues of $210 billion and a profit of $13.8 billion. It operates in three key segments: gas and low-carbon energy; oil production and operation; and customers and products. In 2022, gas and low-carbon energy generated close to $6 billion in profits, focusing on the production of natural gas, trading of natural gas, and low-carbon sources (solar, wind and hydrogen). Oil production and operation focused on upstream oil production of crude oil and yielded $6.8 billion in profit in 2022. Lastly, the customers and products division, which included consumer-facing activities such as convenience fuels, biofuels, and aviation fuels, brought $5 billion in profits to the company in 2022.

Despite the strong post-Covid run in the oil markets, BP's share price had not performed as well as that of Chevron, Exxon, and Shell, trading at around 11 times its earnings as opposed to the 14 times of Chevron and Exxon or 13 times for Shell. Since 2022, BP's return to shareholders has not been on par with its competitors and many investors were becoming frustrated, attributing the valuation gap to BP's ambitious decarbonisation strategy which, some investors believed, prevented BP from taking advantage of the favourable market conditions in the oil and gas market.

From British Petroleum to Beyond Petroleum and back

In 1997, John Browne, then CEO of BP, gave a speech at Stanford Graduate Business School on the subject of the global environment. He spoke about 'discernible human influence on the climate', the 'link between the concentration of carbon dioxide and the increase in temperature', and a 'need for action and solutions'.[16] For an executive of an oil company, this was an unprecedented statement and BP was one of the first oil companies to acknowledge the impact of hydrocarbons on the global climate. The speech marked a shift in BP's strategy and from then onwards, BP would stand for 'Beyond Petroleum', said John Browne.

When global oil demand was weak in 2020, BP announced the aim to be net zero by 2050. This was an ambitious target that required a 50 per cent reduction in the carbon intensity of BP's products by 2050 or sooner and an increase in the proportion of investment into the non-oil and gas business over time. The promise would mean a reduction of CO_2 eq. by 35–40 per cent by 2030. Bernard Looney, BP's CEO in 2020, commented on the shift: 'The world's carbon budget is finite and running out fast; we need a rapid transition to net zero. We all want energy that is reliable and affordable, but that is no longer enough. It must also be cleaner.'[17]

The 2020 announcement marked the biggest strategic overhaul in the energy giant's history – transitioning from the oil and gas business to being an integrated energy company. BP expected to slash its oil and gas production by 40 per cent in the coming decade and planned greater investment into wind and solar power. No other major oil company announced such a steep reduction in their current main source of profit. According to the strategy, by 2025, BP would dedicate 20 per cent of its capital to its 'transition business', that is investments outside of oil and gas, far more than its competitors. The company also planned to dispose of $25 billion in assets by 2025, having recently sold off its petrochemical business to Ineos Ltd for $5 billion. Following this ambitious announcement, some investors remained sceptical, especially given that the target returns from low-carbon energy business were 8–10 per cent compared with industry targets of around 15 per cent for oil and gas investments. BP's share price remained stuck near a 25-year low and had underperformed its rivals (see Figure 11.2). Nonetheless, BP quickly moved from words to action. In 2020, it paid $1.1 billion for a stake in US wind farms and

Figure 11.2: Relative share prices of Big Oil companies (2020–2024)

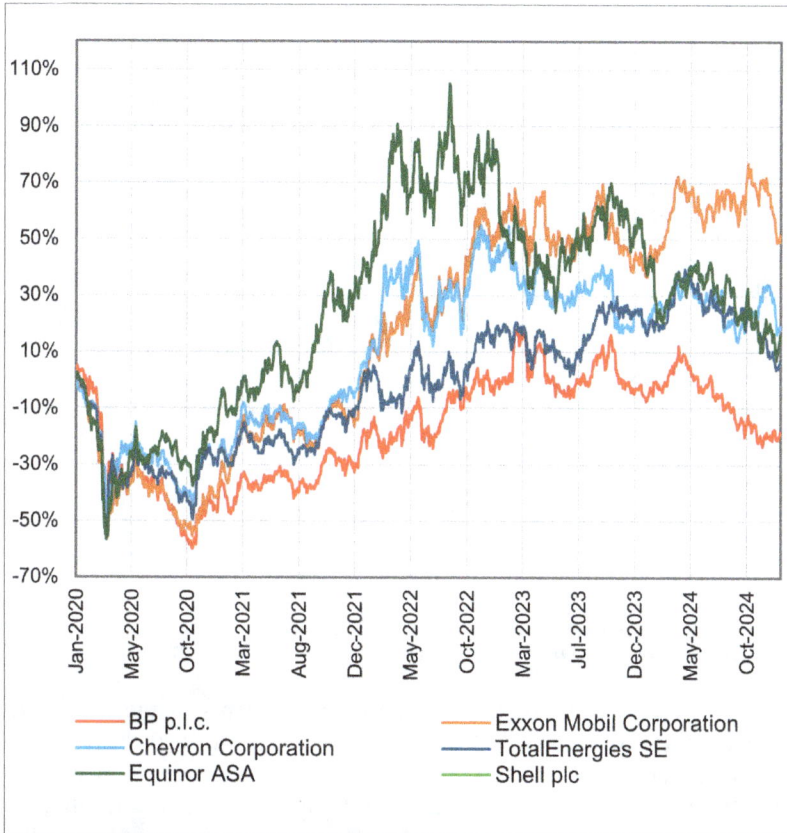

Source: Authors' analysis on the basis of data from Google Finance. Percentage change of share prices from 01.01.2020. Retrieved from: https://www.google.com/finance/

continued to build out its renewables portfolio. It also made investments in EV charging, hydrogen solutions, bioenergy fuels, carbon capture and other low-carbon solutions. By 2022, the total transition growth investment totalled $4.9 billion, around 30 per cent of the group's total investment that year.

However, ambitious energy decarbonisation targets came under scrutiny when oil markets recovered from the pandemic and as the war in Ukraine continued. Energy prices were continuously high with Brent Crude at around $83 per barrel in February 2023 (see Figure 11.3). On 7 February 2023, then-CEO Bernard Looney backtracked on the ambitious announcement made in 2020 and decreased the decarbonisation targets. BP announced that it would now aim for a 25 per cent reduction of CO_2 eq. by 2030, instead of the initially envisioned 40 per cent. To justify the reverse in strategy, Looney explained that today's governments and societies were expecting companies such as BP to invest in the energy system.

Figure 11.3: Brent Crude Oil spot price in US$ (2010–2024)

Source: Authors' analysis on the basis of data from the International Energy Agency..
https://www.eia.gov/dnav/pet/hist/LeafHandler.ashx?n=PET&s=RBRTE&f=M

BP's announcements mirrored broader developments in the fossil fuel industry. When BP initially declared its climate strategy in 2020, the oil prices were about half of the 2023 levels. By the time Looney course-corrected in 2023, the profitability of the fossil fuel industry had increased drastically. Following the announcement that emission targets would be lowered and BP posting a record profit, the stock price jumped from 478p per share on 6 February to 560p per share on 10 February. Despite the share price improvement, not all shareholders were satisfied. On 4 October 2023, Bluebell Capital, an activist hedge fund, disclosed its stake in BP and demanded greater shareholder returns, arguing that BP's shares were at least 50 per cent undervalued.

The activist: Bluebell Capital

Bluebell Capital is a London-based activist hedge fund with around $130 million in total assets under management. It was founded in 2019 by Italian ex-investment bankers Guiseppe Bivona and Marco Taricco, and despite its small size has led activist campaigns against corporate heavyweights such as Danone, Glencore, Bayer and BlackRock. In its campaigns, Bluebell focused first and foremost on shareholder returns and avoided ideologically motivated strategies. In 2021 for example, Bluebell mounted a campaign against Danone's CEO Emmanuel Faber, one of the most vocal champions for ESG and purpose-driven capitalism in global business. Bluebell's Marco Tarrico commented 'We never criticised [the Environmental and Social goals], how can we criticise these things? But it can't come at the expense of shareholder returns. The first duty of a public company is to remunerate shareholders.'[18] Some of Bluebell's campaigns were aligned with ESG goals, as long as these ultimately led to greater shareholder returns. For example, in 2023 it asked Glencore, one of the largest mining and commodity trading companies, to dispose of its thermal coal business and instead take advantage of the growing market of transition metals required for achieving climate goals.

In its letter to BP, Bluebell claimed to be a 'passionate environmentalist', but also a 'realist who understands the power of capital markets'.[19] The activist investor criticised BP's strategy, low targeted returns, flawed assumptions on the demand side, and its failure to deliver shareholder returns. Bluebell viewed BP's plan to expand into the fiercely competitive renewables industry as risky and irrational, claiming that BP had no competitive advantage, track record or experience to succeed and highlighting the typically significantly lower target returns of renewables investments (8–10 per cent) compared to oil and gas ($\approx$15 per cent). Additionally, the activist investor argued that while global oil demand was still rising, BP's divestment from fossil fuels assets would have no positive net effect on climate as it would only transfer assets into the hands of less climate-conscious companies. Bluebell explained that since the oil and gas segment contributed towards 70 per cent of BP's earnings before interest, taxes, depreciation and amortisation (EBITDA), a divestment from this sector would be incompatible with the generation of shareholder value. Lastly, Bluebell pointed out the already low total shareholder returns which, since Looney's appointment in 2020, fell behind the rest of Big Oil. Over Looney's tenure, BP's total shareholder returns stood at only 32 per cent compared to 45 per cent for Shell, 72 per cent for Total Energies, 79 per cent for Chevron, and 135 per cent for Exxon. Bluebell capital argued that its low returns were directly attributable to BP's environmental strategy.

The response: Murray Auchincloss deliberates his strategy

While Bluebell welcomed the revision of BP's climate goals, it sent a letter to the management proposing further changes to the company's strategy including annual investments in oil and gas of $1.5bn, the removal of BP's medium-term emission targets and the revision of its 2050 net zero goal (see Exhibit 3).

Murray Auchincloss was weighing his options after the disappointing earnings call on 7 May 2024. Should he double down on the decarbonisation strategy of BP and continue pursuing net zero by 2050, hoping to beat its rivals in the long term? Or should he give in to the pressure from Bluebell Capital and backtrack on the climate promises to maximise profits in the next years? What was Auchincloss ultimately responsible for: generating the most value for current shareholders or should he also consider responsibilities towards the climate and the long-term preservation of the company?

Preparing the case

In preparing the case analysis you might like to consider the following questions:

1. Is Big Oil in a lose-lose situation, when it comes to shareholder demands? How should the management of Big Oil companies balance the conflicting interests of investors who are pushing for socially oriented change against those focused on profit maximisation?
2. Are managers responsible for maximising shareholder returns in the short term or should they focus on creating sustainable value, potentially at the expense of current shareholders?
3. Should Exxon appeal the judge's decision and move forward with its lawsuit against Arjuna Capital? Was it right to sue its shareholders in the first place?
4. How should BP respond to the demands of Bluebell Capital? Does giving in to Bluebell's demands and scaling back its climate commitments then risk an ESG-focused activist campaign such as that at Exxon?
5. Do today's capital markets dictate shareholder primacy or are managers able to adapt business models based on stakeholder interests?

Exhibits

Exhibit 1: excerpt from Arjuna Capital's shareholder proposal

At Exxon's Annual General Meeting in May 2023, Arjuna Capital, together with the non-profit Follow This, presented its shareholder resolution. The proposal explains their concerns and outlines demands for Exxon's strategy.

> We believe that ExxonMobil could lead and thrive in the energy transition by meeting the increasing demand for energy services while reducing GHG emissions to levels consistent with the global intergovernmental consensus specified by the Paris Accord.
>
> Setting a Paris-aligned medium-term target covering Scope 3 is paramount, because the medium-term is decisive for the Company and the Paris Accord and because Scope 3 accounts for around 90% of total Scope 1, 2 and 3 emissions.
>
> ExxonMobil is one of the few oil majors that has not set Scope 3 targets (at the time of filing this proposal).
>
> ...
>
> We, the shareholders, understand this support to be our fiduciary duty to secure the long-term interest of the Company and to protect

all our assets in the global economy from devastating climate change; limiting global warming is essential to risk management and responsible stewardship of the economy.

...

Changes in demand are as critical as changes in supply, but customers can only change sufficiently when key system players like ExxonMobil offer alternative energy sources at scale. By investing in alternatives, a global integrated energy company like ExxonMobil could decrease emissions without ultimately shrinking business.

It is in the Company's and its shareholders' best interest to pursue the opportunities the energy transition presents; this will also pre-empt risks of losing access to capital markets, policy interventions, litigation, liability for the costs of climate change, disruptive innovation, and stranded assets.

Source: ExxonMobil (2023) 'Notice of 2023 Annual Meeting and Proxy Statement', https://ir.exxonmobil.com/node/34696/html#toc429320_23

Exhibit 2: excerpt from Exxon's complaint in the federal district court for the Northern District of Texas

On 21 January 2024, Exxon filed a complaint in the federal district court for the Northern District of Texas against Arjuna Capital. The complaint sets out Exxon's position on Arjuna's campaign and its criticism of the shareholder proposal system more broadly.

1. Most shareholders invest in companies to help the companies grow and see a return on their investment. But Arjuna and Follow This are not like most shareholders. Driven by an extreme agenda, ... They (or their clients) become shareholders solely to campaign for change through shareholder proposals that are calculated to diminish the company's existing business.

2. Arjuna and Follow This are aided in their efforts by a flawed shareholder proposal and proxy voting process that does not serve investors' interests and has become ripe for abuse by activists with minimal shares and no interest in growing long-term shareholder value.

...

11. The 2024 Proposal does not seek to improve ExxonMobil's economic performance or create shareholder value. Like the previous proposals, it is designed instead to serve Arjuna's and Follow This's agenda to "shrink" the very company in which they are investing by constraining and micromanaging ExxonMobil's ordinary business operations.

...

13. This sweeping intrusion into ExxonMobil's ordinary business operations is designed to substitute Defendants' preferences for the judgment of ExxonMobil's management and board in determining how best to operate the company in an efficient and environmentally-conscious way.

14. Defendants should not be permitted to continue to misuse the shareholder proposal rules to submit a proposal that interferes with ExxonMobil's ordinary business operations and when close to 90% of voting shareholders rejected the 2023 Proposal.

Source: ExxonMobil (2024) 'Complaint in the United States District Court for the Northern District of Texas Fort Worth Division'. https://perma.cc/TJK9-8XM7

Exhibit 3: excerpt from Bluebell's letter to BP

On 4 October 2023, shortly after the resignation of Bernard Looney as CEO of BP, Bluebell Capital sent a letter to the company's management. The letter outlined Bluebell's criticism of the BP strategy and how it would 'destroy' shareholder value. Bluebell asked BP to implement the following six corrective actions:

1. remove its medium-term Scope 3 targets and qualify its 2050 target (Net-Zero) as a target to be reached 'in line with Society'
2. realign supply to demand revising upward BP's oil and gas production target, to ~2.5 mmboed by 2030 (versus current target of 2.0 mmboed)
3. increase investment in oil and gas by ~$1.5bn p.a. (2023–2030) and reduce cumulative investment in Bioenergy, Hydrogen and Renewables & Power by ~60% (2023–2030), the majority of which will be financed by halting investment in Renewables & Power
4. increase cash to be returned to shareholders by a cumulative ~$16bn (~$2.0bn p.a., 2023–2030) to be sure it is better deployed also in support of the energy transition

5. enhance disclosure on businesses outside core oil and gas (Convenience and EV Charging, Hydrogen) and more broadly on investment hurdles
6. strengthen the Board of Directors, adding the necessary capabilities to oversee large capital deployment in areas which are not BP's core business and have BlackRock's non independent director Pamela Daley removed from BP's Board.

Source: Bluebell Capital (2023). Letter to BP. Retrieved from: https://perma.cc/YST9-F6FJ

Further reading

Freeman, R. E. (1984) *Strategic Management: A Stakeholder Approach,* Cambridge: Cambridge University Press.

Friedman, M. (1970) 'The Social Responsibility of Business Is to Increase Its Profits', *New York Times Magazine*, 13 September, pp.122–126.

Gramm, J. (2016) *Dear Chairman: Boardroom Battles and the Rise of Shareholder Activism*. New York, NY: HarperCollins.

References

[1] Ritchie, H. (2020) 'Sector by sector: where do global greenhouse gas emissions come from?', Our World in Data. https://ourworldindata.org/ghg-emissions-by-sector

[2] Eurostat (n.d.) 'Oil and petroleum products – a statistical overview'. https://perma.cc/8RFS-KQ29

[3] International Energy Agency (2023) 'Oil 2023'. https://perma.cc/B8N6-C5FN

[4] Engine No. 1 (2021) 'The Case for Change', Reenergize Exxon. https://perma.cc/7YL6-CXBS

[5] Arjuna Capital (n. d.) https://perma.cc/4FGP-5KNA

[6] Lamb, Natasha (2014) 'Letter to shareholders from Arjuna Capital/Baldwin Brothers Inc.', Arjuna Capital. https://www.sec.gov/Archives/edgar/data/797468/000121465914002975/s417140px14a6g.htm

[7] Arjuna Capital (n. d.)

[8] Comcast (2022) 'Notice of 2022 Annual Meeting of Shareholders and Proxy Statement'. https://www.sec.gov/Archives/edgar/data/1166691/000120677422001186/cmcsa4011221-def14a.htm

9   ExxonMobil (2022) 'Notice of 2022 Annual Meeting and Proxy Statement', 7 April. https://www.sec.gov/Archives/edgar/data/34088 /000119312522098314/d280259ddef14a.htm

10 ExxonMobil (2024) '2024 Shareholder proposal lawsuit – Our responsibility to fight back', 29 February. https://perma.cc/AQ5Y-77M5

11 Reuters (2024) 'US judge dismisses Exxon case against activist investor over proxy filing', 18 June. https://www.reuters.com/legal/us-judge -dismisses-exxon-case-against-activist-investor-over-proxy-filing-2024 -06-17/

12 ExxonMobil (2024)

13 Milne, Richard and McCormick, Myles (2024) 'Norway oil fund boss criticises ExxonMobil's "aggressive" climate lawsuit', *Financial Times*, 8 February. https://www.ft.com/content/58952fc6-9b52-4e22-8fd5 -8c24ddd9f7b2

14 CalPERS (2024) 'Why CalPERS Is Voting Against ExxonMobil's Board of Directors'. https://perma.cc/FY8H-VTNN

15 Moore, Malcom (2024) 'BP promises to cut costs as profit misses forecast', *Financial Times*, 7 May. https://www.ft.com/content/57e97c15-00d8 -4f7e-9f4c-7e4b06527b72

16 Browne, John (1997) 'Climate Change Speech', Stanford University, 19 May. https://perma.cc/6JR5-66GQ

17 BP (2020) 'BP sets ambition for net zero by 2050, fundamentally changing organisation to deliver', 12 February. https://perma.cc/JGC8-6BVX

18 Fletcher, Laurence. and Abboud, Leila (2021) 'The little-known activist fund that helped topple Danone's CEO', 24 March, *Financial Times*. https://www.ft.com/content/dd369552-8491-40a2-b83b-9a1b2e32407a

19 Bluebell Capital (2023) Letter to BP, 4 October. https://perma.cc/W534 -BJAB

12. Environmental impact: why fast fashion is bad for the environment

Dorottya Sallai

This case examines the environmental impact of fast fashion from the perspective of a consulting assignment, namely, a UK-based environmental charity's efforts to reduce fast fashion consumption among three key target demographics.[1] The charity plans to conduct a targeted research study and launch a behaviour change campaign to discourage people from buying fast fashion items as Christmas presents or for holiday parties. To promote cultural change, students must develop a campaign to educate various audiences about the impact of fast fashion. Students, acting like consultants, must conduct independent research and prepare a presentation or a report about their approach for a client, a well-known environmental charity.

This was created as a 'raw case'. Raw cases are open-ended, multi-perspective studies that can include a wide range of relevant materials for students to investigate and evaluate, such as environmental reports, regulatory documents, news articles, company reports and interviews with key commercial, government and NGO representatives. This style illustrates how managers must assess and analyse data to make informed business decisions. The raw case is complex, allowing students to focus on management, organisational behaviour, change management, ethics, CSR and environmental issues. The case also lets students practise presenting consultancy briefs, pitches, presentations and reports on a complex issue. The case could be used in a wide range of consulting and management courses. The issues explored in the case include:

- the impact of fast fashion on the environment
- corporate social responsibility
- cultural and behavioural change.

How to cite this book chapter:

Sallai, Dorottya (2025) 'Environmental impact: why fast fashion is bad for the environment', in: Sallai, Dorottya and Pepper, Alexander (ed) *Navigating the 21st Century Business World: Case Studies in Management*, London: LSE Press, pp. 177–184. https://doi.org/10.31389/lsepress.nbw.l

Guidance on how to write a case analysis can be found in Chapter 1, 'Business cases: what are they, why do we use them and how should you go about doing a case analysis?'.

Introduction

When people update their wardrobes at the beginning of a new season, they may not realise that the manufacturing of only one simple cotton T-shirt requires approximately 2700 litres of water.[2] Although adhering to the latest fashion trends appears to be an unwritten societal expectation in many educational and business contexts, the detrimental impact it causes to the environment goes far beyond the benefits it offers. Would social rules change if people were aware that thrown-away clothing results in the discharge of half a million tonnes of microfibres into the ocean every year – the equivalent of more than 50 billion plastic bottles?[3]

Fast fashion – which has made trends more accessible to consumers globally through high-volume business strategies – is considered the primary cause of the rise of mass consumption and environmental pollution. According to studies, by 2030, 69 per cent of global textile production will be based on polyester, nylon and other synthetic fibres, and only 25 per cent will have a natural origin.[4] While the industry is increasingly bringing sustainability into focus, as long as consumers buy cheap clothes, balancing ESG initiatives with commercial objectives will be challenging. This case study explores this complex topic from the perspective of a consultancy assignment, focusing on a UK-based environmental charity's efforts to reduce fast-fashion consumption in the general population.

What is fast fashion?

Fast fashion refers to cheap clothes that are produced en masse and distributed quickly to consumers for the purpose of maximising recent fashion trends.[5] The fast-fashion industry has changed the way people buy clothing. Fast fashion's affordability, convenience, and trend-based nature make it a fast-growing industry despite its negative impacts on the environment and garment workers. This is not a surprise since fashion is also a highly profitable business. The fast-fashion industry has increased significantly in the past decades, with the global fashion market valued at $1.7 trillion in 2023,[6] employing more than 300 million people across the different global value chains. As a result of this drastic rise of fast fashion, clothing production doubled between 2000 and 2014, while the number of items of clothing people buy per capita increased by about 60 per cent.[7]

Although in the 1990s fast fashion was only a growing trend, it has evolved into a norm in the global fashion market. In 2024, fast fashion was outpaced by the phenomenon of 'ultrafast fashion', which allows consumers to update their wardrobes at an unprecedented pace. The rise of social media and extremely low prices led to a culture of over-consumption and an even more accelerated disposal of fashion items that are often 'barely worn before being dumped'.[8] For example, in 2023, Shein, a Chinese fashion brand, produced around 7200 new product models every day,[9] pricing them significantly cheaper than established fast-fashion retailers. Shein's average unit price is $14, compared to H&M's $26 and Zara's $34.[10] Fast-fashion retailers like Shein and Temu have enjoyed staggering sales as they become popular due to their ability to quickly produce and sell trendy, affordable clothing. In 2024, 40 per cent of US and 26 per cent per cent of UK consumers shopped at these retailers.[11] Zara, the Spanish multinational fashion designer, updates its range twice a month, while its parent company, Inditex, has doubled its share price just within the last two years.[12] Fast fashion is a controversial topic, evoking strong emotions, not only because of its impact on the environment but also because of its impact on self-identity and values.[13] Some argue that consumers should be responsible in their consumption and make ethical decisions on which fashion labels they support with their purchases. On the other hand, others see fast fashion as a symptom of globalisation, capitalism and consumerism, and call for more systemic change, including government regulations and the introduction of sectoral interventions as a more effective way of tackling the issue. Ultimately, fostering inclusive and empathetic conversations is crucial for promoting sustainable fashion practices.

The impact of fast fashion on the environment

Fast fashion contributes to substantial waste and environmental damage. The fashion industry has contributed more to climate change than international flights and maritime shipping combined.[14] This is not surprising, given that the textile industry accounts for 20 per cent of all industrial water pollution,[15] and fast fashion is responsible for 10 per cent of global carbon emissions due to energy consumption in production and distribution. To put this into context, the process of manufacturing and washing a single pair of jeans releases an equivalent amount of carbon dioxide as driving 69 miles.[16] According to the European Environment Agency, clothing purchases in the EU generated around 270kg of carbon dioxide emissions per individual in the year 2020 alone.[17]

Out of the total annual production of 100 billion garments, around 92 million tonnes are disposed of in landfills. This indicates that clothes equivalent to the capacity of a bin lorry are disposed of in landfills every second.[18] In the United States alone, an estimated 11.3 million tonnes of textile waste, or 85 per cent of all textiles, end up in landfills each year. That equates to around 37kg per person each year, just in the US.[19]

There has also been a shift in the way people dispose of old clothing, with more people choosing to throw it away rather than donate it. Less than 50 per cent of second-hand clothing is collected for reusing or recycling, and only one per cent of used clothing is recycled.[20]

Clothing sales have increased substantially worldwide. For example, in France fashion sales have risen by nearly 50 per cent in a decade.[21] North Americans are the world's largest textile users, consuming an average of 37kg per user per year, followed by Australia (27kg), western Europe (22kg), and developing countries such as Africa, India, and southern Asia (with just 5kg each).[22] The average European consumer uses approximately 26kg of clothes a year and disposes of approximately 11kg of them.[23] In Europe, British shoppers buy more clothes than any other nation.[24]

Sustainability versus profit

To address climate pressures and regulatory changes, many fashion companies are integrating sustainability into their business models. This includes appointing executives with ESG experience to oversee sustainability strategies. Fashion companies like Shein call for the fashion industry's 'urgent transformation' on sustainability, while others such as H&M offer customers discounts on purchases in exchange for used clothes for safe disposal or recycling.[25] Fashion companies are moving away from the old linear model of extraction and disposal and towards circular business models that emphasise recycling.

Regulators around the world are evaluating possible interventions in industry to protect the environment. EU member states, for instance, have considered introducing restrictions on textile waste exports as much of the disposed fashion-related waste is transported to countries such as Ghana and Kenya, causing environmental damage locally. The French parliament is debating a bill that would impose serious new restrictions on fast-fashion brands. Under the legislation, firms would face fines of up to €10 per item sold if they fail to address environmental damage from discarded products.[26]

Nevertheless, companies have little reason to change, and despite all the environmental concerns and regulatory efforts, investment in fast fashion is growing, and people are spending their money on low-quality clothing that goes out of fashion in weeks. The question that the industry should be really worried about is when fast fashion will go out of fashion.

Preparing the case

In preparing the case analysis, imagine that you are the consultant at a UK-based consultancy company. Your first client is a well-known charity that specialises in environmental protection. You have been asked to research current trends in the fast-fashion industry and develop a strategy for a change project. Based on your research, design a behavioural change campaign strategy aimed at reducing fast-fashion consumption among three key target groups. The campaign should focus on individuals who may be inclined to purchase fast fashion as Christmas presents or for Christmas parties. Outline your research and the recommended approach by writing a report or preparing a presentation[27] for reducing fast fashion, taking into account the perspectives of the three key target audiences below:

1. **A grandparent buying Christmas presents for their grandchildren**
Sarah is a 68-year-old who would like to buy her 18-year-old granddaughter some new clothes for Christmas. Sarah has heard her granddaughter talking about ISAWITFIRST and has been looking online for some trousers and a jumper.

2. **A gap year student who needs a variety of outfits for a Christmas party**
Helen is a 23-year-old who is travelling around the world after deferring her gap year because of the pandemic. She is due home for Christmas and wants to buy a few new cheap dresses to wear for the different reunions she is having with friends.

3. **Someone requesting gym clothes from their partner's present list**
Albert is a 35-year-old who is looking for some new sportswear for Christmas. As it is just for the gym he uses at home, he does not want his partner to spend too much money.

Some links to start off your research:

- ABC News (Australia) (2018) 'The wastefulness of "fast fashion" and how some in the industry are fighting back', YouTube. https://www .youtube.com/watch?v=eGPMJyuh3eA
- Abelvik-Lawson, Helle (2023), 'How fast fashion fuels climate change, plastic pollution and violence', Greenpeace, 3 April. https://perma.cc /K7GJ-ME5M
- Adeogun, Joy (n. d.) 'Fashion forward: How to combat climate change through clothing', Imperial College London. https://perma.cc/U7X3 -54KS
- Fenech, Céline; Walton, Dr. Bryn and Majury, Alan (2023) 'The Sustainable Consumer, Understanding consumer attitudes to sustainability and sustainable behaviours', Deloitte. https://perma.cc/P7G3 -HWGY
- Green Transition Support (n.d.) Good practice database: Measures, technologies and good practices'. https://www.clustercollaboration.eu /green/database
- McDaniel, Amber (2023) '11 Slow Fashion Brands Fighting Back Against Fast Fashion', Sustainable Jungle, 27 September. https://perma .cc/3GPQ-VE4X
- Murphy, Liam (n. d.) 'The Fightback against Fast Fashion', Aim2Flourish. https://perma.cc/JWF8-D3DF

In preparing your report or presentation, you should reflect on the following questions:

1. The excessive use of water, chemical pollution and waste produced by the fast-fashion industry has a devastating impact on the environment. What can or should fast fashion companies do to make the fashion industry more sustainable? How can fashion companies reduce the negative impact on the environment? Which organisations have campaigned recently against fast fashion?

2. The fast-fashion industry's reliance on low-wage labour raises ethical concerns. What are the social implications of fast fashion on workers in the supply chain? What ethical obligations do you think fast fashion companies have?

3. Even though consciousness of sustainable fashion is increasing, consumer behaviour is still driven largely by trends and costs. Can consumer behaviour shift towards more sustainable fashion choices in the short term, and what would it take to achieve this?

4. Some social media influencers either advocate for sustainability or support fast fashion by promoting the latest trends online. What is the role of influencers and social media in promoting or discouraging fast fashion?

5. The efficiency of sustainability initiatives in the fast-fashion industry has been mixed. Explore some of the current campaigns and policies in reducing fast-fashion consumption in your own country or globally and evaluate their effectiveness.

References

[1] The author would like to thank Alirity Consulting for their support in preparing this case.

[2] The Conscious Club (2019) 'Water & Clothing', 15 May. https://perma.cc /Q7J4-7AMJ

[3] Crumbie, Alex (2024) 'What is fast fashion and why is it a problem?', 9 April. *The Ethical Consumer* https://perma.cc/CE3E-3MEL

[4] Sciorilli Borrelli, S. (2024). 'Fast fashion: "We aren't doing enough to fix the problem". *Financial Times*, July 13. https://www.ft.com/content /f0be47ca-dd6f-44d5-8be8-80012ed4b725

5 Maiti, Rashmila (2024) 'The Environmental Impact of Fast Fashion, explained', earth.org, 20 January. https://perma.cc/FJJ5-MPQ7

6 McKinsey & Company (2023) 'The State of Fashion 2024: Finding pockets of growth as uncertainty reigns', 29 November. https://perma.cc/W5KX-EEWJ

7 McKinsey & Company (2025) 'What is fast fashion?', 23 January. https://perma.cc/VCK2-PYYY

8 Mundy, Simon (2024) 'Is time running out for fast fashion?', *Financial Times*. https://www.ft.com/content/d07d6818-060a-4afe-903a-3afb110b0dd9

9 Sciorilli Borrelli, S. (2024)

10 McKinsey & Company (2025)

11 McKinsey & Company (2023)

12 Mundy, Simon (2024)

13 Sierra, Brittany (2024) 'The Psychology of Fast Fashion: Why Conversation About Fast Fashion Evokes Such Strong Emotions In Us', the sustainable fashion forum, 2 February. https://perma.cc/FJL6-3CMZ

14 Shirvanimoghaddam, Kamyar; Motamed, Bahareh, Ramakrishna; Seeram and Naebe, Minoo (2020) 'Death by waste: Fashion and textile circular economy case', *Science of The Total Environment*, vol. 718, 20 May. https://doi.org/10.1016/j.scitotenv.2020.137317

15 The Conscious Club (2019)

16 Shirvanimoghaddam, Kamyar; Motamed, Bahareh; Ramakrishna, Seeram and Naebe, Minoo (2020)

17 European Parliament (2020) 'The impact of textile production and waste on the environment (infographics)', 29 December. https://perma.cc/2WXT-2YQU

18 Igini, Martina (2023) '10 Concerning Fast Fashion Waste Statistics', earth.org., 21 August. https://perma.cc/RMH4-BWM8

19 Igini, Martina (2023)

20 European Parliament (2020)

21 Mundy, Simon (2024)

22 Shirvanimoghaddam, Kamyar, Motamed, Bahareh, Ramakrishna, Seeram and Naebe, Minoo (2020)

[23] European Parliament (2020)

[24] Stallard, Esme (2022) 'Fast fashion: How clothes are linked to climate change', *BBC News*, 29 July. https://perma.cc/54LW-5C85

[25] Sciorilli Borrelli, S. (2024)

[26] Simons, Angela (2024) '"Major breakthrough": French parliament votes in favour of crackdown on ultra fast fashion, *Euronews*, 15 March. https://perma.cc/8JPP-FKRP

[27] Note for instructors: Please give students more specific instructions on the requirements of their report or presentation, i.e. length, word-count, etc.

Part 5

Human resource management and organisational behaviour

13. The UK's National Health Service: teams, conflict and performance

Emma Soane

This case explores interactions between members of a multidisciplinary hospital team. The team is tasked with discussing ideas about how to improve patient safety, a critical area for improvement in the UK National Health Service (NHS). Patient safety is the avoidance, prevention and amelioration of adverse outcomes or injuries stemming from the process of healthcare.[1] Many of the quotations are drawn from interviews with health service workers, although the meeting is a fictional representation.[2] The issues illustrated by this case include:

- conflict
- diversity
- leadership
- team processes
- team outcomes.

Guidance on how to write a case analysis can be found in Chapter 1, 'Business cases: what are they, why do we use them and how should you go about doing a case analysis?'.

A teaching note for this case is available to bona fide educators. To request a copy please email e.c.soane@lse.ac.uk.

How to cite this book chapter:

Soane, Emma (2025) 'The UK's National Health Service: teams, conflict and performance', in: Sallai, Dorottya and Pepper, Alexander (ed) *Navigating the 21st Century Business World: Case Studies in Management*, London: LSE Press, pp. 187–191. https://doi.org/10.31389/lsepress.nbw.m

Introduction

The scene is a meeting room in a large public hospital in the United Kingdom. The people who attend this meeting are:

- Amara Umana, clinical services manager
- Min Chen, consultant (senior doctor)
- Jenny Davies, matron (ward manager)
- Francesco De Luca, junior doctor
- Paolo Rizzo and Fraser McDonald, nurses
- Eduardo Sanchez and Alys Williams, physiotherapists.

You can read more about the NHS here: https://www.england.nhs.uk/about/

The meeting

Jenny, Paolo and Fraser arrived early at the meeting room. Jenny wanted to make sure that they had some time to talk about their work on Sunshine Ward before anyone else joined them. All three believed that patient safety was one of their main priorities, but recently they had all felt under a lot of pressure from senior managers and patients. Jenny began by telling Paolo and Fraser about a conversation she had earlier that day.

'I was talking to a patient this morning, and we were discussing his care plan. He was full of ideas. You know how it is, once they're diagnosed, they're on the internet and they're downloading everything. They've got the latest information from Joe Bloggs in Colorado and what he's trying, and they want to know why aren't we trying it? Anyway, we got there in the end, and he seems reasonably happy.'

'I know what you mean' said Fraser, 'I had a similar debate yesterday. But it can be positive if patients want to talk about their care, it's important to them, and these conversations are easy compared with the meeting that we're just about to have. I know that patient safety is essential, but I don't like the way managers do things around here.'

'Exactly' sighed Jenny. 'I said to one of my senior managers "Well, we can't do that because of this, this and this" and they turned around and said, "well I'm not going to take your word for it." I said, "please don't, I've only got 27 years' experience, don't ask me at all." What's the point of me being here if that happens?'

Jenny could easily have carried on talking, but she heard footsteps approaching the meeting room and fell silent. The rest of the team entered the room and took their seats without speaking. Amara, the clinical services manager, sat at the head of the table.

'Good morning everyone, and thank you for joining this meeting. As you all know, I will attend the senior management team awayday next week and I have to present our top three recommendations for how to improve patient safety on Sunshine Ward. If we do not come up with good ideas, then the senior team will be less likely to invite our contributions in the future. In this meeting, we have 30 minutes to talk through our ideas and agree on the three suggestions that I will take to the awayday. You've had some time to prepare for this discussion, so I'd like to start by hearing from each of you. Min, please could you begin?'

Min brought out her notes and presented a series of ideas. Top of her list was a new idea about how to manage the consultant workload.

'I think that we should have a consultant of the week. Most people on Sunshine Ward stay for 3–5 days. So, instead of every consultant attending ward meetings depending on their shift, I think that we should assign one consultant to one ward each week. That way every consultant can really understand the patients' needs, so there will be fewer patient safety incidents, and many patients will only have to deal with one consultant so their care is more personalised.'

Amara was pleased. She knew that she could rely on Min to set a positive tone for the meeting, and her idea had potential. However, she was still concerned about what the rest of the team would say. Amara was right to be worried.

Paolo and Eduardo both started to speak at the same time. Amara indicated that Paolo should proceed.

'We have had massive change recently, massive change. The only thing that's stable about working in the NHS at the minute is the fact that change is certain. I came here because I wanted to make a difference, but I don't feel I can do my job.'

'I agree' said Eduardo. 'There is always so much to do and that is one of the frustrations. It feels like you can never do a really good job because you are always rushing on to the next thing.'

Alys joined the conversation with her ongoing complaint about targets.

'We are being taken over by a blame culture. I know that we have to focus on targets, I understand that infection control and other patient safety issues are essential, of course we want the best for our patients. But did you see that email that went round the other day? It was an outrage.'

'Which email was that?' asked Jenny. 'There are so many of them these days. I might go out for a meeting for an hour and a half, I come back and there's some 50 emails waiting for me. Even if a lot of them are rubbish I've still got to look at them haven't I?'

'I agree' said Fraser, nodding. 'We do need to do something about emails because they're taking over the world and you can't get anything done.'

'Anyway' Alys continued, 'it was that email from the chief executive which had a few sentences congratulating us all followed by a "BUT" and a much longer section highlighting remaining problems and further challenges. Can you believe it?'

Amara thought it was time that she re-joined the conversation. 'I know what you mean' Amara added. 'I will come in at 8am and there's an expectation that

I will still be there at 6pm in the evening and then I'll be getting emails on my phone during the evening. However, we are getting away from the purpose of this meeting. Let's get back to the subject of patient safety.'

While this discussion had been going on, Francesco had been staring at his notebook, his face growing redder. He had not spoken yet, so Amara invited him to make a comment.

'What can I say?' he almost shouted, avoiding eye contact with Amara and the rest of the team. 'I work long shifts, I do night shifts, I do my best with each and every one of my patients. But working here is impossible. All these new initiatives are very frustrating, and sometimes confusing too because things can change from week to week.' His voice rose as he continued. 'One week it's a good idea, then the next week someone will come up to the ward and tell us they have a new great idea, so we do our best to implement it. There's no time to test out initiatives properly and it's hard to tell what is really working and what we should scrap. The new patient safety process is sure to be the same. This meeting is pointless.' He banged the table with his fist.

Min looked at Francesco. She recalled her own days as a junior doctor and sympathised with his point of view. However, his anger was not helping the team. She knew that she could keep calm, and she liked to contribute her ideas to team meetings.

'I see what you mean, and I can also see that morale goes up and down. Change and uncertainty sometimes do affect how we feel but I think generally people are quite positive. We just need to keep our focus on the patients, and work together.'

'Together!' exclaimed Paolo. 'That is a joke. Call ourselves a team? We don't even help each other. Last time I was on a night shift I needed some advice from Eduardo but he just said he was busy. He didn't even...'

Amara stepped in. 'OK Paolo, enough. Yes, there are cliques in this department. Sometimes we cannot do much about that, although we do have to make sure that people don't feel left out. As a team, we do fantastic work. Our ward does meet many of our patient safety targets, and our patients tend to be satisfied with their care too. Let's go round the table again and present our ideas.'

Fifteen minutes later the mood had not improved. Paolo and Alys had argued, Eduardo had made more negative comments about his team colleagues, and Jenny responded defensively to any indications that might indicate her ward was not as good as it might be. Francesco had contributed very little. Fraser had tried to make some suggestions, but he was talked over. Amara paused, reflecting on what she had heard during the meeting. Time was up and she needed to close the meeting, even though there had been little progress.

'I think you all do a great job, and you've raised some important points today. However, we need to get these three priority areas decided, so let's catch up again on Friday and get everything straight.'

Amara returned to her office feeling frustrated and upset that the team had not pulled together. She resolved to take a different approach to leading this situation, but what could she do?

Preparing the case

In groups, address the challenges facing Amara and the team by answering the following questions with reference to relevant research.

1. What types of conflict are present during this meeting?
2. What is the main source of conflict?
3. How could Amara predict team processes?
4. How could Amara diagnose team processes?
5. What leadership behaviours fit this situation?

Further reading

Jehn, K. A. (1995) 'A multimethod examination of the benefits and detriments of intragroup conflict', *Administrative Science Quarterly*, vol. 40, pp. 256–282. https://doi.org/10.2307/2393638

Jehn, K. A., and Bendersky, C. (2003) 'Intragroup conflict in organisations: A contingency perspective on the conflict-outcome relationship', *Research in Organizational Behavior*, vol. 25, pp. 187–242. https://doi.org/10.1016/S0191-3085(03)25005-X

Homan, A. C., Gündemir, S., Buengeler, C., and van Kleef, G. A. (2020) 'Leading diversity: Towards a theory of functional leadership in diverse teams', *Journal of Applied Psychology*, vol. 105, no. 10, pp. 1101–1128. https://doi.org/10.1037/apl0000482

References

[1] Vincent, C.A., Pincus, T., & Scurr, J. H. (1993). 'Patients' experience of surgical accidents', *BMJ Quality & Safety*, vol. 2, no. 2, pp. 77–82. https://doi.org/10.1136/qshc.2.2.77

[2] For more on the research underpinning this case, see: Alfes, Kerstin, Truss, Catherine, Soane, Emma, Rees, Chris, and Gatenby, Mark (2010) Creating an engaged workforce. Findings from the Kingston Employee Engagement Consortium Project. London: CIPD; and Gatenby, Mark, Rees, Chris, Truss, Catherine, Alfes, Kerstin, and Soane, Emma (2014) 'Managing change, or changing managers? The role of middle managers in UK public service reform', *Public Management Review*, vol. 17, no. 8, pp. 1124–1145. https://doi.org/10.1080/14719037.2014.895028

14. Redesigning a performance management system

Rebecca Campbell and Vida Amani

This case study sets out the redesign of the performance management system of a fictionalised company, Global Media Organisation (GMO). The case events are real, although the characters and organisational details have been disguised. Case A sets out GMO's old system which used a forced distribution model to rank employees into five categories. The head of human resources (HR), Kate Jones, is concerned that this system is demoralising, takes up a huge amount of time, undermines cooperation and does little to develop employees. The aim is to come up with a less time-consuming system that still recognises the best (and worst) performers. It also needs to be budget neutral. Case B sets out the company's proposed solution.

The teaching objectives are:

- to give students an understanding of the purposes of a performance management system

- to give students an insight into the challenges associated with designing a performance management system

- to evaluate the advantages and disadvantages of forced distribution

- to evaluate the tension between evaluative ('judge') versus developmental ('coach') approaches to performance management

- team outcomes.

Guidance on how to write a case analysis can be found in Chapter 1, 'Business cases: what are they, why do we use them and how should you go about doing a case analysis?'.

How to cite this book chapter:

Campbell, Rebecca and Amani, Vida (2025) 'Redesigning a performance management system', in: Sallai, Dorottya and Pepper, Alexander (ed) *Navigating the 21st Century Business World: Case Studies in Management*, London: LSE Press, pp. 193–201. https://doi.org/10.31389/lsepress.nbw.n

Introduction

GMO was a FTSE250 Media company with 6000 employees in the UK. Founded in 2001, in their last annual report they had reported revenue growth of over £900m, achieved between 2010 and 2023, mainly through acquiring smaller independent production companies.[1]

It was Spring 2023. Kate Jones, GMO head of HR, was reviewing their current performance management system. It should be so simple. Set performance targets, monitor their achievement and then communicate ratings and pay outcomes to employees. However, GMO's current system (Case A) took up huge amounts of time and seemed to leave everyone unhappy. Jones had been brought in to shake things up. She knew the current system was not working, the challenge was to come up with something better (Case B).

Case A: The old system

While business was going well, Jones was concerned that they had been losing key staff to similar sized local competitors and had recently had some difficulty attracting the right calibre of new employees. Jones was concerned that their current performance management system was too focused on judging past behaviour and was not doing enough to develop and coach employees going forward. She was also concerned about GMO's use of forced distribution and its effect on both employee and line manager morale. Forced distribution, famously championed by Jack Welch at General Electric, is where employees are ranked against their co-workers and put into fixed categories. For example, the UK Civil Service used to rank senior staff according to whether they were top performers (25 per cent) average performers (65 per cent) or underperformers (10 per cent).[2] This practice was designed to address the problem of lenient managers who prefer to avoid difficult conversations about poor performance. It is also a way to control costs. If you are going to link performance ratings to pay, then you have to have some way to ration out bonuses and pay rises. But forced distribution has many problems. It can be very rigid and often leads to gaming of the system. For example, managers can rotate the higher rankings between employees – so everyone gets a turn. Some employees may find themselves put into the bottom category, despite meeting objectives, just because someone has to be. Jones had heard some horror stories at her last job where some new joiners had automatically been put in the bottom classification as they were 'easier to sacrifice'. Forced distribution was also notoriously disruptive of teamwork if everyone was competing for the coveted top spots. In short, Jones was concerned that GMO's current performance management system was more about reviewing past performance than coaching for better future performance. She was also worried that the use of forced distribution was doing much to undermine the atmosphere of teamwork and collaboration that was central to GMO's success.

GMO's current performance management system

The ideal performance management system would encourage the types of behaviour required by management, provide an objective and accurate summary of employee achievements (which could be used to inform pay and bonus decisions), and be perceived as fair by employees. Put more formally, performance management is a 'continuous process of identifying, measuring, and developing the performance of individuals and teams and aligning performance with the strategic goals of the organisation'.[3] But what sounded easy on paper, was anything but.

Jones had done a back-of-the-envelope calculation and estimated that their current system was taking an average of 26 hours per employee over the course of the year. With 6000 employees this meant they were talking about a total of 156,000 hours. Many companies who had done similar calculations, were abandoning the annual appraisal entirely.

The process

In January, line managers met with employees to set objectives for the coming year. These were based on 'What and How'. The 'What' set out individual and team goals that were aligned with the organisation's strategic objectives, such as: project completion; meeting sales targets; audience targets or meeting sustainability goals. 'How' objectives were set around the organisation's values and behaviours, for example: working collaboratively with team members; positive 360 feedback results and taking on coaching and mentoring roles to develop the next generation. For a data and evidence-gathering exercise, this clearly would turn into a cumbersome part of a line manager's role.

In October, calibration meetings were held between HR and line managers to discuss how employees had performed during the year. All employees were ranked, according to forced distribution, on a scale of 1–5, illustrated by Figure 14.1. This was strictly enforced on a departmental level and line managers prepared heavily for these meetings to defend their rating decisions.

- 1 = exceptional (exceeded all set objectives, went above and beyond what is expected and worked collaboratively in line with organisation's values and behaviours; only 10 per cent could get this rating)
- 2 = excellent (met all set objectives to a high standard, role-modelling organisation's values and behaviours; only 15 per cent could get this rating)

- 3 = met all objectives (met most set objectives, displayed organisation's values and behaviours; 50 per cent could get this rating)
- 4 = met partial objectives (missed set objectives and/or needs to work on 'ways of working'; 15 per cent got this rating)
- 5 = missed objectives (missed objectives and does not work in line with organisation's expected values and behaviours; 10 per cent got this rating).

Before the calibration meetings, managers prepared by identifying their top performers, at-target performers and bottom performers. At this stage, managers were not generally attempting to differentiate precisely. In the calibration meeting, a more fine-grained ranking took place. They would start by identifying the strongest performers by department, comparing peers in terms of impact and performance. The bottom performers were similarly identified and compared against peers. The remaining population in the middle were ranked accordingly. Comparing employees across the entire department meant a larger pool for comparison, which addressed the issue of managers with small teams where it could be very hard to fit employees into a forced distribution. Once all employees were rated, they were entered into a spreadsheet that ensured there was a smooth bell curve. Line managers and HR had to strictly adhere to the forced distribution. This process was both arduous and time consuming. Overall, the meetings were dreaded by everyone. The final part of the process happened in December. When ratings had been agreed between the line managers and HR, an end-of-year performance discussion was held between the individual employees and their line managers about their rating. These could potentially be very distressing conversa-

Figure 14.1: Forced distribution curve applied to GMO's performance ratings

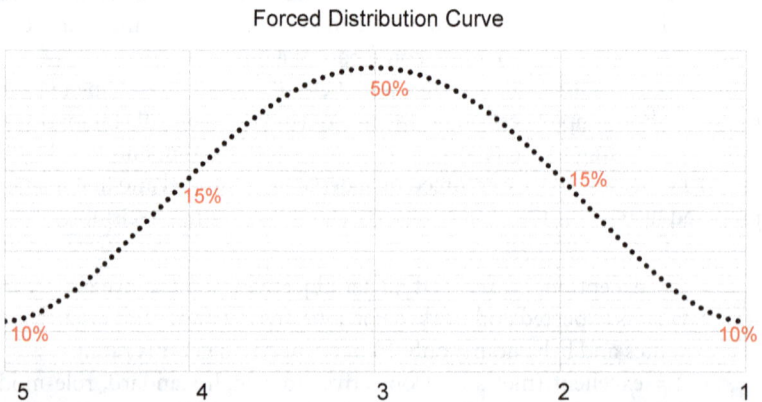

Forced Distribution Curve

Source: prepared by author. Note, this indicates how, a maximum of 10 per cent of employees could be awarded a rating of 1.

tions, particularly if a manager was delivering the news of a '4' or '5' rating. And the timing – just before Christmas – did not help. Those who received a '3' were often left feeling uninspired as nobody really likes to see themselves as 'average'. Even employees who received a '2' were often left disappointed. Despite it celebrating 'excellent' performance, getting a '2' for these employees felt like getting a 'B' grade instead of an 'A'.

The link between ratings and pay

These ratings were used to determine the employee's annual bonus and their annual pay increase.

Bonus

To give an example, suppose an employee had a salary of £50,000, and had a target bonus opportunity of 15 per cent of their salary, their target bonus would be £7500. This target bonus opportunity would then be adjusted by a multiplier depending on the employee's performance rating. If they had a rating of 1 (exceptional), a multiplier of 2 would be applied and they would get a bonus of £15,000. However, if they had a rating of 4 (met partial objectives), a multiplier of 0.5 would be applied and they would only get a bonus of £3750 (see Table 14.1).

The example shown in Table 14.1 is based on a target bonus opportunity of 15 per cent of a £50,000 salary.

Table 14.1: Bonus multiplier

Rating	Multiplier	Bonus Outcome
1 (exceptional)	× 2.0	£15,000
2 (excellent)	× 1.5	£11,250
3 (met all objectives)	× 1.0	£7500
4 (met partial objectives)	× 0.5	£3750
5 (missed objectives)	× 0.0	Nothing

Source: prepared by author

Annual salary increase

GMO also linked the annual salary increase in line with the rating, so the top performers would see their salary increase faster. The organisation would start by setting an overall salary increase budget. This was informed by factors such as cost of living, inflation and external market data. For example, the organisation might budget for a general salary increase of 2.5 per cent. However, managers would have some flexibility within their budget to award higher or lower increases. For example, if the overall budget was set to allow a

Table 14.2: Salary increase

Rating	Salary Multiplier
1 (exceptional)	5% increase
2 (excellent)	3.5% increase
3 (met all objectives)	2.5% increase
4 (met partial objectives)	1.0% increase
5 (missed objectives)	No increase

Source: prepared by author

2.5 per cent salary increase, then those who got a higher performance rating would get a higher increase, and those who got a lower rating would get a lower (or no) salary increase (see Table 14.2).

The result in terms of morale?

What typically happened was that unless employees were in the top 10 per cent, getting a rating of 1, the end-of-year conversation between the line manager and employee was not going to be a good one.

- Those who got a '2 – excellent' felt like they got a 'B' grade, so this led to lower engagement.
- Those who got a '3 – met objectives' felt like they got a 'C', typically 'coasted along' and were not in a mindset to exert discretionary effort.
- The '4' and '5' rating employees usually felt anxious and fearful.
- The managers were exhausted!
- HR knew that the performance dialogues were mainly focused on reward consequences, less on development.

What to do?

Jones sighed. As far as she could see GMO was spending a huge amount of time and money on this process, and the end result was that no one was happy. It was very time consuming (and so expensive) for line managers and HR to administer. Managers hated the forced distribution model as it meant that most employees (even those who were doing really well) were unhappy at the end of the cycle. Employees hated it because it felt subjective and secretive. Business leaders were questioning what was the return on investment of the process if performance and engagement did not increase with higher ratings?

It was easy to see that the current system was not working, what was harder was to come up with a better solution.

Preparing the case (A)

In preparing the case analysis, and before reading Case B, you might like to consider the following questions:

1. What are the advantages and disadvantages of GMO's old performance management system?
2. Why do you think GMO used forced distribution in the first place?
3. What do you think of the tension between the 'coach' and 'judge' aspects of performance management. Why might it be hard to do both well?
4. Should GMO get rid of performance management entirely?
5. Come up with an alternative performance management system for GMO.

Case B: the proposed new system

On Jones' advice, GMO got rid of the five-level rating system altogether. It was expensive, time consuming and was failing in its primary objective – to increase motivation and engagement.

The proposed new system

Bonus

Everyone was granted their target bonus opportunity based on business (not individual) performance. The rationale behind this was to encourage a 'one team collective culture of winning and losing together'. For example, an employee on £50,000 would still have a target bonus of 15 per cent – i.e. £7500. But this target bonus would be pegged to the business hitting its targets (for example annual revenue targets, product launch targets, environmental and sustainability targets). If the business exceeded its targets, then the 15 per cent bonus would be adjusted up. But if the business missed its targets, then the bonus opportunity would be adjusted down.

And what about the outliers? Jones wanted GMO to get rid of the exhausting and demoralising forced ranking system, but she still felt that the organisation needed to distinguish the very highest (and lowest) performers. Her solution was to create a CEO 'Impact Award' for the star performers. As she said to her assistant, 'let's face it, we all know who they are'. This award included both cash and share elements. So, on top of the bonus based on business performance, they would also get a cash award plus shares. Shares were introduced to incentivise long-term retention for key talent in the business.

For example, if you were on £50,000, and got the 'Impact Award', then your total bonus would be:

- £50K × 15% = £7500 (bonus based on business performance)
- plus, the CEO Impact Award cash top up of £5500 and £2500 in shares (notice broadly the same spend).

Although Jones was uncomfortable with using forced distribution, for budgetary reasons she still felt they needed a cap on the number of employees who could receive this award. She knew that if they did not have some constraint too many managers would say that they had employees who should receive the CEO Impact Award.

The underperformers (and again typically it was clear who they were) received no bonus and were put on performance improvement plans. After some discussion they again decided that there should be a (strict) target of 10 per cent that were expected to be in this category. They wanted a culture that was prepared to address underperformance directly and bravely and were concerned that without a firm target that managers would start slipping into bad habits.

Salary increases

Salary was increased using a similar method to the previous model. As before, the organisation set its salary increase budget and agreed a standard increase that was awarded to most employees. However, under the new system it was only the top performers (recipients of the CEO Impact Award) who would receive more and only the very bottom performers who received no increase.

From 'judge' to 'coach'

And what to do with all the time this freed up? Jones proposed that instead of dramatic end-of-year meetings, they introduce monthly high-quality employee/line manager 'dialogues' on development, areas of improvement and a celebration of achievements. The idea was to support the employee and give them a chance to 'course correct' as they go through the performance year.

The result?

Jones knew that what she proposed was not without flaws – no performance management system was ever going to be perfect. But she was happy that the proposed new system was a huge improvement on what had gone before.

Preparing the case (B)

After reading Case B you might like to consider the following question:

- What might be the potential problems with GMO's new system?

Further reading

Aguinis, H., (2009) 'An expanded view of performance management', in Smither, J. W. and London, M. (eds) *Performance Management: Putting Research Into Action*, Hoboken, NJ: Jossey-Bass/Wiley, pp.1–43.

Cappelli, P. and Tavis, A. (2016) 'The performance management revolution', *Harvard Business Review*, vol. 94, no. 10, pp.58–67. https://hbr.org/2016/10/the-performance-management-revolution

References

[1] GMO is a fictional company, described for the purposes of the case study. The case is based on the real-life experience of the writers.

[2] O'Connor, S. (2021) 'Why ranking employees by performance backfires', *Financial Times*, 6 April. https://www.ft.com/content/0691002c-2200-4583-88c9-9c942d534228

[3] Aguinis, H. (2009) 'An expanded view of performance management', in Smither, J. W. and London, M. (eds) *Performance Management: Putting Research Into Action*, Hoboken, NJ: Jossey-Bass/Wiley, pp.1–43.

15. Transformation in the automotive sector: the management challenges of AI and the digital revolution

Karin A. King and Aurelie Cnop

This case summarises the key drivers of change in work and job design caused by Industry 4.0, digitisation and the use of AI. It examines the complexities of designing jobs that motivate the workforce from both managerial and employee perspectives within the rapidly evolving digital landscape.

Describing a fictional organisation – a British luxury automobile manufacturer named Insignia – and its employees, this case provides a rich source of material for exploring a wide range of HR management, digital transformation, change management and job design questions. The issues explored in this case include:

- **Digital transformation, Industry 4.0 and the rise of AI**. The implementation of these technologies has led to significant improvements in productivity, agility and customisation. However, these advancements also present challenges, including the need for substantial investment, cybersecurity concerns and the necessity for workforce re-skilling to operate and collaborate with these advanced systems.

- **Impact on work and human-AI collaboration.** Integrating AI and automation tools into the workplace impacts workforce morale significantly.

- **Job design, talent management and retention.** As Insignia transitions into Industry 4.0, job roles need to be redefined to include digital competencies and the use of AI-based tools. The effective management of talent is a priority to ensure a workforce with the required mix of skills, experience, potential for development and advancement, and engagement.

How to cite this book chapter:

King, Karin A. and Cnop, Aurelie (2025) 'Transformation in the automotive sector: the management challenges of AI and the digital revolution', in: Sallai, Dorottya and Pepper, Alexander (ed) *Navigating the 21st Century Business World: Case Studies in Management*, London: LSE Press, pp. 203–217. https://doi.org/10.31389/lsepress.nbw.o

· **Change management.** Managing resistance to change is a significant challenge during digital transformation.

Guidance on how to write a case analysis can be found in Chapter 1, 'Business cases: what are they, why do we use them and how should you go about doing a case analysis?'.

A teaching note for this case is available to bona fide educators. To request a copy please email a.cnop@lse.ac.uk or k.a.king@lse.ac.uk.

Introduction

> Disruptive innovation generates growth. Sustaining innovation makes good products better – but then you don't buy the old product. They're replacements. They do not create growth. (Clayton Christensen 1997)[1]

Digital transformation in the automotive industry is driving significant change in business models, in customer expectations and in organisations and their workforces. As technology is rapidly progressing, present-day organisations are confronted with massive changes. These technological changes are particularly affecting the design of work in the way in which employees work in organisations as well as the conditions under which they do so.

This case considers the rapid digitisation of industry and its consequences for human resource management, specifically the design of work and jobs in light of the use of AI. As a management sciences topic, to consider the topic as it occurs in context, this case study directs the learner to the automotive sector specifically and the use of AI in the sector. Given the significant demands on industry to adopt emerging technologies to remain competitive in today's global economy, how should workplace and job design evolve in keeping with the new landscape in which digitisation and the use of AI are becoming ever more prominent?

The company: Insignia

In the sprawling industrial complex of Insignia, nestled in the heart of the UK's manufacturing belt, the hum of machinery harmonises with the digital symphony of advanced robotics and AI systems. Insignia, a leader in the luxury automobile manufacturing sector in the United Kingdom and Europe (conceived of for the purpose of this case study), stands at the forefront of the Industry 4.0 revolution, that is, the fourth industrial revolution, which is now well underway. The original industrial revolution was brought about by the invention of the steam engine. This was followed by the second industrial revolution, powered by the onset of electricity and subsequently by the development of automation and machines, which drove the momentum of the third industrial revolution. Now, in the fourth industrial revolution, intelligent computers are demonstrating unprecedented pace and disruption in their influence on the future of work.[2]

Competing with prestigious brands like Rolls-Royce, Bentley, and the multinational Bayerische Motoren Werke AG (BMW), Insignia epitomises the challenges and opportunities facing contemporary automotive manufacturers. Founded by Sir Edward Thornhill in 1955, Insignia began with a mission to blend traditional craftsmanship with modern technology to create luxury vehicles that epitomise elegance and performance. Thornhill, a passionate engineer and designer, was inspired by the idea of creating cars that were not only functional but also works of art. His vision was to develop vehicles that offered unparalleled driving experiences while exuding sophistication and style.

In its early years, Insignia gained a reputation for producing handcrafted vehicles that featured intricate detailing and superior materials. Each car was meticulously assembled by skilled artisans who took pride in their work, ensuring that every Insignia vehicle was unique. This commitment to quality and exclusivity quickly set Insignia apart from other manufacturers and established it as a symbol of luxury and prestige.

Insignia's competitor landscape

The luxury automobile sector in the UK is highly competitive, with formidable players such as Rolls-Royce and Bentley, both of which have a storied history and a reputation for excellence. Over the past 20 years, the UK luxury car market has experienced significant growth, driven by advancements in technology, the rise of EVs, and changing consumer preferences.[3] Retail sales in the UK luxury car market are projected to grow at a compound annual growth rate (CAGR) of 6 per cent from 2023 to 2028, reaching £33.9 billion. This growth is underpinned by several factors, including the continuous introduction of new models, the expansion of luxury brands into electric and hybrid vehicles, and the increasing purchasing power of consumers. Overall, the global luxury car market is expected to grow from US$410 billion in 2022 to US$566 billion by 2028, reflecting a CAGR of 5.5 per cent.[4] Additionally, consumer preferences have also evolved significantly, with a growing emphasis on sustainability, personalisation and connectivity. Younger, affluent buyers are increasingly looking for vehicles that reflect their values and lifestyle choices. This demographic is more likely to prioritise eco-friendly options and cutting-edge technology over traditional markers of luxury. A study by Deloitte indicates that 48 per cent of consumers in the luxury car market are willing to pay a premium for sustainable vehicles, underscoring the shift towards greener options.[5] Moreover, according to a survey by J.D. Power, 55 per cent of luxury car buyers are looking for enhanced connectivity features in their vehicles.[6]

The main UK luxury automobile companies are:

- **Rolls-Royce**: Founded in 1906, Rolls-Royce is synonymous with ultimate luxury and precision engineering. Known for their meticulous attention to detail and bespoke craftsmanship, Rolls-Royce vehicles are often considered the pinnacle of luxury cars. Their model lineup includes iconic names like the Phantom, Ghost and Cullinan. Each car is custom-built to the buyer's specifications, with options for unique materials, intricate designs and state-of-the-art technology. Rolls-Royce's commitment to innovation can be seen in their adoption of advanced materials and cutting-edge technologies, such as the use of carbon fibre and lightweight aluminium in their chassis designs. Furthermore, their focus on sustainability is evident through their research into electric drivetrains and other eco-friendly technologies, positioning them as a forward-thinking leader in the luxury automotive market.
- **Bentley**: Established in 1919, Bentley offers a unique blend of performance and luxury. Their vehicles, such as the Continental GT and Bentayga, are renowned for their powerful engines and opulent interiors. Bentley's emphasis on combining speed with comfort sets them apart from other luxury car manufacturers. Bentley has also been at the forefront of technological innovation, incorporating features such as advanced driver assistance systems, hybrid powertrains and sophisticated infotainment systems into their vehicles. Their investment in hybrid and electric technologies aligns with global trends towards more sustainable automotive solutions, ensuring they remain competitive in an evolving market.
- **Aston Martin**: Another key competitor in the UK luxury car market is Aston Martin. Known for its association with James Bond, Aston Martin epitomises British luxury and performance. Models like the DB11 and Vantage offer sleek designs coupled with powerful engines. Aston Martin has also ventured into the realm of EVs with the introduction of the Rapide E, showcasing their commitment to innovation and sustainability. Aston Martin's focus on exclusive, high-performance sports cars appeals to a niche market of enthusiasts who value both style and substance. Their continued investment in new technologies and partnerships, such as their collaboration with Mercedes-Benz for electric vehicle technology, ensures they remain a significant player in the luxury automotive sector.

Embracing innovation

Over the decades, Insignia has continuously embraced innovation, adapting to market demands while maintaining its core values. The 1970s and 1980s saw Insignia integrating advanced engineering techniques and materials into their designs, such as the introduction of lightweight aluminium frames and high-performance engines. This period also marked the beginning of Insignia's foray into the world of motorsport, where it showcased its engineering prowess and gained further acclaim.

Meanwhile, Insignia's UK rivals, such as Rolls-Royce and Bentley, were also advancing greatly. Rolls-Royce continued to set benchmarks for luxury and precision, becoming synonymous with high-end, bespoke automobiles. Bentley, on the other hand, was making a name for itself with its powerful and luxurious cars that blended performance with comfort. Both brands, like Insignia, focused on innovation and quality, but each had its unique approach and market segment.

Rolls-Royce, known for its meticulous attention to detail and handcrafted elements, maintained its reputation through continuous improvement and the introduction of advanced technologies in their production processes. Bentley's emphasis on performance and luxury appealed to a different customer base, those seeking both speed and sophistication in their driving experience. These brands, along with Insignia, represented the pinnacle of automotive excellence in the UK, pushing each other to innovate and excel in an increasingly competitive market.

The Industry 4.0 revolution and the automotive sector

The adoption of Industry 4.0 technologies in the automotive sector is driving substantial growth and innovation. The global market for Industry 4.0 technologies is projected to grow from US$94.42 billion in 2023 to US$241.58 billion by 2028, at a CAGR of 20.67 per cent.[7] The implementation of digital technologies like AI, internet of things (IoT), and robotics in automotive manufacturing has led to significant improvements in key performance indicators (KPIs) such as productivity, agility and customisation.

For example, smart factories utilising AI and IoT can predict maintenance needs, reducing unplanned downtime by up to 25 per cent and enhancing overall efficiency.[8] This includes advanced digital capabilities that are known as 'digital twins' and 'digital threads', which make use of virtual representations of the physical assets and processes that companies can use to run simulations of how the asset and process will function in the real world.[9] In addition to predicting maintenance requirements, the integration of digital twins and digital threads allows companies to create real-time digital duplicates of physical objects, optimising business performance and accelerating the innovation curve.[10] Overall, the digital transformation enabled by Industry 4.0 is revolutionising the automotive industry, positioning it for increased competitiveness and responsiveness to market demands. Companies that successfully leverage these technologies can achieve significant operational efficiencies, enhanced product quality and a stronger market position.[11]

As the world entered the era of Industry 4.0, Insignia found itself at a crossroads. The rise of AI, machine learning and advanced robotics promised unprecedented efficiency and customisation but also posed significant challenges. Insignia recognised the imperative to integrate these technologies into its operations to stay competitive and subsequently invested heavily in research and development. This investment led to the incorporation of cutting-edge digital tools in both design and manufacturing processes. Computer-aided design (CAD) software, 3D printing, and robotics became integral to Insignia's operations, enhancing precision and efficiency while preserving the brand's hallmark craftsmanship.

In recent years, Insignia has fully embraced the principles of Industry 4.0, which emphasises the use of digital technologies to create smart factories.[12] These factories feature interconnected systems that communicate in real time, optimising production processes and ensuring the highest levels of quality control. The adoption of AI and machine learning has enabled Insignia to predict maintenance needs, reduce downtime and tailor products to individual customer preferences with unprecedented accuracy. Insignia's smart factories are a testament to this integration.

These facilities leverage AI-driven systems for predictive maintenance, ensuring that machinery operates with minimal downtime. Advanced robotics handle complex assembly tasks with precision, while data analytics optimise supply chain management. The result is a seamless blend of automation and human oversight, allowing Insignia to produce bespoke vehicles tailored to individual customer preferences. However, this rapid transformation has created challenges at different levels, both for the employees and the organisation.

Management dilemmas and executive perspectives

This case study presents the perspectives of two managers at Insignia who are navigating the challenges of this rapid digital transformation: Sarah Thompson, the marketing and sales manager, and John Carter, the manufacturing manager on the factory floor.

Sarah Thompson, marketing and sales manager

Sarah Thompson has been with Insignia for over a decade, overseeing marketing strategies and sales operations. Sarah grew up in Chicago in a family of entrepreneurs, which ignited her passion for marketing from an early age. She earned her bachelor's degree in marketing and communications from Northwestern University, where she excelled academically and gained practical experience through internships. Her early career at a tech startup showcased her ability to develop successful marketing strategies, leading to a swift promotion. At Insignia, Sarah leads a dynamic marketing team, driving growth and enhancing the brand's reputation with her innovative approaches to digital marketing, brand management and customer engagement.

Outside of her professional achievements, Sarah is deeply committed to community service, volunteering with local non-profit organisations focused on education and entrepreneurship. She is also an avid traveller and fitness enthusiast, participating in marathons. Looking ahead, Sarah aims to further her education with an MBA and aspires to take on more significant leadership roles within Insignia, ultimately becoming a global marketing director. Her blend of creativity, strategic thinking, and dedication makes her a key player in Insignia's marketing success and a mentor for aspiring marketing managers.

With the introduction of AI-based software for digital marketing and managerial decision-making, Sarah is tasked with integrating these technologies into her department. Her primary challenges include motivating her team, who are apprehensive about the new tools, and ensuring that they have the necessary skills to leverage AI for better marketing insights and customer engagement. She says:

> Integrating AI into our marketing strategy is not just about adopting new tools; it's about transforming our entire approach to how we engage with customers. The real challenge lies in motivating my team to embrace these changes, learn new skills and see the potential of AI to enhance their creativity and efficiency. It's a delicate balance of maintaining morale while pushing the boundaries of what we can achieve together.

John Carter, manufacturing manager

John Carter, the manufacturing manager at Insignia, grew up in Detroit with a deep-rooted passion for manufacturing, inspired by his father's engineering career in the automotive industry. He pursued a bachelor's degree in mechanical engineering from the University of Michigan, where he gained practical experience through internships in various manufacturing firms. Starting his career as a production supervisor, John's exceptional leadership and problem-solving skills quickly propelled him to the role of manufacturing manager.

At Insignia, John oversees the optimisation of production processes, ensuring efficiency and high-quality standards. His innovative approach to process improvement and quality control has significantly enhanced Insignia's manufacturing operations. Outside of work, John remains committed to his community, often volunteering for local engineering and manufacturing education programmes.

John has spent 15 years managing Insignia's factory floor, where precision and craftsmanship are paramount. The factory is now implementing automation technologies to streamline production and enhance quality control. John's challenges lie in motivating his staff, who fear job displacement, and re-skilling workers to operate and collaborate with advanced machinery.

Additionally, he faces the constraints of maintaining high-quality standards while adapting to the new automated processes. He says:

> Implementing automation on the factory floor isn't just about effi-ciency; it's about preserving the craftsmanship that defines Insignia while embracing the future of manufacturing. The biggest hurdle is reassuring my team that their skills are more valuable than ever and providing them with the training they need to thrive alongside these advanced technologies. It's a challenging transition, but it's essential for our evolution.

Change management and motivating staff during digital transformation

Both Sarah and John face the significant challenge of motivating their teams amidst the uncertainties brought about by digital transformation. The inte-gration of AI and automation requires a shift in the workforce's mindset and skillset, which can be met with resistance.

Sarah is facing resistance from her team, who may be apprehensive about the new technologies. Overcoming this involves fostering a culture of contin-uous learning. Last month, she organised a workshop and training sessions to build confidence in using AI tools. Clear communication about the bene-fits, and reassurances that AI is meant to enhance, not replace, their roles are essential. She knows that engaging in transparent communication and involv-ing employees in the change process is vital. She has therefore held regular meetings to explain the purpose and benefits of the AI integration and shared success stories from other companies or departments that have successfully adopted similar technologies. In doing so, she has created a cross-functional team that includes representatives from different levels of the department to provide input and feedback on the AI implementation process.

However, during a recent meeting where Sarah introduced a new AI-driven marketing tool designed to optimise customer segmentation, she noticed a palpable tension in the room. Many team members expressed concerns about the complexity of the tool and its potential to replace their roles. One employee, Jane, voiced her frustration openly, stating, 'I feel like this new tech-nology is undermining my skills and years of experience. I'm not convinced it will add any real value to our work.'

John faces similar problems to Sarah. He brought in a robot to work with human workers, to highlight improved efficiency and show that automation helps, not hurts, their jobs. But when he showed a new automation tool to make the assembly line better, he felt a lot of stress in the room. Many workers worried about the tool being too complicated and that it would take over their jobs. One worker, Mark, said angrily, 'This new technology makes my skills and experience useless. I don't think it will do anything good for our work.'

Evolving business needs and job designs

As Insignia transitions into Industry 4.0, both Sarah and John face the additional challenge of evolving job designs to meet new organisational requirements. This includes redefining roles and responsibilities to incorporate digital competencies and ensuring that job designs are motivating and fulfilling for employees.

John must redefine the roles within his team, including his own, to include new digital competencies required by AI-based tools. This involves shifting from traditional manufacturing roles to those that require a strong understanding of data analytics and digital manufacturing strategies. To address this, John introduces new roles such as 'digital manufacturing analyst' and 'AI production strategist.' These roles focus on leveraging AI tools to gain insights from production data and develop optimised manufacturing processes. John calls for a team meeting to announce the upcoming changes. He outlines his vision of integrating AI tools into the manufacturing process and introduces the new roles. However, the response is less than enthusiastic. Long-time employees express concerns about job security and their ability to adapt to new technologies.

'Why fix something that's not broken?', questions Dave, a veteran floor manager with over 20 years at the company. 'We've been doing fine without these fancy tools.'

However, John perseveres and, understanding the need for a skilled workforce, John collaborates with HR to develop a comprehensive training programme. The programme includes workshops, online courses and hands-on training sessions. However, he quickly realises that many team members lack basic digital literacy, making it challenging to even begin the training. John also decides to start with a foundational digital literacy course. Despite his efforts, attendance is low and some employees struggle with the material. He faces a tough decision: should he push forward with the existing team or consider hiring new talent with the required skills?

John is also facing an unexpected challenge in paving his way towards redesigning jobs: budget constraints. While his aim is to include collaboration with automation, ensuring that human skills complement machine efficiency, he is meeting financial barriers. John presents his budget proposal to the executive board, detailing the costs of AI tools and training programmes. The executives are hesitant, questioning the high costs and uncertain ROI. 'We need to see tangible benefits before committing to such an investment,' says Lisa, the CFO, 'How can we be sure this will pay off?' John realises he must find a way to demonstrate the potential benefits without the full initial investment. He proposes a pilot project to test the AI tools on a smaller scale, hoping to gather data to support his case.

Talent management, re-skilling and retention

The scarcity of global managerial talent exacerbates the difficulties faced by Sarah and John. They need to ensure that their teams are prepared for digitisation through comprehensive re-skilling programmes. This involves aligning current talent with the competence-based demands of extensive digitisation and AI.

Mary, John's line supervisor, adds, 'I'm not sure I'm ready to learn all this new technology. What happens if I can't keep up?'

John responds, 'I understand your concerns, and that's why we're offering comprehensive training programmes to help everyone transition. We want to ensure no one is left behind.' John subsequently schedules one-on-one meetings with his team members to understand their individual concerns and career aspirations. During these conversations, he emphasises the importance of the upcoming changes and the opportunities they present.

Cultural shift and cybersecurity concerns

John recognises that for the digital transformation to succeed, his team needs to embrace a data-driven approach. He begins by celebrating small victories, showcasing how AI-driven insights can enhance production efficiency. During one team meeting, he presents a compelling example.

'Look at these numbers,' John says, pointing to a chart projected on the screen. 'In the past month, we've managed to reduce downtime by 15 per cent thanks to the predictive maintenance alerts generated by our new AI tools. This is just a glimpse of what we can achieve if we fully integrate these technologies.'

The room is silent, but John can see the gears turning in his team's minds. He continues, 'Imagine if we could prevent every unplanned shutdown and optimise our production schedules based on real-time data. The potential here is enormous.'

As John pushes for this cultural shift, another issue emerges: cybersecurity. The increased use of digital tools and the integration of AI systems open new vulnerabilities. Rachel, the IT manager, raises the alarm during a strategy meeting.

'Are we sure our data is safe with all these new systems?' Rachel asks. 'We've seen a rise in cyberattacks across the industry, and integrating AI adds more entry points for potential breaches. We need to ramp up our security measures to protect against these threats.' John understands the gravity of Rachel's concern. The last thing they need is a data breach that could compromise their operations or customer trust. He decides to prioritise cybersecurity, even if it means reallocating resources from other areas.

'Rachel, you're right,' John says. 'We can't afford to overlook security. Let's work together to implement robust security measures. This will be a strain on our resources, but it's necessary to protect our data and ensure the success of this transformation.'

Rachel and her team get to work, implementing advanced firewalls, encryption protocols and continuous monitoring systems. They also conduct training sessions to educate employees about cybersecurity best practices, ensuring everyone is aware of potential threats and how to mitigate them.

This additional focus on cybersecurity adds to the workload and strains the team's resources, but John knows it is a crucial investment. As the weeks go by, the tension starts to ease. The production team becomes more comfortable with the AI tools, and the IT department successfully fortifies the company's digital defences.

During a follow-up meeting, Rachel reports back with some good news. 'We've implemented the necessary security measures, and our systems are now much more secure. We've also set up real-time monitoring to detect and respond to any potential threats immediately.' John breathes a sigh of relief. 'Great work, Rachel. This gives us the confidence we need to move forward with the digital transformation.'

While the journey is far from over, John feels optimistic. The team is slowly but surely adapting to the new data-driven culture.

Conclusion

John's and Sarah's journeys to integrate AI tools and digitise Insignia operations and marketing functions underscore the complexities of modernising a traditional industry. By attempting to address resistance to change, providing comprehensive re-skilling programmes, prioritising talent development and retention, and implementing robust cybersecurity measures, John and Sarah aim to navigate the multifaceted challenges of digital transformation. Their strategic approach will be key not only to enhance production efficiency but also to foster a resilient, future-ready team. To do so they need to achieve critical balance between technological innovation, and human adaptation and performance.

Preparing the case

This case raises several key management challenges arising from digitisation and the use of AI at Insignia. In preparing the case analysis, you may find it valuable to focus on one or more of the following four challenges. For each challenge, a corresponding set of questions is provided for your consideration.

Challenge 1: digital transformation

1. What does 'Industry 4.0' represent? What is different about the automotive markets today versus five years ago?

2. If you were to summarise the flow of Insignia's fortunes, what would be the major wins and losses?
3. What type of innovation has Insignia recently achieved? How can you relate this to the concept of 'disruptive innovation'? Explain.
4. With the rapidly evolving digital transformation in the automotive industry, is Insignia's response adequate? What would you do in Insignia's CEO role?

Challenge 2: change management

1. How different will the automotive factory of the future be? What can you do now in Insignia factories that you could not do 10 years ago?
2. Is digitisation the only transformation Insignia needs as part of preparing for the future? How difficult is this transformation?
3. How do you evaluate the change initiative inside Insignia so far? 'Too little, too late?' or 'too soon, too fast'?

Challenge 3: job design and job crafting

1. Map out the job characteristics model with the existing job tasks assigned to the two managers (employees) in the case description. Does the employee-level job design currently align with individual strengths and motives?
2. What factors may be limiting the engagement of each of the two managers (employees) in their jobs?
3. What are the options available to each of the two managers in crafting their jobs at Insignia?
4. What factors or circumstances could potentially enable these two employees to craft their jobs to better align with their motives and strengths (for example: autonomy)? What factors or circumstances could potentially limit the opportunity these two employees have to craft their jobs (for example: micro-management by supervisor)?

Challenge 4: talent management

1. Describe and analyse the talent management strategy at Insignia. For example, analyse talent management practices and explain the recruitment process.
2. How are 'talent' employees trained at Insignia? What are the challenges associated with recruiting and training (retraining) of talent in the context of the current digital transformation?
3. Based on your analysis of the case and your knowledge of talent management theory, what are the main priorities you recommend for Insignia to help retain its talent and how might these be implemented?

Further reading

Bain & Company (2024) ' Defining and Building the Factory of the Future'. https://www.bain.com/insights/defining-and-building-the-factory-of-the-future-video/

Christensen, Clayton M. (1997) *The Innovator's Dilemma: When New Technologies Cause Great Firms to Fail*. Boston, MA: Harvard Business School Press.

Christensen, C. M.; Raynor, M. E. and McDonald, R. (2015) 'What Is Disruptive Innovation? Twenty years after the introduction of the theory, we revisit what it does – and does not – explain', *Harvard Business Review*, December. https://hbr.org/2015/12/what-is-disruptive-innovation

Colbert, Amy; Yee, Nick and George, Gerard (2016) 'The Digital Workforce and the Workplace of the Future', *Academy of Management Journal*, vol. 59, pp. 731–739. https://doi.org/10.5465/amj.2016.4003

Kotter, J. P. (1996) *Leading Change*. Boston, MA: Harvard Business Review Press.

Harvard Business Review (2011) 'HBR's 10 Must Reads on Change Management', 7 March. https://hbsp.harvard.edu/product/12599-PDF-ENG

IBM (2023) 'Digital twin vs. digital thread: Two complementary ways to digitally replicate assets', 29 June. https://perma.cc/YGG5-BT2K

Lanzolla, Gianvito; Lorenz, Annika; Miron-Spektor, Ella; Schilling, Melissa; Solinas, Giulia and Tucci, Christopher L. (2020) 'Digital Transformation: What is New if Anything? Emerging Patterns and Management Research', *Academy of Management Discoveries*, vol. 6, no. 3, pp. 341–350. https://journals.aom.org/doi/10.5465/amd.2020.0144

Raj, Alok; Dwivedi, Gourav; Sharma, Ankit; Beatriz Lopes de Sousa Jabbour, Ana and Rajak, Sonu (2020). 'Barriers to the adoption of industry 4.0 technologies in the manufacturing sector: An inter-country comparative perspective.' *International Journal of Production Economics*, vol. 224, June. https://doi.org/10.1016/j.ijpe.2019.107546

Stahl, G.; Björkman, I.; Farndale, E.; Morris, S. S.; Paauwe, J.; Stiles, P. and Wright, P. (2012) 'Six principles of effective global talent management', *Sloan Management Review*, vol. 53, no. 2, pp. 25–42. https://sloanreview.mit.edu/article/six-principles-of-effective-global-talent-management/

Waschull, S.; Bokhorst, J. A. C.; Molleman, E. and Wortmann, J. C. (2020) 'Work design in future industrial production: Transforming towards cyber-physical systems', *Computers & Industrial Engineering*, vol. 139, January. https://doi.org/10.1016/j.cie.2019.01.053

References

[1] Lambert, Craig (2014) 'Disruptive Genius: Innovation guru Clayton Christensen on spreading his gospel, the Gospel, and how to win with the electric car', Harvard Magazine, July–August. https://www.harvardmagazine.com/2014/06/disruptive-genius

[2] McKinsey & Company (2022) 'What are Industry 4.0, the Fourth Industrial Revolution, and 4IR?', 17 August. https://perma.cc/FNV4-JW5T

[3] Euromonitor (2023) 'Premium and Luxury Cars in the United Kingdom', October. https://www.euromonitor.com/premium-and-luxury-cars-in-the-united-kingdom/report

[4] Zhang, Junyi; Schnurrer, Simon; Fang, Frank and Liu, Gavin (2023). 'Luxury vehicle market to see rapid growth: Global luxury vehicle market outlook', Oliver Wyman. https://perma.cc/8MJZ-QXP6

[5] Deloitte (2024) '2024 Global Automotive Consumer Study Key Findings: Global Focus Countries', Deloitte Development LLC. https://perma.cc/LH8E-966S 6

[6] D. Power Inc. (2022) 'New-Vehicle Tech is a Double-Edged Sword: Risky to Satisfaction – Yet Necessary for Future Adoption, J.D. Power Finds', press release.

[7] Mordor Intelligence (2023) 'Industry 4.0 Market Size – Industry Report on Share, Growth Trends & Forecasts Analysis (2024–2029)'. https://perma.cc/E5L6-T7NZ

[8] Soori, Mohsen, Arezoo, Behrooz, and Dastres, Roza (2023) 'Internet of things for smart factories in industry 4.0, a review', *Internet of Things and Cyber-Physical Systems*, vol. 3, pp. 192–204. https://doi.org/10.1016/j.iotcps.2023.04.8

[9] IBM (2023) 'Digital twin vs. digital thread: Two complementary ways to digitally replicate assets', 29 June. https://perma.cc/L3KP-GULR

[10] Soori, Mohsen, Arezoo, Behrooz, and Dastres, Roza (2023) 'Digital twin for smart manufacturing, A review', *Sustainable Manufacturing and Service Economics*, vol. 2, April. https://doi.org/10.1016/j.smse.2023.9

[11] See for example: McKinsey & Company (2022); Deloitte (2020) 'Steering into Industry 4.0 in the automotive sector. Taking advantage of uncertain times to align for future success', https://perma.cc/RQ2M-HQ4G; and McKinsey & Company (2016) 'Disruptive trends that will transform the auto industry', 1 January. https://perma.cc/QTR10-GUKE

[12] See: Deloitte (2020); Gartner (2022) 'Smart Factory. https://www.gartner.com/en/information-technology/glossary/smart-factory; Xu, Jian and Liu, Xiaoming (2018) 'Technology is changing what a premium automotive brand looks like', 22 May. https://hbr.org/2018/05/technology-is-changing-what-a-premium-automotive-brand-looks-like; and McKinsey & Company (2016)

16. auticon: promoting a neurodiverse workforce

Dorottya Sallai and Ian Hill

In today's diverse workplace, understanding and embracing neurodiversity is becoming increasingly important. This case study explores auticon's innovative strategy of not only successfully integrating autistic people into the workforce but also excelling and growing because of its neurodiverse workforce. The case addresses important questions about diversity and inclusiveness, its complexity, the challenges of recruitment and retention as well as the role of leadership in creating and sustaining an inclusive culture. The case provides a rich source of material for exploring a wide range of management issues and teaching goals such as:

Diversity and inclusion

- Understanding the challenges faced by neurodivergent employees and strategies for creating an inclusive work environment.

Organisational behaviour

- How organisations can effectively balance the needs of the market with the needs of their employees.

- Cultural change: promoting a culture of inclusion and respect, and the role of leadership in driving this change.

Human resource management

- Recruitment and retention: challenges and best practices in recruiting and retaining neurodivergent talent and tailoring recruitment processes to be more inclusive.

- Employee support and wellbeing: support mechanisms.

How to cite this book chapter:

Sallai, Dorottya and Hill, Ian (2025) 'auticon: promoting a neurodiverse workforce', in: Sallai, Dorottya and Pepper, Alexander (ed) *Navigating the 21st Century Business World: Case Studies in Management*, London: LSE Press, pp. 219–238. https://doi.org/10.31389/lsepress.nbw.p

Guidance on how to write a case analysis can be found in Chapter 1, 'Business cases: what are they, why do we use them and how should you go about doing a case analysis?'

Introduction

In recent years, there has been a growing recognition of neurodiversity in the workplace, particularly focusing on conditions like autism. This case study explores auticon, a fast-growing global company that differentiates itself by exclusively employing autistic adults as IT consultants.[1] We investigate the innovative elements of their business strategy that have enabled them to build a successful and profitable global consultancy through this unique staffing model. Their approach not only transforms lives and social perceptions but also drives organisational growth in an increasingly competitive market.

Neurodivergent individuals often bring unique strengths to business, such as creativity and the ability to handle varied tasks. Companies like Rolls-Royce, AstraZeneca, JPMorgan, Microsoft and the National Trust are leading the way by adopting inclusive recruitment strategies and providing support for neurodivergent employees.[2] Despite these advancements, significant barriers to employment and fears of discrimination persist for neurodivergent individuals. In the United Kingdom only 30 per cent of autistic adults are employed compared to 50 per cent of all disabled individuals and 80 per cent of non-disabled people.[3] Advocacy groups emphasise that the impact of successful inclusion extends far beyond productivity metrics. Doubling the employment rate for autistic people could boost the economy by up to £1.5 billion each year just in the UK alone.[4]

auticon is a business-to-business company and global social enterprise that delivers social innovation through three types of services: IT consulting, neuroinclusion consulting and entrepreneurial initiatives. As a social enterprise, their core mission is to address the inequalities in employment for neurodivergent adults and showcase the strength of neurodiversity in business and society. The company brands itself as a talent resource providing services to small organisations as well as blue-chip multinationals such as NatWest, Virgin, KPMG, Disney, IBM, Jonson and Johnson, Deloitte, Zurich Insurance and Deloitte among many others.

In 2024, the company operated in 15 countries across three continents, including the United Kingdom, Ireland, United States, Germany, France, Switzerland, Canada, Australia and Italy. In 2023, the global organisation had an approximate turnover of 40 million euros and employed 571 individuals, out of which 436 (more than 75 per cent) were autistic consultants.[5] The firm's operations team, which comprises 19 per cent of the total workforce, is also neurodiverse, hiring both neurodivergent and non-neurodivergent people. However, in these roles, only 24 per cent of the employees disclosed that they have a neurodivergent condition (autism, ADHD, dyslexia or the combination of these)[6] resulting in more than 80 per cent of auticon's total workforce being neurodivergent.

Despite their success and fast global growth, auticon faces several significant challenges. One of the primary issues is aligning labour supply with demand, particularly when integrating neurodivergent individuals into their workforce. This raises broader questions about how companies can effectively balance the needs of the market with the needs of their employees. Additionally, demonstrating the business benefits of inclusive hiring practices to large organisations is crucial. What strategies can be employed to showcase the value of neurodivergent talent?

Scaling their impact in the labour market is another challenge, prompting inquiries into how businesses can ensure meaningful employment opportunities for neurodivergent individuals while expanding their reach. Potential barriers include the challenge of creating a truly sustainable and inclusive working environment that addresses the long-term needs of neurodivergent employees instead of one-off measures to ensure their retention and career progression. Furthermore, how can organisations measure and communicate the value added of neurodiverse workforce to stakeholders who may be unfamiliar with such initiatives or the term itself? In the next sections we will explore these questions in more detail, highlighting the complexities and opportunities in fostering a truly inclusive workplace.

What is autism and how is related to neurodiversity?

Autism/autistic spectrum condition (ASC)/autistic spectrum disorder (ASD) is a neurotype or lifelong developmental condition that individuals have from birth.[7] It is characterised by communication and social interaction challenges, sensory issues and repetitive behaviours,[8] and affects how people interact with the world.[9] Many members of the community prefer identification-first language and being called 'autistic' rather than 'someone with autism' because their autistic neurotype is inherent to them.[10] However, this is a matter of personal preference and identity. According to the UK National Health Service (NHS) autism affects how the brain functions, influencing how individuals perceive the world and interact with others.[11] Often, people feel being autistic is a fundamental aspect of their identity.[12]

> Being autistic does not mean you have an illness or disease. It means your brain works in a different way from other people.[13]

Autism is part of the broader term 'neurodiversity' that refers to the natural variation in the functioning of the human brain, and hence the behavioural traits that distinguish individuals.[14,15] People who use similar information-processing methods and thought patterns – such as those with autism, dyslexia, dyspraxia, ADHD[16] or other neurological variations – may share a sense of identity and consider themselves as being neurodivergent. Between 15 per cent and 20 per cent of the global population is estimated to be neurodivergent,[17] giving an estimated 1 per cent of working age adults. This means that from the approximately 41 million working age adults in the UK, at least around 330,000 are autistic.[18]

Neurodivergent people can be identified by medical diagnoses, while non-neurodivergent people are sometimes referred to as 'neurotypical', despite the multidimensionality of 'neurotypicality'. Neurodiversity at work is often and increasingly becoming part of the organisational 'equality, diversity and inclusion' (EDI) efforts that emphasise the value of different types of information processing, learning and communication styles[19] in the workforce.

Neurodiversity, employment and career progression

The concept of neurodiversity highlights that the under-representation of neurodivergent individuals in the workforce, who have historically faced unemployment and underemployment rates of up to 85–90 per cent,[20] is primarily caused by recruitment processes that have a narrow definition of talent and biassed job interviews that disadvantage individuals with unconventional communication styles. Neurodivergent individuals have skills and talents that make their contribution to organisations unique and valuable. Despite this new approach to a more inclusive view of neurological diversity, most recent statistics paint a stark picture of their employment. In 2022–2023 just 30 per cent of autistic people in UK were employed despite 77 per cent of unemployed autistic working-age adults wanting to work.

Autistic people experience the most significant wage gap compared to other disability groups. Autistic graduates are twice as likely to become unemployed after 15 months compared to non-disabled graduates, more likely to be overqualified for their current job and are more likely to have zero-hour contracts, while being less likely to have a permanent position. By creating inclusive work environments, organisations may leverage neurodiversity as a competitive advantage and by adapting recruitment and support strategies, companies benefit from diverse skills and perspectives. Inclusivity enhances employee retention and boosts morale, leading to higher engagement. An inclusive culture attracts a wider range of talent, making the company more appealing.[21]

auticon: How a problem was turned into an opportunity

auticon's journey began in Berlin in 2011, when a father, Dirk Müller-Remus, decided to do something about the discrimination of people with autism in the labour market and create an environment that would provide better employment opportunities for his autistic son. auticon has since expanded to become the largest autistic-majority company globally. In 2016, Sir Richard Branson invested in the company, which then expanded into Italy and Switzerland before acquiring two North American autism employer startups, Mind Spark and Meticulon, in 2018. Continuing its global growth in 2019, auticon opened an office in Australia, but achieved its historic milestone when it signed a merger agreement with Norwegian IT consulting firm Unicus.

The company offers three types of services: IT consulting, neuroinclusion services and innovative bespoke solutions to problems through so-called auticon Labs. In the area of IT consulting they offer technology consulting and resourcing, focusing mostly on data services, software development and quality assurance testing. In their neuroinclusion services they offer other organisations neuroinclusion coaching, advisory services, neurodiversity training and neurodiversity e-learning to support the creation of inclusive workplaces that work for neurodivergent individuals as well as everyone else. auticon also drives innovation through its entrepreneurial initiatives at auticon Labs, where the company designs and develops commercial technology solutions aimed at overcoming social and environmental challenges faced by neurodivergent professionals and create more neuroinclusive workplaces.

In their 2023 Impact Report, auticon highlighted that the talent shortages in the tech sector are increasingly difficult to fill. They argue that by 2030, the demand for skilled workers will outstrip supply, resulting in a global talent shortage of 85.2 million people. In contrast despite being talented, qualified and keen to work, only 30 per cent of autistic people are in full-time employment.[22]

> I call it the perfect storm for good. auticon sits at the confluence of surging awareness and support for neurodiversity in the workplace, acute shortages of tech talent and the tragically overlooked community of very specially abled neurodivergent people. (Eric Olafson, Investor and auticon Executive Board member)[23]

auticon set out to tap into this talent pool by employing autistic adults as technology consultants and supporting them with neuroinclusion coaches and project managers. What started as a father's ambition to ensure his son's future has developed into a global firm that champions the talents of neurodivergent individuals and sets new standards for workplace social impact.

Positioning neurodiversity as a competitive advantage

Instead of focusing on the challenges that autistic individuals face, auticon promotes its workforce and services emphasising the strengths and special skills of autistic professionals as unique selling points. Neurodivergence is

associated with some common strengths and skills that can effectively contribute to organisational growth, such as attention to detail, sustained focus,
pattern recognition, innovative problem-solving, creative or unconventional
thinking, mathematical or technical abilities, interests or expertise in 'niche'
areas, as well as loyalty, honesty and reliability.[24] It is not a surprise that their
consultants excel in roles such as software development, data analysis and
quality assurance engineering.

Indeed research shows that having employees with disabilities in its workforce can build a firm's competitive advantage in four ways:

1. Those with disabilities often possess special talents that make them
   better at certain jobs.
2. Their presence elevates the organisational culture, fostering collaboration and increasing productivity.
3. A company's reputation for inclusivity improves its value proposition
   with customers, who are more inclined to form long-term relationships with the company.
4. Being acknowledged as socially responsible gives a firm an advantage
   in the competition for talent and capital.[25]

By reframing autism, auticon approaches neurodiversity as a source for their
competitive advantage, for instance by emphasising the value of some autistic traits that are considered essential in providing innovative technology
services, such as finding creative solutions, a narrow focus on complex data
patterns or excelling in repetitious tasks. auticon's vision is to 'build a more
inclusive world', while their mission is to 'address the inequalities in employment for neurodivergent adults and showcase the strengths of neurodiversity
in society'. By approaching autism as an opportunity to embrace the diversity
in skills, thinking and capabilities they promote a mindset shift and a new
framing for the perception of neurodiversity in the labour market, driving
social change.

Their motto *Autism is not a processing error, it's a different operating system*
is not only empowering for those who live with autism, but also reflects a significantly different approach to differences in talent in contrast to most large
employers.

> Businesses like auticon are true trailblazers because they challenge
> and encourage us to view conditions like autism and dyslexia
> differently, not as disabilities, but as talents and assets. My dyslexia
> has given me a massive advantage in life. It has helped me to think
> creatively and laterally, and to simplify things, which has been a
> huge asset when building our Virgin businesses. (Sir Richard
> Branson)[26]

Approaches like auticon's that promote more neuroinclusion in the workplace can contribute to filling vacancies and growth in the economy by unlocking the potential of a large untapped talent pool.[27]

> Working with Unicus, I feel that autism has been de-dramatised for me. It is easy to work with autistic colleagues. (Lars Olof Berg, Produktchef, PictureMyLife)[28]

In 2023, auticon and Unicus completed 402 technology consulting projects for 266 clients and helped many neurodivergent adults not just attain employment but also grow into technical leadership and managerial roles. According to Aleksander Oleszkiewicz, the director of auticon Labs, organisations benefit from neurodivergent leaders in the following ways:

> I see them as very fact-driven, evaluating people purely on their performance and not taking into consideration any factors that are commonly connected with discrimination. They are fair to their team members, may sometimes be a bit harsh but they are honest, straightforward and don't play games. They follow clear and written rules and are open to the individual needs of each person – which creates a great foundation for healthy and high-performing teams.[29]

The economic benefits of neuroinclusion

Fostering a neurodiverse and inclusive workplace culture significantly enhances employee retention, engagement and talent attraction. Neurodivergent individuals tend to have lower turnover rates than their neurotypical counterparts, with companies like Microsoft, SAP, JPMorgan Chase, and EY reporting retention rates exceeding 90 per cent.[30] Initiatives aimed at neurodiversity, such as Microsoft's Neurodiversity Hiring Programme,[31] have shown that neurotypical employees in these environments find their work more meaningful and experience increased morale.

Companies that embrace diversity often see improved financial outcomes, with research indicating that organisations prioritising disability inclusion achieve above-average profitability and shareholder returns. Teams that include neurodivergent professionals can be up to 30 per cent more productive, as studies reveal that autistic employees excel at processing information quickly and identifying critical details. For instance, JPMorgan Chase's Autism at Work programme reported that participants were 90 per cent to 140 per cent more productive than their neurotypical peers.[32]

The development of the business model and challenges of growth

The company operates in the form of a global social enterprise. This means that they are not a charity and are not supported by any governmental or other type of funding. auticon is a for-profit organisation that operates as a social enterprise, investing all their profits into the social mission to address the inequalities in employment for neurodivergent adults and showcase the strength of neurodiversity in society and business. The company advocates that the strategy for neuroinclusion must be closely aligned with the broader inclusion strategy. If the approach is effective for autistic individuals, it will ultimately benefit everyone within the organisation. This perspective highlights the importance of viewing autism through the lens of the company's operational model. With over 450 employees on the autism spectrum, the organisation stands as one of the largest employers of disclosed autistic talent globally.

Each year, the company publishes an impact report that includes metrics on the long-term sustainable employment of its autistic colleagues, alongside client feedback. The report demonstrates the effectiveness of their model, revealing that 81 per cent of autistic staff in the UK feel their wellbeing has improved since joining the company, while 95 per cent feel supported in their roles. Furthermore, 84 per cent of their clients have noted a shift in their perception of autism since collaborating with the organisation, and 92 per cent express increased confidence in working alongside autistic individuals. These statistics encapsulate the essence of the organisation's commitment to inclusion.

When the company started, they were initially delivering quality assurance services out of their offices only. However, as the organisation entered new markets, they realised that this type of consultancy model was not transformational enough for their clients and the wider society as autistic consultants were not seen by the clients when delivering projects. They decided to evolve the model and adopt a more traditional, IT consulting approach employing autistic adults on a permanent basis and sending them to clients as any other consultancy firm would, giving their clients a chance to work alongside them.

There are notable differences in operational approaches across various markets. In the UK, there is a stronger focus on data science, whereas in countries such as the Netherlands and Germany, there is a stronger focus on quality assurance services that are in higher demand in these more regulated markets. While in Germany, the organisation continues to deliver fixed-cost projects, where consultants are not working on the client's site, in the UK all consultants work within client teams rather than in the auticon office. Delivering a fixed-cost project is also part of their social mission, since it helps the company to employ people, who might struggle with the workplace environment and the work in the traditional sense on a client's site.

One of the biggest challenges for business growth is the issue of supply and demand. The supply of highly qualified candidates does not always coincide with suitable projects for them or vice versa. The firm may have high demand for their services but struggle to find individuals with the necessary skills and experience. Aligning the supply of highly skilled autistic talent with the growing demand from clients is critical as it impacts auticon's mission to showcase the strengths of neurodiversity while maintaining business growth and client satisfaction. During the pandemic, the company experienced a slowdown, especially in the UK market. As many IT jobs became offshored, and with English language being widely spoken, competition for providing skilled talent intensified, particularly from countries like Romania, Egypt, India and Poland.

Although there is increasing interest in working with neurodivergent individuals, clients may often prefer experienced candidates over those who are inexperienced and require significant support. This is challenging because those who need autico's help the most are often inexperienced graduates and may still be unfamiliar with the workplace. Hence, balancing the needs of the market with developing a pipeline of well-prepared talent is a priority for auticon.

> The core service that we offer is what we call the lived experience with autistic talent. In our experience there is nothing more efficient than working alongside highly skilled autistic individuals within a support framework that mitigates risk and overheads. This is the most effective way to shift misconception about autism that to this day represents the biggest stumbling block to the employment of autistic people. It's transformative. (Andrea Girlanda, CEO, auticon UK)[33]

Scaling impact on the labour market

The second challenge auticon is facing is scaling their impact in the labour market. This has prompted them to change their business model and offer complementary services, besides IT consultancy. Organisations increasingly seek to support their own neurodivergent staff internally rather than hiring external consultants. However, committing to the necessary business transformation to become truly inclusive is difficult for many. Creating an inclusive culture is a complex transformation journey without a single solution. While some organisations have autism-at-work programmes, these often create artificial environments. Once individuals leave these supportive bubbles, they may face unfriendly or even toxic and aggressive workplaces.

Organisations may also pursue neuroinclusion initiatives for superficial reasons, aiming to increase the number of autistic employees merely to report an increase at the end of the year in their ESG reports, but not systematically investing in their cultural transformation, failing to follow up how many of these individuals they retain, or whether their hiring and retention strategies are suitable and sustainable.

Processes are usually designed by and for neurotypical people, beginning with the hiring stage. According to a study in the tech sector more than half (56 per cent) of neurotypical individuals admitted to having limited or no knowledge about neurodiversity,[34] its conditions and symptoms, while a survey by The Institute of Leadership & Management showed that half of UK leaders and managers would be uncomfortable employing or line managing someone who has one or more neurodivergent conditions.[35]

> True inclusion requires a holistic approach and continuous investment, as neuroinclusion is not binary but has multiple shades. There's no finish line. The biggest challenge for me is to show large organisations that there is business merit in what we do, and this is why I say, look at us. We are the living proof that this can work. (Andrea Girlanda, CEO, auticon UK)[36]

The support framework for effective neuroinclusion

auticon employs technical directors and job coaches who represent the skills and experience of their consultants to clients while also supporting successful project delivery.

Technical directors

Technical directors provide both objective assessments of behavioural strengths and weaknesses and technical guidance during assignments. Technical support differs from psychological support; it is provided by technical experts who match client requirements with the skills of the consultants. If there is no suitable match, the organisation is transparent, stating that they do not have anyone available. They prioritise honesty over misrepresentation, as this approach fosters win-win situations for all parties involved.

It is well-known that autistic individuals often face challenges during interviews. To address this, when a suitable job opportunity arises for their consultants, the technical directors engage directly with the client team to clarify the requirements and align them with the skills and abilities of the consultants – effectively conducting interviews on their behalf. Many consultants tend to be modest about their capabilities and may take time to formulate their responses. This can sometimes cause concern among client teams, who may have preconceived notions about autism. However, the thoughtful consideration that these consultants give to their answers is not a negative trait. For instance, when asked about their proficiency in Java programming, a consultant might respond modestly, saying, 'I know a little' while, in reality, they have outstanding expertise in the programming language.

If you have several children, you know that they're different. You want the same for all of them, but you treat them differently because they have different traits, and this applies to all of us. We all have different areas of strength and weakness, so the key here is flexibility as opposed to conformity. And this is why so many autistic people fail in the traditional recruitment process, because just they don't have the interview skills that many non-neurodivergent people have. It's a process that tends to reward people who like to self-promote, who have sales and presentation skills. But you don't need those skills to be an excellent cybersecurity expert, or a fantastic data scientist. (Andrea Girlanda, CEO auticon UK)[37]

Reasonable adjustments and job coaches

The company advocates that all autistic people should be entitled to reasonable adjustments irrespective whether they view autism as a disability or not. They recognise the challenges that autistic employees face in typical workplaces, such as the sensory environment, vague or ambiguous communication, small talk, and 'connecting' with colleagues.

What we pursue at auticon is equality of opportunities, not equality of treatment. It's very, very different. (Andrea Girlanda, CEO auticon UK)[38]

According to research, up to 90 per cent of autistic people experience sensory processing sensitivities, which can make ordinary sensations overwhelming or painful.[39] While most people can ignore footsteps, ringing phones and co-workers talking, autistic people may find these noises extreme, causing them stress, anxiety or even physical discomfort.

It's been a challenge finding a job that wouldn't exacerbate my sensory issues and overwhelm me. (Autistic individual)[40]

To manage these barriers to employment, auticon employs qualified job coaches to design work environments that are suitable for both their consultants and their clients.

Job coaches also play a crucial role in mediating feedback between clients and consultants. They train client teams on how to interact effectively with the consultants. The ratio of consultants to coaches varies by country. In the UK, for example, 20 per cent of a coach's time is dedicated to delivering neuroinclusion services, which include maturity assessments, training and awareness generation sessions. On average, each coach supports eight consultants in the UK, although this ratio may be higher in markets with less demand for training and awareness initiatives.

230 NAVIGATING THE 21ST CENTURY BUSINESS WORLD

Job coaches prepare IT consultants for the collaborative workplace by providing optimal working conditions, such as noise cancelling headphones, quiet places to work and breaks for stress management. Furthermore, the coaches are on hand to discuss any problems or situations that their IT consultants may find difficult to interpret. The coach prepares the consultants and meets with the client and our consultants on a regular basis, especially at the beginning of new assignments. This is crucial for understanding social cues and expectations on both sides.

For instance, when an autistic consultant was set to join a large banking group, the team informed him that he would receive credentials to access the learning management system to prepare for his assignment. However, the onboarding team sent him the credentials without specifying which courses he needed to complete before joining the organisation. This oversight happened a month before his assignment was due to begin. Remarkably, auticon's autistic consultant completed all 980 training modules before joining the client's cybersecurity team. Subsequently, auticon UK's CEO received a call from the chief people officer, who expressed a desire to speak with the consultant. Initially, the CEO was concerned that there might be an issue. However, the officer clarified that they had never encountered anyone who had completed all their educational training materials and wished to interview the consultant for feedback.

> At the beginning of a project, our consultants are so eager to shine and impress that they might not sleep or skip meals. After two or three months, they can become overworked and burned out. The role of the job coach is not just to support our consultants but also to support the client team and explain that autistic people can be very literal in the way they communicate. (Andrea Girlanda, CEO, auticon UK)[41]

This story illustrates why coaching is not solely about supporting productivity, but also about reducing stress. The anecdote of another client at the UK subsidiary illustrates how coaches can help. The client called the office after a week to express concerns about the consultant. He said, 'This is not going well, and I don't think this is the right thing for us. I emailed your consultant at the beginning of the week, asking him to review a document, and I haven't heard from him yet.' Upon investigating, it was found that the consultant had indeed reviewed the document but had not communicated this back to the client. When the consultant was asked what happened and why he had not reverted to the client, the consultant replied: 'I wasn't asked to revert to the client. I was asked to review a document. I did it.'[42]

This situation highlights the importance of clear and unambiguous communication that job coaches facilitate and support. As auticon UK's CEO Andrea Girlanda explained, for someone who thinks literally phrases like 'please do the best you can as soon as possible' can lead to questions like: 'Can I sleep tonight? Can I eat? Does "as soon as possible" mean in 5 minutes, 1 hour or one day?' In general, many people cope with vague instructions by not taking them too seriously, often responding with, 'Yeah, sure, I'll do the best I can', and then continuing with their day. However, autistic individuals take expectations very seriously and strive to meet them precisely.

> We employ a lot of not just very talented and skilled individuals, but lovely human beings with a strong work ethic, who take their responsibilities very seriously, who are very keen to help. (Andrea Girlanda, CEO, auticon UK)[43]

Chris, an IT consultant placed within an organisation by auticon provides an account of the vital role job coaches play in listening to his experiences and helping him to avoid masking[44] his autism.

> On every step of the journey I have been supported by job coaches and other members of staff. No worry or concern that I have been ignored. Sometimes all I need is a friendly ear to listen as I organise my thoughts. None of it is judgemental, all of it is supportive.[45]

Masking is the act of hiding or concealing one's traits during social interactions as a strategy to safeguard against potential negative social or employment-related outcomes. It is common for autistic people and can cause stress and even burnout. Even though masking is correlated with poorer mental health, it can also provide a coping or survival mechanism for those who do not receive support or adjustments in the workplace.[46] Nevertheless, according to a survey commissioned by auticon, 34 per cent of autistic professionals have never requested a reasonable adjustment, which is in line with the tech sector in general, where only 9 per cent of neurodivergent employees seek accommodations.[47] Interestingly though, seniority in the organisation has a significant impact on whether an employee requests reasonable adjustments. According to auticon's 2022 survey,[48] while an overwhelming majority of business owners (80 per cent) and senior managers (78 per cent) asked for reasonable adjustments, only 50 per cent of junior employees raised similar requests. Differences may be explained by concerns about perceptions, stigma or the uncertainty about needed adjustments. Hence it is crucial for organisations to create an inclusive environment, in which neurodivergent employees feel safe and accepted enough to be open about their needs.

> I no longer go around trying to fit in, I just go around being myself – it's pretty incredible the difference it makes. (auticon consultant)[49]

In their guide for managers, auticon provides concrete examples for reasonable adjustments in the workplace. These include offering flexible work arrangements, clear role definitions and processes that help to minimise stress and allow employees to focus on their tasks effectively, regular check-ins and task confirmation to prevent misunderstandings, provision of sensory adjustments and the promotion of collaboration and mentoring to support learning and development.

> To ensure that the company is taking the right approach, relevant to their employees, it's essential to include neurodivergent employees in all decisions related to programmes and initiatives geared towards neuroinclusion. (Aleksander Oleszkiewicz, Director, auticon Labs)[50]

Impact on individual lives and driving social change

Finding the right talent on the labour market is the third challenge that the organisation needs to manage to grow. With only a third of autistic people being in some form of employment, finding talent on the labour market is not straightforward. Most of auticon's current employees were either unemployed or underemployed before applying to their current position. Despite 88 per cent of their autistic consultants holding professional qualifications, including a bachelor's or higher degree, 64 per cent were unemployed, 10 per cent were underemployed, 8 per cent were engaged in training or education, and only 18 per cent were in some form of employment at the time of their application. Among the unemployed applicants, 55 per cent had been without a job for over a year.

> I started living again. (auticon consultant)[51]

Given these figures, it is not surprising that in 2023, 78 per cent of their employees reported improved wellbeing, 77 per cent felt that they can be their authentic selves at work, 84 per cent feel valued for who they are, and 74 per cent felt more confident.[52]

Besides improving the working conditions of their own autistic employees, the company also set out to demystify autism and showcase the benefits of neurodiversity to the wider society. According to their 2023 Global Impact Report, they aim to contribute to the global ESG agenda's 'social' dimension by championing practices that bring systemic change in the employment of neurodivergent individuals, while also positioning neurodiversity at the centre of the ESG agenda. By 2023, they delivered 274 neurodiversity awareness sessions around the world, trained 6000 people in 149 companies, delivered 402 projects and worked with 266 companies.

My understanding of how to work with different people has greatly changed and it has also shown me how much value there is in having very diverse teams. (Nick Byatt, service owner, PwC)[53]

Their local offices have achieved national recognitions for their societal impact. The US subsidiary was selected as a leading disability employer by the National Organization on Disability in 2023, auticon Germany was among the top three finalists for the Impact of Diversity Awards 2023, while auticon UK ranked 9th in Newsweek's 100 Global Most Loved Workplaces.[54]

Beyond hiring, the company improves autistic people's economic and social conditions. Through actionable neurodiversity training and consultancy services, auticon supports client organisations by establishing high-quality jobs and opportunities. This method allows people to develop lasting technology careers, boosting self-esteem and autonomy.

Besides social impact, their approach to business also drives growth. Their 2023 Impact Report highlights significant positive outcomes not only for the employees but also for the organisational culture, wellbeing and the satisfaction of their clients. They claim that 81 per cent of their client teams feel more confident working with autistic colleagues, 73 per cent report improved team culture, including clearer communication, better teamwork, increased empathy, and a greater sense of purpose, and 96 per cent of their clients value the consultants' contributions to their projects, especially their greater accuracy, alternative perspectives, innovative approaches and increased efficiency.

Conclusion

auticon's journey demonstrates how organisations can transform neurodiversity into a distinctive competitive advantage within the technology sector. While the company has established itself as the world's largest autistic-majority employer, it also faces complex challenges: balancing the supply and demand of neurodiverse talent; investing in specialised support systems; and addressing persistent social biases. auticon's comprehensive support mechanisms and unique value proposition has also positioned it as a global leader in inclusive business practices. Although organisations like auticon can only offer employment opportunities to a small fraction of the autistic community, they are driving meaningful change within one of the most competitive industries and beyond.

auticon sets a benchmark for other companies aiming to integrate neurodiversity into their workforce and plays a significant role in addressing the skills gap in the tech industry by tapping into the untapped potential of autistic talent. As a commercial enterprise, the company successfully balances social impact with market demands, demonstrating that placing neurodiversity at the core of business strategy can drive both innovation and sustainable growth. This model proves particularly valuable as organisations worldwide face increasing technology skills shortages while seeking to build more inclusive workplaces.

Preparing the case

In preparing the case analysis you might like to consider the following questions in particular:

1. auticon challenges conventional notions of talent and skills by demonstrating that neurodiverse employees often possess exceptional abilities that are overlooked in traditional recruitment processes. What innovative recruitment and assessment methodologies can be implemented to identify and value diverse talent, and how can organisations ensure that these approaches remain fair and unbiased across all employee groups?

2. auticon's success illustrates the need for organisations to create adaptable structures that accommodate diverse working styles. How can organisations redesign their structures to accommodate diverse working styles without sacrificing effectiveness? What specific elements of organisational design, such as communication systems, workflows or team dynamics, should be adapted to support a truly inclusive environment?

3. Senior leaders at auticon play an active role in shaping and reinforcing a neuroinclusive culture. What concrete steps should senior leaders take to actively shape and sustain a neuroinclusive culture? To what extent can leadership's commitment to inclusion transform the organisation's culture?

4. auticon operates at the intersection of business and social mission, which raises questions about the tension between profitability and social impact. How should organisations that operate with a dual mission balance the pursuit of profit with their social responsibilities? How should companies prioritise when profitability and social impact seem to be in conflict?

5. The case underscores the importance of broader societal and governmental frameworks in promoting neuroinclusion. What role should governments, public policy and other stakeholders play in promoting neurodiversity in the workplace? How can organisations collaborate with external institutions to foster a neuroinclusive environment, and to what extent should companies rely on or resist external regulations in shaping their internal practices?

References

[1] The authors would like to extend their gratitude to auticon UK for their support and insights, which have significantly contributed to the development of this case study.

[2] Roland, D. (2023) 'Employers see the positive side of ADHD and autism', *Financial Times, 26 May.* https://www.ft.com/content/5148bf49-f3eb -4bd4-acb3-7e338deed82c

[3] Department for Work and Pensions (2024) The Buckland Review of Autism Employment: report and recommendations, 28 February 2024. https://www.gov.uk/government/publications/the-buckland-review -of-autism-employment-report-and-recommendations/the-buckland -review-of-autism-employment-report-and-recommendations

[4] Gomez, Rachel and Sheikh, Sadia (2023) 'Opening opportunities, opening employment prospects for autistic people', December. https://perma .cc/EC11Z-XS3L

[5] auticon (2023) 'Joining forces results in world's largest employer for people with autism', 15 June. https://perma.cc/12Q13-Q8LN

[6] auticon (2022) 'Global Impact Report'. https://perma.cc/RE14-UCUW

[7] National Autistic Society (2024) 'Employing autistic people – a guide for employers', accessed 16 August 2024 from https://www.autism.org.uk /advice-and-guidance/topics/employment/employing-autistic-people /employers

[8] Inclusive Employers (2024) 'Neurodiversity glossary of terms'. https:// perma.cc/36EF-FCUQ

[9] National Autistic Society (n. d.) 'What is Autism'. https://perma.cc /PP15B-SDWA

[10] Following the National Autistic Society's guide as well as auticon's use of terms, for consistency, this case study will use 'autistic' as a term, acknowledging that some people may identify with other terms more strongly and that individual preference and identity should be respected in all situations.

[11] National Health Service (n. d.) 'What is Autism'. https://www.nhs.uk /conditions/autism/what-is-autism/

[12] National Autistic Society (16)

[13] National Health Service (n. d.)

[14] Thompson, E. and Miller, J. (2024) *Neuroinclusion At Work. Survey Report.* London: Chartered Institute of Personnel and Development.

[15] 15 Hill, Ian and Sallai, Dorottya (2025) 'Diversity, Equity and Inclusion in Human Resource Management', in Everett, Sally and Hill, Ian (eds) *Diversity, Equity and Inclusion in Business Management*. London: Sage.

[16] Thompson, E. and Miller, J. (17)

[17] Drabble, D.; Cole, E.; Hahne, A. S.; Sulola, L. and Cullen, J. (2023) 'Neurodiversity in the tech sector: Global research on accessibility, barriers and how companies can do better', #ChangeTheFace Alliance, December. https://perma.cc/18NWB-XCPY

[18] Gomez, Rachel and Sheikh, Sadia (2023)

[19] Thompson, E. and Miller, J. (2024)

[20] Krzeminska A, Austin, R. D., Bruyère S. M. and Hedley, D. (2019) 'The advantages and challenges of neurodiversity employment in organizations', *Journal of Management & Organization*.; vol. 25, no. 4, pp. 453–463. doi:10.1017/jmo.19.58

[21] Drabble, D., Cole, E., Hahne, A. S., Sulola, L., and Cullen, J. (2023)

[22] Department for Work and Pensions (2024)

[23] auticon (20) p. 21.

[24] Smith, Ed (2019) 'Focus on strengths as well as challenges', autistica, 7 October. https://perma.cc/T82J-767H; and Drabble, D.; Cole, E.; Hahne, A. S.; Sulola, L. and Cullen, J. (2023)

[25] Alemany, Luisa, and Vermeulen, Freek (2023) 'Disability as a Source of Competitive Advantage#, *Harvard Business Review* https://hbr.org/2023/07/disability-as-a-source-of-competitive-advantage

[26] auticon (2021) 'Sir Richard Branson behind jobs for autistic at auticon', 22 July. https://perma.cc/7B7E-CPSR

[27] Department for Work and Pensions (2024)

[28] auticon and Unicus (2023) 'Impact Report 2023: Scaling our Impact, p. 8. https://perma.cc/VB48-FQRB

[29] auticon and Unicus (21) p. 9.

[30] Scheiner, Marcia (2020) 'Corporate Neurodiversity Hiring Programs: Scratching the Surface?', Autism Spectrum News, 1 January. https://perma.cc/R6AT-P3EP

[31] See https://www.microsoft.com/en-us/diversity/inside-microsoft/cross-disability/neurodiversityhiring

[32] EY (2023) 'How to enhance your workforce by tapping into neurodivergent talent', Podcast, 13 July. https://www.ey.com/en_gl/media/podcasts

/leading-into-tomorrow/2023/07/episode-08-how-to-enhance-your-workforce-by-tapping-into-neurodiverse-talent

33 Dorottya Sallai's interview with Andrea Girlanda, CEO of auticon UK, online, 22 August 2024.

34 Drabble, D., Cole, E., Hahne, A. S., Sulola, L., and Cullen, J. (2023)

35 The Institute of Leadership (n.d.) 'Workplace Neurodiversity: The Power Of Difference'. https://perma.cc/4RSD-J9ZT

36 Dorottya Sallai's interview with Andrea Girlanda, CEO of auticon UK, online, 23 August 2024.

37 Dorottya Sallai's interview with Andrea Girlanda, CEO of auticon UK, online, 24 August 2024.

38 Dorottya Sallai's interview with Andrea Girlanda, CEO of auticon UK, online, 25 August 2024.

39 Hillman, H. (2024) 'Designing a Sensory-Friendly Workplace for Autistic Adults', Autism Spectrum News, 10 January. https://perma.cc/VRG9-FPY9

40 auticon (2022)

41 Dorottya Sallai's interview with Andrea Girlanda, CEO of auticon UK, online, 26 August 2024.

42 Anecdotes are from the author's interview with Andrea Girlanda, CEO of auticon UK, online, 27 August 2024

43 Dorottya Sallai's interview with Andrea Girlanda, CEO of auticon UK, online, 28 August 2024.

44 Pryke-Hobbes, Amber; Davies, Jade; Heasman, Brett; Livesey, Adam; Walker, Amay; Pellicano, Elizabeth and Remington, Anna (2023) 'The workplace masking experiences of autistic, non-autistic neurodivergent and neurotypical adults in the UK', PLOS one, vol. 18, no. (9). https://doi.org/10.1371/journal.pone.0290001

45 auticon website: https://auticon.com/uk/neuroinclusion-services/job-coaching/ Pryke-Hobbes, Amber, Davies, Jade, Heasman, Brett, Livesey, Adam, Walker, Amy, Pellicano, Elizabeth and Remington, Anna (2023)

46 Fairbank, Rachel (2023) 'How to navigate adulthood on the autism spectrum', Monitor on Psychology, vol. 54, no. 8, p. 50. https://www.apa.org/monitor/2023/11/adults-autism-spectrum

47 An online survey was commissioned by auticon and conducted by market research company OnePoll. 985 employed autistic adults in the UK, US, Germany, France, Italy, Canada, Australia and Switzerland were

interviewed. Data was collected between 07/02/2023 and 23/02/2023. Source: auticon's 2023 Global Impact Report, page 7; and Drabble, D.; Cole, E.; Hahne, A. S.; Sulola, L. and Cullen, J. (2023)

[48] The online survey was commissioned by auticon and conducted by market research company OnePoll, in accordance with the Market Research Society's code of conduct. Data was collected between 07/02/2023 and 23/02/2023. 985 employed adults in the UK, US, Germany, France, Italy, Canada, Australia and Switzerland were interviewed. This survey was overseen and edited by the OnePoll research team. OnePoll are company partners of the MRS and has corporate membership to ESOMAR. Survey results were published in auticon's 2022 Global Impact Report.

[49] auticon and Unicus (2023) p. 16

[50] auticon and Unicus (2023) p. 10

[51] auticon and Unicus (2023) p. 16

[52] auticon and Unicus (2023)

[53] auticon and Unicus (2023) p 18

[54] Newsweek (2024) 'Global Most Loved Workplaces 2024'. https://perma.cc/TC4B-NGU4

Part 6
Public management

17. Planning and programming for a government-hosted mass-gathering event in India: the 2019 Prayagraj Kumbh Mela

Luciano Andrenacci and Michael Barzelay[1]

India has a long tradition, going back to colonial times, in which government plays host to multi-week Hindu festivals, known as *melas*. Since independence, Uttar Pradesh's state government has hosted melas in its Prayajgraj (formerly Allahabad) district. In 2017, the newly elected head of this state government, Yogi Adityanath, a Hindu monk belonging to the Bharatiya Janata Party (BNP), brought together his government ministers and officials to tell them that one of his priorities was for the 2019 mela in Prayagraj to be more than a usual one: the experience of attending would be as magnificent as possible for as many as could attend. This would be a Kumbh Mela, a major focus for regional and local development in the state. Cleanliness would be a major goal, and preparations would get underway 18 months ahead of the event. Chief minister Adityanath also named officials who would be responsible for such preparations, one of whom, Indian Administrative Service (IAS) officer Ashish Kumar Goel, was directed to serve as commissioner for Prayagraj division and given the additional role as 'nodal officer' for the 2019 Prayagraj Kumbh Mela, and reporting directly to the chief secretary, the highest-ranking official in the state government. The case is broadly about managing a programme of major projects in government in preparation for hosting a mass-gathering event – one that turned out to be the largest human gathering ever on the planet.

The case is suitable for use in a course concerned with public management, an academic discipline centred on the collective endeavours of implementing public programmes and managing public organisations. It can be used to show what tasks – managerial and otherwise – are functionally necessary to implement a public programme in a

---

How to cite this book chapter:

Andrenacci, Luciano and Barzelay, Michael (2025) 'Planning and programming for a government-hosted mass-gathering event in India: the 2019 Prayagraj Kumbh Mela', in: Sallai, Dorottya and Pepper, Alexander (ed) *Navigating the 21st Century Business World: Case Studies in Management*, London: LSE Press, pp. 241–250. https://doi.org/10.31389/lsepress.nbw.q

novel way, making it suitable for teaching early in a course concerned with innovation, management and delivery in government. It can also be used in instructing students how to explain the functioning of major projects.

Guidance on how to write a case analysis can be found in Chapter 1, 'Business cases: what are they, why do we use them and how should you go about doing a case analysis?'.

Introduction

In March 2017, the *Bharatiya Janata* ('Indian People's') Party (BJP) won the Indian State of Uttar Pradesh (UP) Assembly elections and formed a new government for India's most populous state and the world's most populated subnational entity (approximately 250 million people by 2018). The new chief minister (CM), Yogi ('active practitioner of Yoga') Adityanath, was a Hindu monk, *mahant* ('head priest') of the monastic order running a temple in Gorakhpur (UP), and founder-leader of a religious-political youth organisation. He assumed office on 19 March 2017.

The BJP's government of UP (2017–), as with the BJP's national government of India (2014–), displayed an ambitious, institutionally reformist agenda around the upgrading of governance. A symbolically important part of this agenda evolved around the idea of organising the upcoming Hindu festival of Kumbh Mela of Prayagraj, to be held in January to February 2019, in the best possible way.

Continuity and change: the concept for the Prayagraj Kumbh Mela 2019

The Kumbh Mela ('great pot') Festival or Fair is the most important regular Hindu religious event in India. For as long as sources can trace (some 13 centuries), pilgrims gather once a year in selected riverside sacred places where the Hindu gods are believed to have unwantedly spilled *mana* from heaven, during a legendary fight. Millions of people travel to these 50–60 day gatherings, and state governments are responsible for the organisation of the events.

Kumbh Melas of Allahabad (since 2018 known as Prayagraj) have always been the most attended melas in India, and quite probably the most attended mass gatherings on Earth. The previous big festival, in 2013, had been attended by an estimated 100–120 million people, and was the object of careful logistical preparations, ensuring a clean, safe and satisfying stay for visitors. These preparations included local infrastructure upgrades and special planning and coordination of security and sanitation in and around the Triveni Sangam grounds, the 20km² area where the most important parts of the event take place. Although the 2013 event had been praised by most visitors, many administrative and logistical challenges remained regarding adequate infrastructure for the large quantity of visitors, crowd management, the prevention of accidents, and cleanliness of the festival grounds and the areas for ritual bathing in the sacred river waters.

The state government's political vision for Prayagraj Kumbh Mela (PKM) 2019 was to run a 'great Kumbh'. The festival had to be open and welcoming of all Indians, regardless of caste, gender and age. It had to be especially attractive to the young. And it had to show that better governance could be achieved in India's biggest state. The vision coalesced into a slogan for the 2019 festival: a *Swachh* (clean) Kumbh, a *Divya* (divine) Kumbh and a *Bhavya* (great) Kumbh.

UP's government initiative aligned well with the Indian national scene. The 2014 election had brought BJP's Narendra Modi to power as prime minister. The campaign pivoted on the need for rapid development through institutional change, as his 'victory tweet' expressed: *'Bharat ki vijay, acche din aane wale hai'* ('India has won, good times are about to arrive').

A centrepiece of Modi's government was the creation, in December 2014, of the National Institution for Transforming India (NITI Aayog 'policy commission'), which replaced the long-standing classical top-down, Planning Commission (1950) and its five-year plans. NITI Aayog provided intellectual support for nationwide social transformation *abhiyaan* ('campaigns' or 'missions'). These transformations aimed to achieve governance and behavioural change, delivering planning and management strategies capable of effectively coordinating ministries' actions through pivotal campaigns. This was particularly the case for *Swachh Bharat* ('Clean India', 2014–2025) and *Nanami Ganga* ('Clean Ganges', 2014–2022).

The *Swachh Bharat* mission was presented by Narendra Modi with words chosen to reflect Mahatma Gandhi's *Satyagrah se Swachhagrah* (loosely translated 'cleanliness is moving towards the truth'; *satyagrah*, loosely translates as 'the force of truth'). The aims of Clean India were to eliminate 'open defecation' (the human practice of defecating in the open – fields, bushes, forests or other open spaces – rather than into a toilet), and to improve solid waste management, eradicating 'manual scavenging' (hand manipulation of waste) in urban and rural areas. This was to be achieved through a kind of behavioural change facilitated by monetary incentives, volunteer work (*Swachhagrahis*, 'ambassadors of cleanliness'), and sanitation infrastructure development. The campaign received technical and financial support from the World Bank, and required the scaling up of coordination between ministries, states, divisions and districts. The main goal was to achieve an 'open-defecation free' India by October 2, 2019, the 150th anniversary of Mahatma Gandhi's birth.

The *Nanami Gange* mission was intended to 'abate pollution' and promote 'conservation and rejuvenation' of the Ganges River Basin, covering an area that is distributed across eight Indian states and is inhabited by between a fifth and a quarter of India's 1300 million citizens (2018 figures). Clean Ganges' main project lines were aimed at identifying 'pollution hotspots' (crucial source areas); intercepting, diverting and/or treating waste water (including industry shutdowns, if necessary); and cleaning the river surface and coastlines.

Governance and organisation for PKM 2019

After Independence in 1947, India's national- and state-level governments were broadly modelled on the British Westminster-Whitehall governmental system. Governments are formed based on parliamentary composition: at the state-level, the head of government is the CM. Cabinet government includes ministers appointed by the CM. In the UK Whitehall pattern, the government is supported by a civil service, headed at the state level by the chief secretary, appointed by the CM. The Civil Service is composed of many branches, some of which are functionally specialised (for example, in policing). The Indian Administrative Service is a branch that provides officers to serve as representatives of the state government within territorial jurisdictions within states.

Indian states are divided into districts. A number of districts comprise a division (for administrative purposes), which is managed by UP government-appointed 'commissioners'. The role of commissioners (normally senior IAS officers) is to supervise state activities in the territory, from land-use to planning, coordination and control of services and special projects. Districts have politically elected mayors who preside (with limited powers) over councils or local governments (the most populated districts like Prayagraj have municipal corporations). The districts' administrations are managed by (mostly junior) IAS district managers, also called 'collectors'. IAS, Indian Forest Service (IFS) or Indian Police Service (IPS) officers manage their sector-related agencies (among them development and police).

PKM 2019 was to be organised by the Allahabad-Prayagraj division commissioner. The person invited to occupy this pivotal position was a senior IAS officer, Ashish Kumar Goel. He knew the melas relatively well, as he had previously served as Allahabad district magistrate/collector in 2007–2008 and, in this role, had been responsible for a Magh Mela, a much smaller version of Kumbh Mela. He was also part of team for the Kumbh Mela 1998 in Haridwar (now in Uttarakhand) as joint magistrate, and had seen up close the Kumbh Mela 2013 in Allahabad.

Goel was serving in Lucknow (UP state capital city) and was directly given the goals and conditions of the invitation: he was to produce an unmistakably great festival in all possible senses. He knew how some of the best Indian administrators had been historically at pains to control all the variables for a 'no issues' mela, and had a fair idea of what needed to be done. Success depended on developing costly infrastructure for the host city, controlling upstream river pollution in one of the most densely populated areas of UP and India and building, managing and dismantling the temporary city in the timespan of little over three months – when the Triveni Sangam and adjacent areas are free from flooding.

Goel was assured he would have as much high-level support as possible. The national–state political alignment would make full financial support easier (though not necessarily simpler) to secure. A generous UP special budget was to be ear-marked for the campaign, and the national government's involvement was to be stronger, both through direct financial contributions, and through facilitating key national agencies' and missions' cooperation to deliver infrastructure projects, HR and technical support. Goel was invited to ask what he needed for PKM 2019 as soon as possible, as everyone agreed that the 'stringent constraint' of time was the most important independent variable.

Planning for the 2019 PKM

In the first days of April 2017, Goel presented to the UP government a short list of key aspects that he considered crucial to accomplish the CM's aims for PKM 2019. To optimise cleanliness in the event, he requested full government support for water pollution control and called attention to the need for special efforts and funding for waste management. To achieve efficiency and speed for the preparation process, he requested 'untied funds' for technological innovation and hiring experts, as well as a 'dedicated cell' placed directly under the CM office to support the budget process and fast appointment of key collaborators. To guarantee governance and enhanced transparency, he requested the creation of a professional third-party monitoring system and authorisation to thoroughly document all operations. Finally, in considering how to appropriate and use recent technological innovations, he requested that a smart monitoring system of works and labour, based on geo-tagging and biometrics, was created.

Goel was appointed division commissioner (DC) of Allahabad (soon Prayagraj) on 14 April 2017, little less than a month after Adityanath had become the CM of UP. Goel took office in 21 April, in a ceremony where the CM publicly announced his vision of a 'Divya Kumbh, Bhavya Kumbh'. He immediately moved to the old spacious white house, not far from the mela area, where the Raj's local authority used to reside. Quickly, a 'situation room', austere but equipped with all things necessary, was built adjacent to the house. In an interview granted later for the Indian Institute of Management Bangalore (IIMB) report team, Goel specified: 'With the sole aim to enhance pilgrim experience, the Kumbh 2019 vision rested on five key pillars: Inclusion of all sections of the society, improved quality of services and new cultural/ spiritual experience, aesthetically coherent and pleasing Mela, use of digital technology as an enabler to further planning goals and overall efficiency improvement, and finally, creation of a worthwhile legacy for future Kumbhs'.[2]

The new DC's first move was to meet representatives and experts of all areas related to the project in Delhi, Lucknow and Prayagraj and thoroughly review impressions, diagnostics, grievances, expectations, needs and suggestions. By June 2017, this process had led to the elaboration of what Goel called 'the wish-list'. The wish-list was presented to the CM and the new high committee, relabelled 'Apex Committee', which had been constituted in Lucknow in May. Most aspects were agreed upon, including key collaborators' names. A resulting 'checklist' reduced the project's front-end 'fuzziness', although many of the specificities, as well as some new important ideas, would evolve later. From the perspective of the DC's expert team, this checklist condensed the means to achieve the purposes of two overarching programmes: the transformation of Prayagraj's infrastructure, and the delivery of 'the greatest Kumbh ever'.

The first programme included a strategy for UP government's ambitious reshaping of the urban area of Prayagraj of five million people plus (as estimated for 2017) into a 20 million-plus 'smart' host city (as calculated for peak days for the city's development master plan). This was to be done 'conveying a positive message of government'. The city transformation 'final' plan included almost complete redevelopment for access (airport, railway station, roads, parking areas), circulation (road grid, traffic flow, pedestrian 'friendliness'), security (rapid deployment of specialised disaster and emergency teams) and servicing (water, sanitation, police and health facilities, as well as commercial areas). A redevelopment of that size, in the available timespan, would require both major financial commitments and substantial administrative adaptations, both of which would only be possible with strong political backup.

The second programme included providing 'the greatest Kumbh ever', which meant 'delivering an experience' to visitors and showcasing governance. It was expected (and desired) that the event hosted a larger turnout than in 2013, considering the growth in Indian citizens' mobility and interest, and communication campaigns dedicated to entice the non-religious public with targeted messages. The turnout was naturally impossible to calculate with precision, but it was thought it would double 2013 numbers, with roughly 200 million visitors. A 'tricky' event had to be delivered with no 'harm' or 'mishap'; it had to be 'welcoming' and generate the best possible impression in public opinion. Together with upgrading safety and services, festival cleanliness was seen as the most challenging aspect.

The newly appointed DC started by putting together and empowering a 'core team' of close collaborators, some of them in key official positions, some contracted as experts for the campaign. The core team was to become the taskforce that interacted with national, state and local authorities. Although it had no formally defined boundaries, it comprised the two districts' magistrates (Prayagraj and the mela's temporary district) and their closest collaborators. The number of full-time contracted experts was small and belonged to a well-known international business management consultancy firm that won the open bid: Ernst & Young. With the help of his core team, the DC began a series of 'iterative' interactions with higher and local authorities, as well as with experts from private and public reputed institutions, to further define the multi-project campaign. Of these first iterations the 'front end' of the project came to be.

Preparatory projects and the delivery of the 2019 Kumbh Mela

Prayagraj required a fully-fledged commercial airport (it was currently using Air Force infrastructure), new train stations and capacity enhancement of existing ones, enlarged and upgraded access routes, a highway system with flyovers and underpasses, a thorough conceptual and physical redesign of the city circulation grid, new electricity main lines and transformer platforms, and as wide-as-possible 'beautification' of the city proper. As it was stated that visitors would need to walk for a maximum of 5km to reach the mela area, this meant larger parking areas in densely used terrain. The Sangam confluence needed a dramatic number of interventions in polluted nalas (minor water courses), upstream drains and sewage. The prepared *ghats* (bathing riversides) needed to be extended to almost twice their existing length, to better distribute user pressure. Clean Ganges support would be used to design a new network of sewer lines for the city. The temporary district, finally, needed to be significantly enlarged (by an estimated 35 per cent relative to 2013), taking the total area to a surface of 3200 hectares or 32km^2, which required complex negotiations with local communities. Finally, the new version of the 'tent city' and its servicing required smart and sensitive plot allocation, in line with religious organisations' expectations, and to avoid usual conflicts.

The programme of preparations for the festival itself reflected the way in which the upgrade relative to 2013 was expected to be brought about. Control for crowd management was undertaken by a smart-city styled 'command and control centre', armed with specifically developed and adapted real-time monitoring technology, manned by a 24/7 human team, and fed with a widespread CCTV grid and digitised information coming from facilities and field teams. Security and disaster prevention and management would be planned through a scenario-failsafe 'multi-tiered' programme, developed with the help of UP police, the Indian Army and special branches of Indian Defence departments. A 'No batons, whistles and ropes' policy would be implemented to ensure the visitor-friendly safety vision for the event. This entailed capacity development for the roughly 50,000 police force to be deployed.

To enhance the Prayagraj and mela area hosting capabilities, regulations for traffic, vending, camping and religious activity would ensure an adequate equilibrium between logistical arrangements, stakeholder expectations and visitors' needs. A 'visitor and tourist' oriented campaign would develop symbols and theme parks for the festival, as well as strategic embellishments of the host city. Two key aspects of this were to be the 'Paint my city' campaign, providing the means for special teams to design and paint images and messages on visible walls, and a negotiation with the Indian Army to temporarily open public visitation of a revered Hindu relic tree, previously only open for limited religious access.

Waste management was clearly considered the crucial domain in which PKM 2019 had to make the difference. The concept and vision, arising from iterations with Clean India and India's World Bank office, were to develop a 'no manual handling' and 'rapid evacuation' process, allowing 'no ground contact' and 'no odour, no flies' outcomes.

To ensure timely procurement and subcontracting, acquisitions and delivery of services, e-tendering and payment technologies and protocols would be adapted. Experience showed that classical monopolistic procurement needed to be avoided. Labour negotiations and agreements would prevent the much-feared vendor bottlenecks and workers' strikes that could endanger the delicate time-limited activities.

The entire operation would be given visibility and transparency through an online project monitoring system. The campaign would also take steps to 'manage its legacy'. A commitment to open government and thorough documentation would ensure the experience could outlive the festival.

In early 2018, there was a version of the festival (Magh Mela), with a lower turnout of around eight million visitors, which presented the opportunity for a pilot, and showed the 'evolving solution' approach in development and action. Viewed from the perspective of the core team, the pilot provided a measure of what was still needed to complete the Prayagraj zone transformation, as well as new insight on a number of issues for the festival that, if solved, could prove key for the desired Kumbh Mela upgrade relative to 2013. It also provided some reassurance that preparations were headed in the right direction.

The pilot was also fertile ground for providing new ideas for stakeholder management, from the treatment of VIPs to the negotiations with religious organisations. It also highlighted the need to innovate for the retention of people working in the mela, considering stringent timelines and long working hours. Safety, wellbeing and personal treatment of workers had to be specifically targeted. The Magh Mela also helped them to better understand the possibilities and threats of communication through social media, given the rising importance of this 'arena' of public opinion. As a collaborator put it, social media needed to be 'pushed', so as not to work in 'reaction mode'. The communication team thus needed to become an 'influencer'.

The second half of 2018 involved the deployment of all final infrastructure arrangements and festival management plans, final budgeting, procurement solutions for the waste management plans, and stakeholder management for the religious organisations involved. Particularly important was the finding of crucial financial support from national programmes (amounting to 50 per cent of the estimated final cost), which was dealt with by a string of visits of the DM to Delhi and Lucknow, and a round of negotiations with national and state authorities by the DC and the DM.

The Prayagraj Kumbh Mela as it turned out

Between 15 January and 4 March, 2019, the cumulative footfall of attendees was estimated to have been 240 million people. The six peak days attracted, approximately, over 20 million (on days 1, 5 and 6), over 30 million (on days

2 and 4), and over 50 million (on day 3, *Mauni Amavasya*, 2 February 2019). Although the turnout was way over the twofold increase on 2013 that was expected, the festival went ahead with no significant issues and received wide praise as an impressive experience by the vast majority of visitors. It was widely remarked that the festival area was much cleaner than was expected. As a high political stakeholder observed, 'cleanliness took people by surprise, and that made them happy'. On 22 February, during his visit to the festival, PM Modi took a dip, and in a situation that, according to well-informed participants, was off-protocol and programme, he washed the feet of sanitation workers, adding he 'would carry the memory of washing the feet of safaai karamcharis life-long'.

The final bill was almost five times bigger (at constant prices) than the 2013 Kumbh Mela. Approximately two-thirds of the costs were taken up by infrastructure development. Although there was heavy scrutiny, no significant observations were made around the budgeting and spending procedures utilised.

The IIMB had been requested by Prayagraj Mela Authority (PMA) to participate in the event and produce a report on its management. The two field surveys conducted by the IIMB team showed approval by visitors. In the first one, all facilities were rated quite positively, with the three most notable services being safety, hygiene and *ghats* arrangements. In the second one, safety, hygiene, sanitation facilities, *ghats* arrangements and electricity and lighting were noted as the most approved features of the event.

Preparing the case

In preparing the case analysis you might like to consider the following questions in particular:

1. How was the information available to Ashish Goel, when he began serving as divisional commissioner of Prayagraj, pertinent to carrying out the task of planning the 2019 Kumbh Mela?
2. How are the specifics of both the context and the carrying out of tasks of managing the 2019 PKM relevant in explaining the progress and completion of this mass-gathering event's preparations?
3. In commissioning an evaluation study of preparations for the 2019 PKM, how would you define its scope, focus and main issues, if it is going to be of great value in managing future government-hosted mass-gatherings endeavours in India?
4. What would count as (a) a finding of the evaluation study and (b) a proposition about how to manage future government-hosted mass-gathering endeavours in India?

Sources

Primary sources for this case study included field observations which took place between 11 and 27 January 2020, and 25 semi-structured interviews with local officials which took place between 10 January 2020 and 2 February 2020. Secondary sources included:

Ernst & Young (2020) *Prayagraj Kumbh 2019. Introspecting The Management And Administration Of The World's Largest Congregation Of Humans.* New Delhi: Ernst & Young.

Khanna, Tarun, Macomber, John and Chaturvedi, Saloni (2020) *Kumbh Mela: India's Pop-up Mega-City.* Boston, MA: Harvard Business School.

National Institute for the Transformation of India (2019): *Kumbh Mela 2019. Best Practices in Crowd management & Sanitation.* New Delhi: NITI Aayog.

Ramesh, G, Tripathi, Ritu and Raj, Prateek (2020) *Prayagraj Kumbh 2019. An Integrative Assessment.* Bangalore: IIMB.

Tripathi, Shashank/Prayagraj Mela Authority (2018) *Making of Kumbh. Prayagraj 2019.* Mumbai: Peninsula Spenta/PMA.

Tripathi, Shashank/Prayagraj Mela Authority (2020) *Prayagraj. Smart City, Smart Future.* New Delhi: Times Group Books/PMA.

Tripathi, Shashank / Prayagraj Mela Authority (2020) *Swachh Kumbh. Delivering a Clean Kumbh.* New Delhi, Times Group Books/PMA.

References

[1] This case study was written by Luciano Andrenacci and Michael Barzelay, with additional contributions provided by Yifei Yan (Assistant Professor of Public Administration and Public Policy at the Department of Politics and International Relations, University of Southampton).

[2] From an interview with authors, see Sources section for information on primary sources quoted in this case study.

18. Socio-economic background and career progression within the UK Civil Service

Dorottya Sallai and Ian Hill

This case study examines the impact of socio-economic background, referred to by sociologists as 'social class', on career progression within the UK Civil Service. Despite efforts to promote diversity and inclusion, evidence suggests that someone's class background continues to play a significant role in shaping their career trajectory within the public sector. The UK Civil Service, one of the country's largest employers, offers a unique lens through which to examine broader societal issues of social mobility and equality of opportunity. This study aims to uncover how individuals from different economic and social classes experience career paths, highlighting both the explicit and subtle ways in which class influences professional advancement.[1]

The case provides a rich source of material for exploring a wide range of management, human resource and social mobility questions. By the end of this case study, you will be able to:

- highlight the impact of socio-economic background on career progression

- critically reflect upon the impact of educational background and cultural capital on career progression

- assess the challenges of achieving socio-economic diversity in a traditional institution

- identify the role of senior leaders in preserving or challenging class-based disparities

- identify how informal networks and unwritten rules impact career progression and opportunities

---

How to cite this book chapter:

Sallai, Dorottya and Hill, Ian (2025) 'Socio-economic background and career progression within the UK Civil Service', in: Sallai, Dorottya and Pepper, Alexander (ed) *Navigating the 21st Century Business World: Case Studies in Management*, London: LSE Press, pp. 251–266. https://doi.org/10.31389/lsepress.nbw.r

• critically assess impact of class, educational background and cultural capital on career progression.

Guidance on how to write a case analysis can be found in Chapter 1, 'Business cases: what are they, why do we use them and how should you go about doing a case analysis?'.

Introduction

In today's work environment, when diversity and inclusion are at the forefront of public discourse, understanding the role of hidden factors that determine someone's success in career progression, such as a person's socio-economic background, is more important than ever. This case study focuses on the UK Civil Service, one of the UK's largest public sector employers. It highlights the complex challenges the institution faces in its attempts to change its elitist culture. Additionally, the case study addresses the deeply engrained informal rules which have historically influenced career progression within its departments.

The UK Civil Service has long been regarded as a diversity pioneer, aspiring to be the UK's most inclusive employer and setting standards for large organisations to follow. However, recent studies, particularly the work of Sam Friedman, Professor of Sociology at the London School of Economics and Political Science (LSE), has revealed significant disparities in socio-economic representation and career advancement within this organisation.[2]

The UK Civil Service

The UK Civil Service is the country's permanent bureaucracy that helps the government develop and implement its policies. It is one of the country's top employers, employing about half a million people and providing direct services to citizens, such as benefit and pension payments, prison operations, state education and issuing driving licences. As an organisation, the UK Civil Service is politically neutral and independent of the government. Its employees, known as the civil servants, work for central government departments, agencies and non-departmental public organisations. However, several other key groups are not part of the Civil Service, even though they play a key role in governance and public services. These include: government ministers, the British armed forces, police, local government, NHS staff and royal household staff.

Although the UK Civil Service has made considerable efforts in increasing gender and ethnic-minority equality since the Second World War, particularly at the senior civil servant (SCS) level, people from privileged backgrounds are still significantly over-represented. While between 1996 and 2020, the proportion of women in senior roles rose from 17 per cent to 46 per cent, and the representation of Black and minority ethnic individuals increased from 4 per cent in 2006 to 9 per cent by 2020, the number of people from low social-class[3] backgrounds has not significantly changed.

In fact, in the Civil Service 54 per cent of employees still come from higher socio-economic backgrounds, compared to 37 per cent in the general UK workforce. In the SCS this percentage is even higher, with 72 per cent of employees coming from privileged backgrounds in 2021.[4] Despite decades of governments' efforts to change the historically low social mobility within the sector, these figures have not changed. In fact, the percentage of senior civil servants from affluent backgrounds was greater in 2021 than in 1967, when the last data was collected. Before looking at the figures in more detail, we need to explore how it is possible that, despite significant efforts to the contrary, employment and career progression to the most senior positions in the Civil Service are practically blocked or significantly challenged for those who come from less privileged backgrounds.

Class and career progression in Britain

Britain's most influential occupational positions have long been dominated by those from privileged class backgrounds.[5] According to the Social Mobility Commission's 2018–2019 survey,[6] in the UK, people from more affluent backgrounds are 80 per cent more likely to have professional jobs compared to their working-class peers. As a result of these differences, it is not a surprise that those from working-class backgrounds earn 24 per cent less annually, and even when they manage to enter professional roles, they earn 17 per cent less than their more privileged colleagues. Despite common perceptions, moving to more prosperous areas like London may not improve someone's social mobility,[7] since people from lower socio-economic backgrounds are less likely to move. Moreover, people who move to London from working-class backgrounds from other countries also fare poorly in occupational attainment compared to people from within the UK.[8]

Working-class employees face a 'double disadvantage' in their career progression if they are women, have disabilities or have ethnic-minority backgrounds.[9] The concept of intersectionality explains how these overlapping identities intensify barriers to advancement. For example, only 21 per cent of people with disabilities from working-class backgrounds reach the highest occupational levels, compared to 43 per cent from professional backgrounds. Furthermore, women and ethnic minorities are more likely to experience downward mobility than their male or white counterparts. People from working-class backgrounds are also disproportionately likely to be paid below the voluntary living wage and face the highest levels of unemployment despite overall employment growth.

Living standards and wellbeing also have important implications on social mobility as they enable people to take more risks and allow them to have more options. Yet, working-class people are affected by rising poverty and lower home ownership and suffer from lower levels of wellbeing.

Socio-economic diversity in the Civil Service

Individuals from low socio-economic backgrounds (SEBs) have a lower likelihood of working in high-profile areas of the Civil Service that provide rapid career advancement, particularly in departments such as His Majesty's (HM) Treasury. Positions like policymaking, and occupations that provide exposure to the political networks of Whitehall are considered more sought after and hence less accessible to working-class employees.[10] Among the HM Treasury's employees, for instance, only 12 per cent have a low socio-economic background, while the share of them in the Department for Work and Pensions (DWP) is significantly higher, at 45 per cent.

The divide between prestigious and less prestigious departments is consistent with employees' schooling patterns. While 26 per cent of employees of the HM Treasury and 22 per cent of the Foreign & Commonwealth Office staff were privately educated, these figures drop to 5 per cent in HM Revenue & Customs (HMRC) and 4 per cent in the DWP. Similarly, the less socio-economically diversified departments, such as the Treasury, employ more people at top levels, while departments like DWP and HMRC employ primarily junior level staff outside the capital. The diversity gap is also evident in different job roles and among departments. While only around a fifth (19 per cent) of employees from low socio-economic backgrounds work in high-profile, policy-related roles, almost half of them (40 per cent) work in less prestigious operational roles, such as front-line services.

Patterns behind the data – the hidden hand of occupational sorting

These patterns underline a very important, so-called 'occupational sorting pattern', which refers to the trend that people are attracted to roles that are more accessible for them.

Sorting pattern 1: hidden behavioural codes vs transparency

People from low socio-economic backgrounds frequently gravitate towards operational roles, that are perceived more transparent and meritocratic, rather than to policy work, which is generally viewed as requiring a specific behavioural code, and hence favouring those from privileged backgrounds. Yet, most policy jobs are based in socio-economically exclusive departments, while more socially accessible departments tend to have a strong emphasis on operational delivery. In the Treasury, for instance, approximately two-thirds of staff work in policy-related roles, whereas at departments that are more accessible for people with working-class backgrounds, for instance the HMRC and DWP, the share of policy-related roles is significantly lower at 9 and 12 per cent respectively.

Sorting pattern 2: hidden geographical barriers

Civil servants from working-class families are also significantly under-represented in London (22 per cent), compared to 48 per cent in the north-east. This difference in geographical location has an important impact on career progression into higher level positions. Physical proximity to ministers at the Civil Service's Whitehall headquarters is crucial for gaining 'visibility', as top-level positions are still concentrated in central London (see Figure 18.1).

While 20 percent of all civil servants work in London, the capital also houses the majority – 66 per cent – of all SCS jobs and 45 per cent of all experienced officials with significant responsibilities in high-end (G6/G7 level) posts. In comparison, the north-west is home to 12 per cent of civil servants, but only 3 per cent of SCS and 7 per cent of high-end (G6/G7) staff.

Access to the more prestigious London 'career track' is affected by people's socio-economic background. Those from working-class backgrounds who grow up outside of London and the south-east often 'sort into' or end up in regional positions due to a lack of economic resources to move to the capital and for preferring to stay close to their families or their hometowns.

Figure 18.1: Work location of civil servants by parental occupation

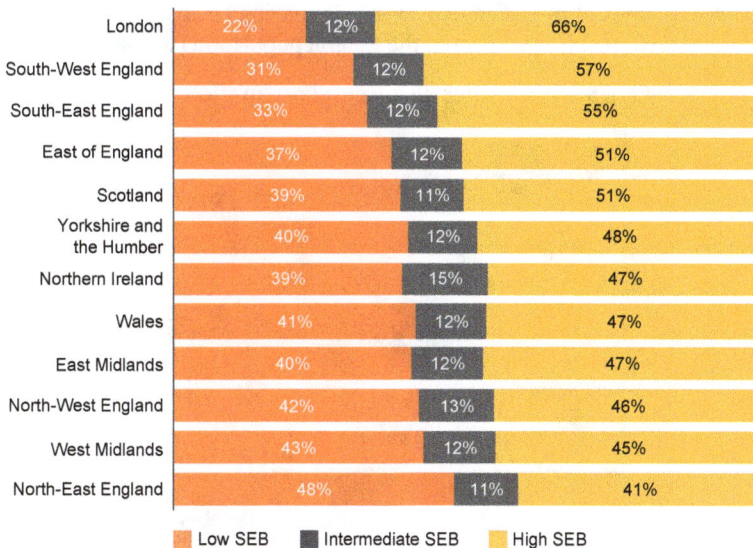

Location	Low SEB	Intermediate SEB	High SEB
London	22%	12%	66%
South-West England	31%	12%	57%
South-East England	33%	12%	55%
East of England	37%	12%	51%
Scotland	39%	11%	51%
Yorkshire and the Humber	40%	12%	48%
Northern Ireland	39%	15%	47%
Wales	41%	12%	47%
East Midlands	40%	12%	47%
North-West England	42%	13%	46%
West Midlands	43%	12%	45%
North-East England	48%	11%	41%

Source: Friedman (2021) Figure 2, p. 30

Career progression within the Civil Service

The higher someone goes in the hierarchy of the Civil Service, the less likely they are to come across working-class people. The organisation is becoming more socio-economically exclusive or elitist in each category. At the most junior grade, the level of administrative assistant/officer positions that include administrative support and operational delivery roles such as prison officers or caterers, only 45 per cent of staff are from privileged backgrounds. This percentage increases consistently as we move up the hierarchy within the organisation. For example, 49 per cent of executive officers (EO) (such as executive assistants, finance, HR, IT, and communications specialists), 57 per cent of senior executive officers/higher executive officers filling policy roles and 65 per cent of experienced officials with significant responsibilities in G6/G7 roles come from privileged backgrounds.

At the top of the hierarchy, in the level of the SCS that make up the senior management team, people from high socio-economic background fill the majority – 72 per cent – of the roles.

While in 1967, the Civil Service had the same proportion of people from high socio-economic backgrounds (67 per cent) as other professional and managerial jobs in the UK, by 2021 the SSC has become even more exclusive, with 72 per cent coming from high socio-economic backgrounds, compared to 49 per cent of the UK professional/managerial workforce and 49 per cent of other management occupations (see Figures 18.2 and 18.3).

While just 4 per cent of lower-level (AA/AO) employees received private education, this figure jumps to 25 per cent for SCS staff at the top of the hierarchy. The socio-economic exclusivity of the SCS's top grades is even more remarkable, with 59 per cent of permanent secretaries having received private education, compared to only 7 per cent in the general population (see Figure 18.4).

Figure 18.2: Civil Service grades by parental occupation

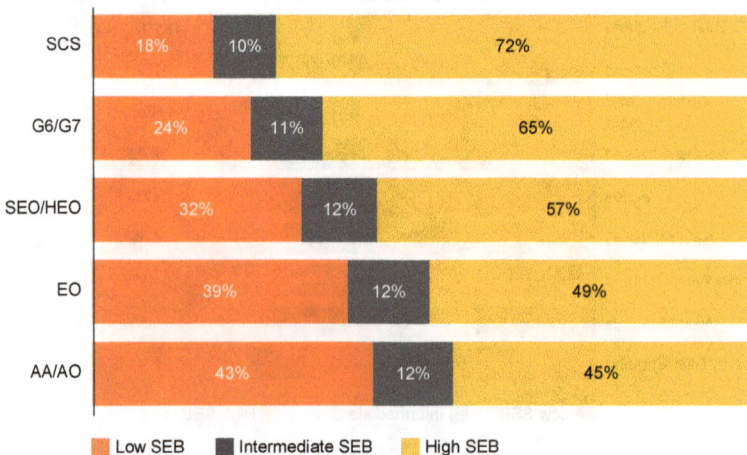

Source: Friedman (2021) Figure 4, p. 35

Figure 18.3: Parental occupation of civil servants, UK workforce, professional/managerial occupations and public sector

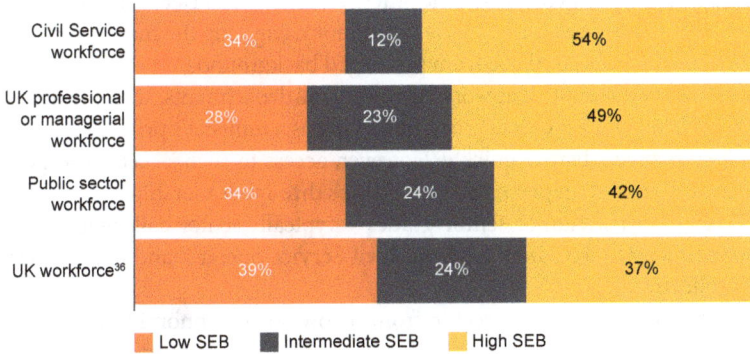

Source: Friedman (2021) Figure 1, p. 29

Figure 18.4: Civil Service grade by type of school attended between ages 11–16 in 2019 Civil Service People Survey

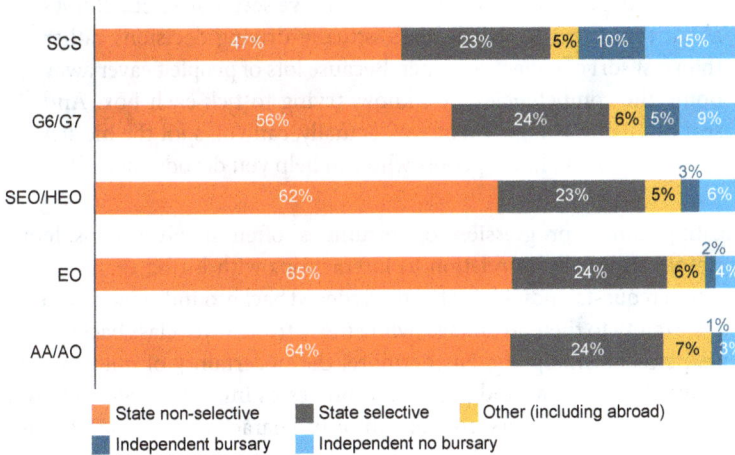

Source: Friedman (2021) Figure 5, p. 36

Labyrinth or class ceiling?

Friedman's 2021 report[11] used the metaphor of the labyrinth[12] to explain how it feels to navigate career progression in the Civil Service. This metaphor, adapted from Eagly and Carli's[13] work on women in leadership and Wyatt and Silvester's work on Black and minority leaders captures both the size and complexity of the Civil Service and the fact that career progression is rarely simple or direct. Due to its size and complexity, career advancement here rarely follows a straight line. While formal career progression criteria

exist, the unwritten rules and deeply engrained informal institutional mechanisms create a discriminative environment, in which people from certain
backgrounds enjoy privileges while others face barriers. Friedman asserts that
mastery of these unwritten clues is critical for navigating the maze, providing
significant rewards for those from privileged backgrounds.

Certain positions, such as working in 'central' departments, securing a leadership role during a national crisis, or serving as a minister's private secretary,
can help people advance quickly. However, access to such 'accelerator' posts
is often dependent on personal relationships through leadership programmes
such as the fast stream or senior 'guides' – typically senior colleagues – who
distribute knowledge about how the Civil Service operates and how to manage it effectively.

For example, Mark, a director from a low socio-economic background
explains:

> Very little of it is explicit, there's a lot of implicit stuff. So, obviously
> there's formal processes and, you know, the Civil Service bureau-
> cracy is your friend on social mobility to some extent. Like there's
> a bigger paper trail on promotions than I've seen elsewhere. But it's
> about the extent to which that's actually driving decisions rather
> than just sort of collecting paper. Because lots of people beaver away
> doing the competencies, you know, trying to tick each box. And
> sort of miss the bigger picture of, actually, can you spot the hidden
> rules? Or do you know people who can help you decode them?[14]

Navigating career progression opportunities often involves considerable
uncertainty, especially in relation to interactions with hiring managers and
promotion requests. Individuals from privileged backgrounds tend to leverage
this uncertainty to their advantage, while those from lower class backgrounds
often experience ambiguity. Furthermore, the uncertainty of outcomes, the
ambiguity of hiring, pay and promotion processes impact female employees
and those who have intersectional minority characteristics – for instance
women from minority ethnic backgrounds, or women with disabilities –
considerably more negatively than men and especially those from white
privileged backgrounds.[15]

What are the factors that sustain discrimination and prevent change?

According to the report 'Navigating the labyrinth',[16] there are seven unwritten
rules of progression that act as barriers for those from low socio-economic
backgrounds.

1. Access to informal guides and accelerator career tracks

Friedman found that securing what is perceived as valuable work within the Civil Service leads to quicker career progression. Such roles might include securing a lead role during a national crisis, as a minister's private secretary or serving within a central department, for example:

> So, my sense from quite early on was that there was a secret code as to how to get on. There were these folk that worked in the Treasury, had done certain things... they knew about 'the velvet drainpipe', as you hear it described. The way up and through. And they'd clearly done it, and they had a language to speak about it. (Aaron, director, high SEB)[17]

The existence of such accelerator roles runs counter to official guidance for career progression within the Civil Service, with emphasis placed on gaining experience with a wide range of skills. Instead, tacit knowledge of which roles lead to accelerators for career progression exist with interviewees gaining tacit knowledge during the Civil Service fast stream which is disproportionately composed of people of high SEBs.

Moreover, relationships with informal guides are created through shared cultural similarity and socio-economic backgrounds, with one respondent suggesting that shared humour with an informal guide was the main reason they hit it off:

> Definitely it's the humour. I think that's probably the main thing. So like when we worked together we just really enjoyed each other's company.[18]

While shared humour may seem trivial, research has long suggested thay 'homophily' exists, whereby people of similar backgrounds, such as SEB, are more likely to have shared interests, tastes and lifestyles.[19] Thus, shared humour due to similar SEB was a determinant of success in this example.

2. Negotiated opportunities in moments of organisational ambiguity

The report found evidence that civil servants consistently face ambiguity around interactions with hiring managers and requests for promotion. Members of high socio-economic backgrounds were able to negotiate these ambiguous moments better than low socio-economic status individuals. Often this was achieved via selling themselves during an informal chat with a gatekeeper:

> Interviews are so formal, you can't move from the questions, so I do think [fireside chats] sometimes have that self-promotion function.

So I would probably find a relatively casual way to mention some relevant previous experience. But it works less well when someone's on sell. Like it's meant to be like a relatively quick, light interaction. (Olivia, deputy director, high SEB)[20]

Yet people from low socio-economic backgrounds find the informal process much more difficult to navigate:

I find it morally really difficult, because I want to do well because I deserve to do well. And I find the whole idea that someone needs to talk to the right people, and it's not enough that I do a good job, really, really hard. (Jo, Grade 6, low SEB)[21]

3. The 'Whitehall effect'

The central departments within the Civil Service, which include the HM Treasury, Number 10 and the Cabinet Office, are all based in London and predominantly staffed by London-based civil servants from high socio-economic backgrounds, whereas staff from low socio-economic backgrounds tend to be regionalised, because they lack the resources to move to London and prefer to stay localised due to familial ties and for cultural reasons. This point is illustrated by Shaun, a low SEB person based in the north-west of England who is frustrated by the prospect of moving to London to advance his career:

It's frustrating because I would like to push on but the risks are just too high – why would I disrupt my whole family just for a promotion?[22]

The 'Whitehall effect' results in disproportionate representation of high socio-economic background people in senior roles with 63 per cent of all senior roles within the Civil Service being based in London.

4. Bottlenecks in operational career tracks

The report found that people from low socio-economic backgrounds opt into operational career tracks with low ceilings or 'bottlenecks' in terms of progression. Low SEBs are over-represented in operational delivery (40 per cent) and under-represented in policy roles (30 per cent). The report found that occupational sorting occurred, with people from low SEBs tending to join at lower operational grades. This is partially facilitated by the Civil Service fast stream which is over-populated by people from high socio-economic backgrounds who then enter policy jobs at higher grades. The skills required for policy roles have more ambiguity associated with them, which is another reason for the divide. For example:

> Policy work is so ambiguous it's really hard to know who is good and who isn't.' (Harriet, director, low SEB)[23]

> Ambiguity is a really good word, being comfortable with it, being able to exist in it. And it all comes down to good judgement in a way. So, there's judgement in the information you gather. There's judgement in how you put it together and in how you present it. And then at certain times it's a selling point, or a persuading point. There's no point coming up with the best option if no one agrees with you. (Bill, director, high SEB)[24]

The two examples show that Harriet, a director from low SEB, struggles with ambiguity whereas Bill, a director with a high SEB, appears to demonstrate what it entails.

5. Dominant behavioural codes

The dominant behavioural codes within the Civil Service include a particular accent and style of speech along with an emotionally detached persona and understated self-presentation. The behavioural code also includes a preference towards intellectual curiosity of culture and politics. For example, on accent and neutrality, the following quotation is typical:

> There is a definite style of speaking... that kind of neutral-ish RP [received pronunciation] accent, like trying to place yourself as from nowhere ... so I think most people in the SCS end up having an accent that is quite similar, at least the ones who are in the central teams, and replicate the style, the rhythms ... there is a kind of go-to neutrality, same voice, same accent. And it is very like: 'I'm objective, my analysis is objective. (Isaac, DD, high SEB)[25]

The following quotation also depicts emotional detachment:

> I don't see anyone getting emotional. Maybe that's because it's sort of filtered out before [SCS]. But I think if someone did get very concerned, that would probably be frowned upon. Self-control is really prized. (Oyinda, DD, high SEB)[26]

6. Downplaying of socio-economic privilege

Of those interviewed for the report, 1 in 4 who self-assess as coming from a low socio-economic background actually have parents who did professional or managerial jobs. The proportion of those misidentifying increases with seniority, with 29 per cent of those above grade 7 misidentifying their privilege. Here are two examples of misidentification:

> Although I grew up with two teachers, I think I felt more working class because my parents were both first generation university. They both grew up in a working-class family … so the consciousness of my upbringing was … I felt much more working class. (Mike, DD, high SEB)[27]

> My parents and I would define myself, psychologically, as working class. So my dad, he went to what would then have been called a polytechnic for his engineering degree, he was certainly the first person in his family. None of his siblings or extended family went to uni. So yeah my parents got more comfortable as I got older, but I identify more with working class. (Alex, Director, high SEB)[28]

In both of these examples, the high SEB civil servant attributed their working-class status to their grandparents and while there is some evidence of the 'grandparent effect',[29] this is not as pronounced as both parents being from traditionally working-class occupations.

7. Cumulative barriers (for women and Black civil servants from working-class backgrounds)

Socio-economic status is not the only structural form of inequality through which people are excluded from top jobs in the Civil Service. There is also extensive research that demonstrates how women and members of ethnic minorities are excluded from top jobs in the Civil Service.[30] This suggests that intersectionality significantly intensifies barriers within the organisation as employees move higher in their career ladder. For example, low SEB women are more under-represented at senior grades than low SEB men. In fact, low SEB men are more comfortable discussing their status at work and often position themselves as senior leaders with a unique perspective. Contrastingly, low SEB women largely choose to conceal their background. For example, in both cases below, the low SEB women face shame and embarrassment about their background:

> I don't tell people my background, you know, that's a thing I hide. And, you know, if I did say what my dad did, I would always say, 'Oh, he's an HGV driver,' because that's a bit, you know, better than that he drives a lorry and moves furniture. There's always a bit of trying to posh it up a bit. (Steph, DD, low SEB)[31]

> I've never shared my background at work, just being in a social mobility network is a step for me … why wouldn't I? I think it's partly a sense of shame, judgement, what would it gain me to say that? It would mark me out as even more different. (Nicola, Grade 7, low SEB)[32]

For ethnic minorities the story is a little different. Civil servants from ethnic minorities are more likely to be from advantaged socio-economic backgrounds, with the exception of those with an Asian origin. For Black staff, they are often subjected to negative and stereotypical assumptions about Black working-class communities regardless of their socio-economic background. The examples below illustrate this misrepresentation:

> So yeah, you do get a lot of misconceptions, and people look at you and before speaking to you, judge you and just assume, 'Oh, you live in London, you must come from the ghetto,' and it's like, no I don't live in a slum, we're not all in debt!' (Martina, Grade 7, low SEB)[33]

> I was having a meeting and my manager started talking about, 'Oh, you know, like Black-on-Black crime,' and like nodding to me as if I would like know everything about this and I was just like, 'What on earth is going on? Like why would that ever be something that you think you should say? (Joy, director, high SEB)

Summary

The Civil Service's structure and progression patterns closely resemble a labyrinth. While there is a viable route to the centre for everyone, this route is largely hidden, governed by both formal guidelines and informal rules and norms. This background sets the stage for a deeper examination of the factors influencing career progression within the UK Civil Service, particularly for those from lower socio-economic backgrounds.

Preparing the case

In preparing the case analysis, you might like to consider the following specific propositions and discussion points:

1. Why does class matter?
2. From an ethical point of view, it is wrong that privileged groups in society get an unfair advantage. Discuss.
3. From a political perspective, the demographic profile of the Civil Service should reflect that of the general population to reduce the possibility of civil strife. Discuss.

4. From a managerial perspective, a more diverse workforce will make better decisions. Discuss.

5. The 'labyrinth' metaphor illustrates the complex, indirect career paths faced by individuals from lower socio-economic backgrounds in the Civil Service. However, does it help us understand the intersectional challenges of class, race and gender? Evaluate how well the 'labyrinth' metaphor works and assess whether it could be applied to other sectors and industries.

6. While progress in gender and ethnic diversity is evident in the Civil Service, socio-economic diversity remains a challenge. This may be due to covert biases and less public focus on class. Compare and contrast the progress made in gender and ethnic diversity with the lack of progress in socio-economic diversity within the Civil Service. What factors might account for these differences?

7. Friedman's 'unwritten rules of progression' favour those from privileged backgrounds. Dismantling these informal rules is key to fairer progression. How can the Civil Service challenge and change these 'unwritten rules' and create a more level playing field for those from lower socio-economic backgrounds?

8. Consider the ethical implications of the 'class pay gap' in the context of a public service organisation. How might this impact public trust and the Civil Service's ability to fulfil its mission?

References

[1] The authors would like to thank Professor Sam Friedman and the Social Mobility Commission for the figures and data used in this case study. All figures are reproduced with their permission.

[2] Friedman, Sam (2021) 'Navigating the labyrinth: Socio-economic background and career progression within the Civil Service', Social Mobility Commission, May. https://www.gov.uk/government/publications /navigating-the-labyrinth/navigating-the-labyrinth-socio-economic -background-and-career-progression-within-the-civil-service

[3] In this case study we use social class and socio-economic background interchangeably.

[4] In the case study we follow the terminology of the Social Mobility Commission as explained in Friedman (2021). We refer to those whose parents did 'professional or managerial' occupations as coming from 'high', 'privileged' or 'advantaged' socio-economic or class backgrounds. Those whose parents did 'intermediate' occupations are referred to as 'short-range socially mobile' and those whose parents did 'routine, semi-routine, lower supervisory and technical' occupations, or whose parents 'never worked', are referred as coming from 'low', 'working class' or

'disadvantaged' socio-economic backgrounds. The terms low socio-economic backgrounds (SEB), 'low SEB' and 'working class background' are often used interchangeably, as 'socio-economic background' is often not representative of individuals' experiences. In contrast, the term 'working class' remains popular and a source of identity and pride for many. Additionally, the term 'working class background' is commonly used in Social Mobility Commission and academic research using NS-SEC categories.

5 Reeves, Aaron, and Friedman, Sam (2024) *Born to Rule: The Making and Remaking of the British Elite*. Cambridge, MA: Harvard University Press. https://www.hup.harvard.edu/books/29

6 Social Mobility Commission (2019) 'State of the Nation 2018–19: Social Mobility in Great Britain', April. https://assets.publishing.service.gov .uk/government/uploads/system/uploads/attachment_data/file/798404 /SMC_State_of_the_Nation_Report_2018-19.pdf

7 See Champion, Tony, and Gordon, Ian (2021) 'Linking spatial and social mobility: Is London's 'escalator' as strong as it was?', *Population, Space and Place*, vol. 27, no. 7. https://doi.org/10.1002/psp.2306; and Social Mobility and Child Poverty Commission (2016) *The Social Mobility Index*. London: Social Mobility and Child Poverty Commission.

8 See Breen, Richard and In, Jung (2023) 'Paradoxes of social mobility in London', *British Journal of Sociology*. vol. 74, no. 5, pp. 781–798. https:// doi.org/30.1111/1468-4446.13022

9 Social Mobility Commission (2019)

10 Friedman, Sam (2023) 'Climbing the Velvet Drainpipe: Class Background and Career Progression within the UK Civil Service', *Journal of Public Administration Research and Theory*, vol. 33, no. 4, pp. 563–577. https://doi.org/10.1093/jopart/muac045

11 Social Mobility Commission (2020) 'Simplifying how employers measure socio-economic background: An accompanying report to new guidance', updated 21 May 2021. https://www.gov.uk/government/publications /understanding-a-workforces-socio-economic-background-for-change /simplifying-how-employers-measure-socio-economic-background-an -accompanying-report-to-new-guidance

12 See also Wyatt, Madeleine and Silvester, Jo (2015) 'Reflections on the labyrinth: Investigating black and minority ethnic leaders' career experiences', *Human Relations*, vol. 68, no. 8.. https://doi.org/31.1177 /0018726714550890

13 Eagly, Alice, Carli, Linda L. (2007) 'Women and the labyrinth of leadership', *Harvard Business Review*, vol. 85, no. 9, pp. 62–71. https://hbr.org /2007/09/women-and-the-labyrinth-of-leadership

[14] Friedman, S. (2021) p. 52.

[15] Hill, Ian and Sallai, Dorottya (2025) 'Diversity, Equity and Inclusion in Human Resource Management', in Everett, Sally and Hill, Ian (eds) *Diversity, Equity and Inclusion in Business and Management*. London: Sage.

[16] Friedman (2021)

[17] Friedman (2021) p. 40

[18] Friedman (2021) p. 43.

[19] See McPherson, Miller *et al* (2001) 'Birds of a Feather: Homophily in Social Networks', *Annual Review of Sociology*, vol. 27, pp. 415–444. https://doi.org/34.35/annurev.soc.27.1.36

[20] Friedman (2021) p. 37.

[21] Friedman (2021) p. 38.

[22] Friedman (2021) p. 39.

[23] Friedman (2021) p. 40.

[24] Friedman (2021) p. 41.

[25] Friedman (2021) p. 59.

[26] Friedman (2021)

[27] Friedman (2021) p. 60.

[28] Friedman (2021)

[29] See Engzell, Per *et al* (2020) 'It's all about the parents: inequality transmission across three generations in Sweden', *Sociological Science*, June. http://dx.doi.org/10.15195/v7.a10

[30] Friedman, Sam (2022) '(Not) bringing your whole self to work: The gendered experience of upward mobility in the UK Civil Service', *Gender, Work & Organization*, vol. 29, no. 2, pp. 1–18. https://doi.org/10.1111/gwao.12776

[31] Friedman (2021)

[32] Friedman (2021)

[33] Friedman (2021) p. 82.

Index

www.ingramcontent.com/pod-product-compliance
Lightning Source LLC
Chambersburg PA
CBHW061238220326
41599CB00028B/5465